Fifty Years of the Concept Album

Fifty Years of the Concept Album

From the Beatles to Beyoncé

Eric Wolfson

BLOOMSBURY ACADEMIC
NEW YORK • LONDON • OXFORD • NEW DELHI • SYDNEY

BLOOMSBURY ACADEMIC
Bloomsbury Publishing Inc
1385 Broadway, New York, NY 10018, USA
50 Bedford Square, London, WC1B 3DP, UK
29 Earlsfort Terrace, Dublin 2, Ireland

BLOOMSBURY, BLOOMSBURY ACADEMIC and the Diana logo are trademarks of Bloomsbury Publishing Plc
First published in the United States of America 2024

Copyright © Eric Wolfson, 2024
For legal purposes the Acknowledgments on p. ix constitute an extension of this copyright page.

Cover design by Studio Auto

All rights reserved. No part of this publication may be reproduced or transmitted in any form or by any means, electronic or mechanical, including photocopying, recording, or any information storage or retrieval system, without prior permission in writing from the publishers.

Bloomsbury Publishing Inc does not have any control over, or responsibility for, any third-party websites referred to or in this book. All internet addresses given in this book were correct at the time of going to press. The author and publisher regret any inconvenience caused if addresses have changed or sites have ceased to exist, but can accept no responsibility for any such changes.

Whilst every effort has been made to locate copyright holders the publishers would be grateful to hear from any person(s) not here acknowledged.

A catalog record for this book is available from the Library of Congress.

ISBN:	HB:	978-1-5013-9181-1
	PB:	978-1-5013-9180-4
	ePDF:	978-1-5013-9183-5
	eBook:	978-1-5013-9182-8

Typeset by RefineCatch Limited, Bungay, Suffolk
Printed and bound in Great Britain

To find out more about our authors and books visit www.bloomsbury.com and sign up for our newsletters.

To Scott for the journey and Michael for the destination

Contents

Acknowledgements ix

Introduction: Ramblin' on My Mind 1

Part 1 The Founding Era (1967–9)

1 We Hope You Will Enjoy the Show: *Sgt. Pepper's Lonely Hearts Club Band* 15

2 This Day Will Last a Thousand Years: *Days of Future Passed* 24

3 We Are the Other People: *We're Only in It for the Money* 32

4 The One That Rambles on for a Million Miles: *Electric Ladyland* 40

5 Amazing Journey: *Tommy* 47

Part 2 The Golden Era (1970–4)

6 God Knows Where We're Heading: *What's Going On* 57

7 I Am On a Lonely Road and I Am Traveling: *Blue* 65

8 We'll Have Superman for President: *Thick as a Brick* 72

9 Like a Regular Superstar: *The Rise and Fall of Ziggy Stardust and the Spiders from Mars* 79

10 And If the Band You're in Starts Playing Different Tunes: *The Dark Side of the Moon* 86

Part 3 The Modern Era (1975–89)

11 Tear the Roof off the Sucker: *Mothership Connection* 95

12 Fairy Tale High: *Once Upon a Time . . .* 103

13 There's No Returning on This Chartered Trip Away: *Zen Arcade* 110

14	As Soon as You're Born You're Dying: *Seventh Son of a Seventh Son*	117
15	This Is a Recording: *3 Feet High and Rising*	124

Part 4 The Postmodern Era (1990–9)

16	I Wanna Be Mesmerizing Too: *Exile in Guyville*	135
17	I Am the Silencing Machine: *The Downward Spiral*	143
18	I Feel Like Death Is Fuckin' Callin' Me: *Ready to Die*	151
19	A Handshake of Carbon Monoxide: *OK Computer*	158
20	I Chose to Use My Heart: *The Miseducation of Lauryn Hill*	166

Part 5 The New Millennium (2000–16)

21	I've Been Taken for Lost and Gone and Unknown for a Long, Long Time: *SMiLE*	177
22	All Across the Alien Nation: *American Idiot*	184
23	If You Want to Be Free: *The ArchAndroid*	192
24	The One in Front of the Gun Lives Forever: *good kid, m.A.A.d city*	200
25	Won't Let My Freedom Rot in Hell: *Lemonade*	208

Conclusion: When Everybody Who Is Lonely Will Be Free	216
Works Cited	223
Index	239

Acknowledgements

This book began as a one-term independent study when I was still in college; I have now spent over half of my life working on it, so some acknowledgements are long overdue.

Thanks first to my beautiful and amazing wife Annie, and our three children, Charlie, Elsie, and Trixie, all of whom were so supportive, patient, and considerate when giving me "Daddy writing time."

Thanks to Leah Babb-Rosenfeld and all the fantastic people at Bloomsbury, including Rachel Moore and her excellent design staff.

Thanks to Greil Marcus, Dave Marsh, Robert Gordon, and Jim Dawson for giving me advice about this project over the years in its various iterations.

Thanks to Sarah Tomlinson and Margaret Welsh, two great writers who were willing to spitball ideas at any hour of the day.

Thanks to Dean Michael Murphy and Ginny Delaney, who supported this project from early on.

Thanks to the twenty-five artists featured in this book and their incredible music: the Beatles, the Moody Blues, Frank Zappa and the Mothers of Invention, the Jimi Hendrix Experience, the Who, Marvin Gaye, Joni Mitchell, Jethro Tull, David Bowie, Pink Floyd, Parliament, Donna Summer, Hüsker Dü, Iron Maiden, De La Soul, Liz Phair, Nine Inch Nails, the Notorious B.I.G., Radiohead, Ms. Lauryn Hill, Brian Wilson, Green Day, Janelle Monáe, Kendrick Lamar, and Beyoncé.

And thanks to my late mother, Elizabeth Wolfson, who always encouraged me with this project and helped me appreciate the simple joy of putting on an album.

Introduction: Ramblin' on My Mind

On April 10, 1967, Paul McCartney visited Brian Wilson at a Hollywood recording studio. Wilson was the leader of the Beach Boys, who had released the landmark album *Pet Sounds* less than a year earlier. He now toiled away on *Pet Sounds*' follow-up, "a teenage symphony to God" he called *SMiLE*, which was already several months overdue. When McCartney arrived, Wilson was working on a light-hearted ode to healthy eating called "Vege-Tables," and he invited McCartney to munch on some celery as part of its rhythm track. McCartney happily obliged, and then sat at the piano to play "She's Leaving Home." Wilson was amazed by the beauty of McCartney's song, which would appear a few months later on the Beatles' *Sgt. Pepper's Lonely Hearts Club Band*. Compared to the music McCartney played, which was taken from an album that was largely finished and being mixed down, Wilson's music sounded tentative and incomplete. "You'd better hurry up!" McCartney reputedly called out before leaving the studio, in a gesture of friendly competitiveness.

But it was too late. After countless hours in the studio, Wilson lost his way with *SMiLE* and didn't finish it until thirty-seven years later; meanwhile, *Sgt. Pepper* was released in the spring of 1967 to widespread acclaim. *Sgt. Pepper* marked the first major rock album grounded in a conceptual structure that went beyond a mere collection of pop songs and to be recognized as such. The rock music world virtually changed overnight. The editors of *CashBox*—a now-defunct music industry magazine that once rivaled *Billboard*—noted this less than three weeks after *Sgt. Pepper*'s release. On May 20, 1967, *CashBox* featured a lead editorial titled "Another Old Way Out The Window." They write how not too long ago, soon after a performing artist had a hit single, "a label would have in its possession a number of sides—usually of questionable substance—that could speedily be added to the hit single (and, of course, its flipside) and—presto!—an LP was on the market." But this was all changing. "While the old-way generally meant an LP that offered the hit act in a rather generalized manner," they continued, "the present trend enables the producer of his recordings to take his cues from the successful recording and build an entire LP concept behind it."[1] In time, the "LP concept" became codified as the concept album.

The earliest use of the term "concept album" I can find in print is from the October 25, 1961, issue of *Variety*. It appears in a small, uncredited piece titled "Korvette Mulls Own Indie Label" about a discount department store chain starting a new record division. The company's buyer speculated that "the line would most likely be a standard-priced set up and would probably specialize in 'concept' albums like singalongs, percussions and whatever particular strong trend develops."[2] Outside of a short-lived record label in the mid-1960s called Concept LPs, I cannot find the term again until after *Sgt. Pepper*'s release.

On November 19, 1967, Topy Malagaris wrote in *The Chicago Tribune* about the Chicago music scene. She interviewed a few record producers who "agreed that to become a best seller, a record must be a hit if a single, and must have a concept if an album. They gave the Beatles' 'Sgt. Pepper's Lonely Hearts Club Band' album as an example of a concept album."[3] No further explanation of what constitutes a concept album is given. A definition appears a month later in the December 9, 1967, issue of *Record World* when discussing the Rolling Stones' *Their Satanic Majesties Request*. "Rather than merely a collection of unrelated songs," the unknown writer explains, "their new LP (which was nine months in the making) is a concept album, 'an integrated and ethereal experience with cosmic quality.'"[4]

The Oxford English Dictionary defines the concept album as "a (rock) album featuring songs which express a unified theme or idea."[5] The earliest example *OED* cites is a *New York Times* article from June 2, 1968, by legendary rock critic Paul Nelson entitled "'Rock Is Too Serious,' Say The Who." Published exactly one year after the Beatles' *Sgt. Pepper's Lonely Hearts Club Band* was released in America, the album hangs over rock music like an albatross. Nelson writes:

> It may or may not be true that "Sgt. Pepper's Lonely Hearts Club Band" has made the themeless rock LP obsolete, but certainly no one can minimize the influence of the Beatles' masterwork in terms of album conceptualization, intellectualism, and structure. Although the death notices for the random rock collection may be greatly exaggerated, it is more than coincidence that such recent releases as "The Who Sell Out" ... fit squarely into the mainstream of the new "concept album" genre.

At this point, the implications of the concept album were still up for grabs. "Having a form for an album seems to be what is happening," the Who's Pete

Townshend explained, "and we wanted a form for ours which would be ... very humoristic."[6] Ironically, as Townshend chastised rock for taking itself too seriously, the Who were about to begin recording *Tommy*, the first major rock opera—and for some, the archetypal "serious" rock album.

Oddly, it appears that *Rolling Stone*, the epicenter of rock journalism, didn't use the exact term "concept album" until their June 8, 1970, issue. In it, Greil Marcus penned an infamous review of Bob Dylan's *Self-Portrait*, which is now far more famous for its opening words—"What is this shit?"—than for its use of "concept album" buried deep within. As Marcus parses through what the album signifies, he suggests at one point that "'Self-Portrait' is a concept album from the cutting room floor."[7] When I wrote Marcus to ask about his use of this term and its origins, he responded: "I have no idea where the term originated. If I was using it in 1970 then it was already a commonplace [term]."[8] Indeed, the use of the word had been in the rock lexicon for roughly three years by then—and was familiar enough to causally throw away in a passing aside about an inscrutable album. It was already both an achievement and a put-on.

The concept album had roots far deeper than rock and roll music. A decade after Thomas Edison invented the phonograph in 1877, German-American engineer Emile Berliner patented the gramophone, which used discs instead of cylinders to hold and play recorded sounds. In 1904, Columbia Records introduced the first two-sided disc; the following decade, discs would overtake cylinders in the first media format war. The 78-revolutions per minute (RPM) 10-inch shellac disc became the default standard unit of recorded sound, holding about four minutes on each side. This worked fine for singles, but anything longer had to be packaged in multi-disc set. The term "record album" was coined because the boxy solution resembled something closer to a classic photo album than to the slick 12-inch package we're used to today.

At first albums were only for classical music, but by the end of the 1930s, things began to change. In April 1938, a musical operetta called *The Cradle Will Rock* was released on Musicraft Records, in which members of the original Broadway cast performed their parts while composer-librettist Marc Blitzstein narrated the work to fill in the story. Today, it is generally considered the first cast recording album. The record is just that, a *record*—the preservation of a stage play that condensed the work into an album that could be followed as a narrative. *The Cradle Will Rock* not only paved the way for the album as a vehicle of storytelling, but for every cast album ever since. Rodgers and Hammerstein's *Oklahoma!* solidified the genre, when the original 1943 Broadway cast and orchestra recorded a six-disc album soundtrack of the show; it became the first album to sell over a million copies. The musical soundtrack became a cornerstone of the album industry, with musical, film, and television soundtracks providing the best-selling album of nearly every year until rock and roll emerged as the most popular album genre in the mid-1960s.

The earliest precursor to the modern rock concept album is Woody Guthrie's *Dust Bowl Ballads*, a two-volume 78-RPM album that consisted of a combined twelve songs on six discs. Recorded and released by RCA Victor in 1940, *Dust Bowl Ballads* featured Guthrie performing solo with his acoustic guitar and harmonica, singing songs he wrote while traveling throughout the Great Depression's Dust Bowl. But *Dust Bowl Ballads* is more than an album—it's a historical document. This was a song cycle of ballads about real dust storms and the people on which they wreaked havoc. But what could have been an endless litany of dust, death, and destruction is saved by Guthrie's versatility. There are many sobering songs, but also flashes of humor ("Talkin' Dust Bowl Blues"), reimagined spirituals ("I Ain't Got No Home in This World Anymore"), outlaw songs ("Vigilante Man"), oral histories ("The Great Dust Storm"), and even a two-part epic ("Tom Joad," based on *The Grapes of Wrath* film). Although *Dust Bowl Ballads* was not promoted by RCA and sold fewer than a thousand copies in its initial release, its influence in hindsight has been incalculable. Every singer who picks up an acoustic guitar and a harmonica rack from Bob Dylan and Johnny Cash on down to Bruce Springsteen and Beck are a disciple of this album.

Dust Bowl Ballads was an artistic and commercial outlier—it only sold to an exceedingly small folk intelligentsia and would not be heard by any sort of critical mass until the folk music revival of the mid-1960s. The postwar public typically opted for what we now call "The Great American Songbook"—well-crafted songs written by professional songwriters who once populated the New York City offices of Tin Pan Alley—which were then interpreted by jazz singers and pop crooners. Among the most prescient of these latter recording artists was Frank Sinatra. In March of 1946, Sinatra released his first album, *The Voice of Frank Sinatra*, on Columbia Records. Sentimental ballads like "You Go to My Head," "These Foolish Things (Remind Me of You)," and "(I Don't Stand) A Ghost of a Chance (With You)" help to craft an intimate, lovelorn listening experience that held together like few pop albums before. While Sinatra did not write these songs—they were all pop standards—he approached them in a way that conveyed a greater mood that reached beyond the songs themselves.

At the time, Sinatra was recording for Columbia Records, which was also exploring the artistic potential of the album. In 1948, Columbia introduced the 33⅓ long-playing record with microgroove technology, which allowed for more songs to fit on the side of a record with better fidelity. Although this format is now associated with the 12-inch record, which holds about twenty minutes per side, initially 12-inch records were only used for classical music. Popular music releases were issued as 10-inch records, which held about twelve minutes per side. The first popular music album ever released in the new long-playing format was an LP reissue of *The Voice of Frank Sinatra*, containing four songs on each side. The future of recorded sound now spun at 33 and a ⅓ revolutions per minute.

Despite Sinatra's initial success, by the early 1950s his popularity was in decline and he was dropped by Columbia. Sinatra staged a comeback in 1953, which led to a new deal with Capitol Records. In 1954, his first album for Capitol, *Songs for Young Lovers*, was a set of playful tunes of new love, featuring arranger Nelson Riddle conducting the orchestra. A following album, *Swing Easy!* continued the trend, with one key distinction—Riddle, who largely had only conducted the orchestra on *Songs for Young Lovers*, now also wrote the arrangements. Both albums were issued as 10-inch, eight-song discs.

Sinatra's third album for Capitol, *In the Wee Small Hours*, broke the mold. Released in April 1955, the album was Sinatra's first 12-inch long-playing record, which allowed for nearly fifty minutes of music, spread across sixteen songs. For the first time, Sinatra had the space to inhabit his album and set the scene for the listener like an installation artist. For his part, Riddle kept the arrangements soft and sparse, matching Sinatra's desolate tone. Sinatra sings like the last patron of a late-night bar closing all around him, nursing one more drink and smoking one last cigarette, lost in a reverie of regret and sorrow. Sinatra was at the peak of his powers as a singer, his voice having grown deeper and more conversational than in his earlier period, which allowed him to shade his vocals with a masterful nuance. Sinatra would collaborate with Riddle to release many other classic theme albums from *Songs for Swinging Lovers!* in 1956 to *Sings for Only the Lonely* in 1958 and beyond, but *In the Wee Small Hours* was the first and most influential.

With Sinatra leading the way, the concept album rolled on, although the term had not yet codified. Many places used the term "idea album." In *Billboard*'s "Dealer-Jockey Report" for March 1956—an advertising page from Columbia Records slyly designed to look like a tip sheet—the label promotes pop singer

Peggy King's *Wish Upon a Star* album: "Did you know that Columbia's 'WISH UPON A STAR' album is a true-to-life musical biography of a young singer's rise to fame? The circumstances could belong to almost any top female vocalist today, but in this case it is the authentic history of Peggy King. It's not just an assortment of songs but an 'idea' album with musical and story continuity."[9] In this phrase, it's the concept that drives the album.

This is not the case for a similar term also used in this period: "album concept." On September 9, 1957, *Billboard* reviewed French composer Guy Luypaerts' *Music of the Danube*: "These sides comprise music one might hear along ... the noted river. This in itself is a good album concept, lending itself to merchandising and giving the clerk something to talk about."[10] Despite being the inverse of "concept album," the term "album concept" wasn't as strong because the emphasis was placed on the concept, not the album. The result is a term that sounds more like the concept is one aspect of the greater album, as opposed to the engine powering the album.

In the new decade, ambitions only grew. On September 5, 1960, Capitol Records took out an ad in *Billboard*, which declared: "An exciting, unique album by Nat King Cole: 'Wild Is Love,'" promising something "completely new in concept with unlimited merchandising opportunities."[11] A week later, Capitol Records ran a new ad, which described about how "each song a different facet of a delightful romance" and is "woven into a refreshing love story, charmingly narrated by Nat himself."[12] In the September 19th issue, *Billboard* reviewed the album: "Here's a really de luxe [sic] hunk of packaging including a 24-page bound-in book containing a story all about young love. It has loads of photos of gorgeous gals and the song titles ... are based on the page by page episodes in the story."[13]

Wild Is Love stood out not only because it offered a complete narrative listening experience with both story narration and photographs illustrating it, but it was seen as potential source material for a Broadway musical starring Cole. While the musical didn't come to fruition, a television special was made based on this album and featured Cole, though it didn't air in America until 1964. *Wild Is Love* then flips the script on how albums are made. Instead of musicals conceived for the stage and made into soundtrack albums, here was an album conceived as a story that could be turned into musical, paving the way for concept albums-turned-musicals like the Who's *Tommy* and Green Day's *American Idiot*.

By the end of the 1950s, one of the most fruitful genres for the concept album was country music. With its recurring themes of trains, honky-tonks, and the

Wild West, it was only natural to step from the single song to the full-length album. Among the first and most influential albums was Marty Robbins' 1959 release *Gunfighter Ballads and Trail Songs*. Mixing classic cowboy songs with originals like "Big Iron" and his signature "El Paso," Robbins conjured an easy western terrain, with a smooth polish that belied his tales of death and an unforgiving landscape. A few months later, the Louvin Brothers released *Satan Is Real*. While the album is best remembered for its over-the-top cover—featuring the white-suited Louvin Brothers in the fiery pits of hell standing in front of a 12-foot-tall cartoon cutout of Satan—the music inside was no joke: twelve testimonies to the power of Christian religion and the perils of the devil.

However, the country singer of this period who most closely associated with the genre's concept albums is Johnny Cash. In 1960, Cash released *Ride This Train*, which documents a train ride through American land and history. Released a month before Nat King Cole's *Wild Is Love*, the songs are linked by Cash's spoken interludes setting up each song. By the mid-1960s, Cash was well on his way of making classic theme albums for Columbia: the labor songs of *Blood, Sweat and Tears* (1963), *Bitter Tears: Ballads of the American Indian* (1964), and *Johnny Cash Sings the Ballads of the True West* (1965). All were commercial hits and put Cash on the creative forefront of the album industry.

While Johnny Cash explored the American West through his albums, instrumental jazz was at the forefront of a more subtle kind of exploration. Jazz had long been a hotbed of album innovation at least since Duke Ellington's extended *Black, Brown and Beige* suite (1946) and Benny Goodman's *The Famous 1938 Carnegie Hall Jazz Concert* (1950), both of which showed the potential of musical statements on the 78-RPM album and the 33⅓ album, respectively. By the end of the 1950s, albums such as Miles Davis's *Kind of Blue* (1959) and Charles Mingus's *Mingus Ah Um* (1959) were among the greatest and most creative albums of their time. Each one reached a level of unity and sophistication far beyond the typical collection of songs on an album.

The story of the jazz concept album could comprise an entire book. And just as *Sgt. Pepper* blew things wide open in the rock world, John Coltrane's *A Love Supreme* played a similar role in jazz. Recorded in a single day—December 9, 1964—and released the following month, it remains one of the finest albums ever made. With Coltrane's tenor saxophone leading the way for Jimmy Garrison's bass, Elvin Jones's drums, and McCoy Tyner's piano, the album was conceived as a four-part pilgrimage through music and prayer: "Part 1: Acknowledgement," "Part 2: Resolution," "Part 3: Pursuance," and "Part 4: Psalm." "This album is a humble offering to Him," Coltrane wrote in the original liner notes. "An attempt to say 'THANK YOU GOD' through our work, even as we do in our hearts and with our tongues. May He help and strengthen all men in every good endeavor." In using secular music as a vehicle to reach sacred understanding, *A Love Supreme* paved the way for albums like the Who's *Tommy*, Marvin Gaye's *What's Going On*, and *The Miseducation of Lauryn Hill*, as well as any other works that used the long-playing record as a means of crafting a transcendental spiritual experience.

A Love Supreme came out in January 1965. For much of the year that followed, the two biggest rock influences of the decade—the Beatles and Bob Dylan—inspired each other to make some of rock and roll's finest music. The Beatles absorbed the musical (and medicinal) lessons of Bob Dylan, as they were amazed by his introspective folk music. Meanwhile, Dylan was inspired by the Beatles to return to rock music after abandoning it for folk in the early 1960s. The following months would find Dylan creating his rebirth as a rock and roll icon—releasing songs like "Subterranean Homesick Blues" and "Like a Rolling Stone," and "plugging in" for a controversial live set at the 1965 Newport Folk Festival.

Meanwhile, the Beatles spent 1965 deepening their sound and widening their musical pallet, delivering *Rubber Soul* in early December. More than any other rock album before it, *Rubber Soul* felt of one piece—a more mature, mellower feel that was adventurous in sound and unified in spirit. From the cryptic, sitar-filled "Norwegian Wood (This Bird Has Flown)" to the effortless pop of "Michelle," the evocatively dire "Think for Yourself," and the bittersweet "In My Life," every track had its own identity without disrupting the flow of the whole work. Beatles producer George Martin recalled that *Rubber Soul* reflected "a new, growing Beatles to the world. For the first time we began to think of albums as art on their own, as complete entities."[14]

Brian Wilson noticed the change. "A whole album with all good stuff . . ." he remembered marveling at *Rubber Soul*. "I suddenly realized that the recording industry was getting so free and intelligent. We could go into new things—string quartets, autoharps, and instruments from another culture. I decided right then: I'm gonna try that, where a whole album becomes a gas. I'm gonna make the greatest rock 'n' roll album ever made!"[15] Wilson set about making his album in the mold of his producer hero Phil Spector, who stacked countless tracks of instruments and voices to create his signature "Wall of Sound" in classics like the Crystals' "He's a Rebel" and the Ronettes' "Be My Baby." But where Spector mostly used this technique to craft singles, Wilson used it to build an album, *Pet Sounds*.

The resulting music of "Wouldn't It Be Nice," "Sloop John B," and "God Only Knows" is absolutely stunning. Some call *Pet Sounds* a concept album—and I for one hear it as a single narrative—but the album's creators were focused more on mood than narrative, never intending it to be a single story about two lovers. In the end, *Pet Sounds*, like *Rubber Soul*, is an essential stepping-stone to the rock concept album, but is not quite one in and of itself.

So, what *is* a concept album? For our purposes here, a concept album is an album that takes you on a journey by virtue of its unifying mood, theme, narrative, and/or underlying idea. When we talk about concept albums, we are talking about art, which generally requires some degree of intention on the part of the artist. There are some common traits for a concept album. They are generally a studio album or new songs recorded by one artist, as opposed to a live album or a compilation gathering older songs by one or more artists. A concept album's songs often run together in one or more suites, and sometimes have a central song or theme that is reprised before the end (often in the second-to-last or final song). Finally, the concept album usually has artwork tying the work together. To keep things from getting too unwieldy, I stuck with what I term popular music—which is essentially rock, pop, soul, and hip-hop. Albums from other genres like jazz, country, and reggae were considered but ultimately left out to keep things streamlined.

As we have seen, the concept album was not a format invented by rock and roll, but rather a loose structure that rock music built upon and perfected. Rock music came from its own rambling tradition—including train-hopping brakemen like Jimmy Rodgers, blues journeymen like Robert Johnson, western folk musicians like Woody Guthrie, north-bound blues singers like Muddy Waters, and wandering lost souls like Hank Williams—all of whom collectively helped to birth a music that was as restless as their itinerant lives. For a music that came from a thousand endless roads, rock and roll was the sound of breaking free. When Elvis Presley sang "I'm leaving home, now, baby!" on his first single, "That's All Right" in mid-1954, he took the history of the music with him.

And so it was until rock music lost its own path towards the end of the 1950s, with nearly all of its key figures hitting a dead-end: Elvis was in the Army, Chuck Berry was in jail, Little Richard was in the ministry, Jerry Lee Lewis was in disgrace, and Buddy Holly was in the graveyard. A new generation emerged with music epitomized by songs like Dion's "The Wanderer," which took a once-dangerous music and sanitized it as empty fun. Several major new movements would save rock and roll in the mid-1960s—namely, the influences of the Beatles and their British Invasion counterparts, as well as Bob Dylan and his folk-steeped contemporaries. The key element for the rock concept album was the introduction of psychedelic drugs, which internalized traveling done through rock music from a literal physical journey into a surreal psychological one. While Robert Johnson once famously sang about rambling on one's mind, the rock concept album introduced rambling *in* one's mind. The concept album provided a format in which one could take an extended "trip" through music without ever having to ingest a hallucinogen. Through the concept album, rock and roll transcends itself from a music to be enjoyed to a music to be *experienced*, and the album is the canvas for this expression.

But this isn't a book of the greatest or most influential concept albums (although it includes many of them). These are simply twenty-five examples of the concept album spread across a half century to map the artform's development. I chose one album per artist, while also trying to get a wide variety of artists and styles. There are omissions you may find unforgiveable—*The Kinks Are the Village Green Preservation Society,* Yes's *Tales from Topographic Oceans,* Randy Newman's *Good Old Boys,* or Genesis's *The Lamb Lies Down on Broadway,* all of which and more were strongly considered for this book—but this is not intended to be the end-all, be-all history of the concept album. Instead, it is the opening of a conversation, the first steps of a greater journey. This is a story of fifty years of artists reaching back and forth through time in an extended dialogue, contributing their own innovations and creativity to the dialogue. In other words, it's not so much a narrative as it is a collective journey—one that takes the most popular technological artifact of recorded sound, the long-playing rock and roll record, and spins it into art.

Notes

1 *CashBox,* 3.
2 Unknown, 49.
3 Malagaris, 10A–13.
4 *Record World.*
5 OED.
6 Nelson, 20 D.
7 Marcus.
8 Greil Marcus, email message to author, November 10, 2021.

9 Columbia Records, advertisement, 31.
10 "Music of the Danube," 38.
11 Capitol Records, advertisement, 25.
12 Ibid., 22.
13 "Wild Is Love," 47.
14 Miller, 230.
15 Badman, 104.

Part One

The Founding Era (1967–9)

1

We Hope You Will Enjoy the Show: *Sgt. Pepper's Lonely Hearts Club Band*

For decades, the Beatles' *Sgt. Pepper's Lonely Hearts Club Band* was the default "greatest album of all time." In 1978, fifty worldwide critics were polled for the first major international "greatest albums" list and *Sgt. Pepper* came out on top. In 1987, the experiment was repeated and *Sgt. Pepper* held its place on top, even as the rest of the top ten shifted beneath it. That same year, *Rolling Stone* ranked the 100 greatest albums of the past twenty years, with *Sgt. Pepper* at #1. A decade later, a list compiled by the UK's Channel 4 and *The Guardian*, crowned *Sgt. Pepper* the "Album of the Millennium." When *Rolling Stone* celebrated rock and roll's fiftieth anniversary in 2003 with "The 500 Greatest Albums of All Time," *Sgt. Pepper* was once again at the head of the list. And in 2007, the Rock and Roll Hall of Fame teamed with the National Association of Recording Merchandisers to create a list of "The Definitive Albums" that yet again placed *Sgt. Pepper* at #1.

But as the polls became more frequent towards the end of the millennium, *Sgt. Pepper* proved less infallible. The Beatles' own *Revolver* began inching out *Sgt. Pepper*, alongside list stalwarts like the Beach Boys' *Pet Sounds* and Marvin Gaye's *What's Going On*, and newer albums like Nirvana's *Nevermind* and Radiohead's *OK Computer*. Tellingly, the *New Musical Express*—which helped start the #1 *Sgt. Pepper* trend in one of the earliest greatest albums lists from 1974—threw down the gauntlet in 2013 when they made their own list of "The Top 500 Greatest Albums of All Time" and placed *Sgt. Pepper* at #87. But the true changing of the guard came when *Rolling Stone* compiled a new Top 500 list in 2020, *Sgt. Pepper* had fallen to #24. This time, Marvin Gaye's *What's Going On* made the top spot, while *Sgt. Pepper* wasn't even the highest *Beatles* album, now beaten out by both *Abbey Road* (#5) and *Revolver* (#11).

So, while the Beatles themselves remain secure in popular culture, *Sgt. Pepper's Lonely Hearts Club Band* does not. For many modern listeners, the album sounds hermetically sealed off like a museum piece. Not only do most people think that it isn't the greatest album of all-time, but that it isn't even the greatest Beatles album of all-time (it's now often considered to be *Revolver*). Like George Washington or *Citizen Kane*, *Sgt. Pepper* is easy to respect, but hard to love. And yet, *Sgt. Pepper's Lonely Hearts Club Band* must be discussed, if only because it was a complete game-changer. It was the tipping point at which the concept album situated itself in the popular consciousness by virtue of the Beatles' creativity, talent, and timing.

In early 1967, the Beatles had two of their best songs in the can: "Strawberry Fields Forever" and "Penny Lane." Under pressure from their record label to release new material, their producer, George Martin, released both songs as a double A-sided single in a move he later described as "the biggest mistake of my professional life."[1] Not only did this kill the momentum of the Beatles' current project—shaping up to be an album about childhood memories and aging—but it left them stranded in terms of its creative development.

It's jarring to realize that only four years earlier, the Beatles recorded their first album in a single day. But things were moving fast for the group as new influences for John Lennon (psychedelic drugs), Paul McCartney (classical music), and George Harrison (Eastern religion) shaped their perspective, while Ringo Starr held everything together with his increasingly creative drum fills. But with recent releases like Bob Dylan's *Blonde on Blonde*, the Rolling Stones' *Aftermath*, and the Beach Boys' *Pet Sounds*—the latter of which McCartney openly called "the greatest album of all time"—if the Beatles were to keep up, they would have to outdo their own best work.[2]

The notion for their archetypal rock concept album came from McCartney. "I thought it would be nice to lose our identities, to submerge ourselves in the persona of a fake group," he explained. "We could make up all the culture around it and collect our heroes in one place."[3] McCartney had recently returned from a trip to America where his thinking was influenced by Ken Kesey's Acid Tests and the counter-culture movement. His songwriting partner noticed this too. "The whole West Coast long-named group thing was coming in," remembered Lennon, "when people were no longer the Beatles or the Crickets—they were suddenly Fred and His Incredible Shrinking Grateful Airplanes."[4] In Lennon's eyes, it was the surreal silliness of the names that caught his attention, while McCartney was on to something bigger: "At the time there were lots of groups with names like 'Laughing Joe and His Medicine Band' or 'Col. Tucker's Medicinal Brew and Compound'; all that old Western going-round-on-wagons stuff, with long rambling names."[5]

McCartney's words tap into a greater sense of what was going on here, specifically in his use of the words "Medicine" and "Medicinal" in his faux-band names. Long before the psychedelic rock scene, medicine men journeyed America as part of the traveling medicine show. These shows crisscrossed the countryside throughout the nineteenth and early twentieth centuries, hawking magical drugs and providing wild entertainment, held together by "old Western going-round-on-wagons stuff" like actual wagon trains and "long rambling names" like Hamlin's Wizard Oil Company or the Kickapoo Indian Medicine Company.

Take the testimony of McCartney's vocal idol, Little Richard, about hitting the road in the mid-1940s:

> When I started getting into all this trouble at home, I left and joined up with Dr. Hudson's Medicine Show. I didn't tell anybody I was going. I just went. Doc Hudson was out of Macon, and he used to sell snake oil. He would go into towns, have all the black people come around, and tell them that the snake oil was good for everything. Well, they would believe him. But he was lying. Snake oil! I was helping him lie.[6]

When McCartney refers to the new American "groups with names like 'Laughing Joe and His Medicine Band,'" he is just as suspicious of their music as Little Richard was of Doctor Hudson's snake oil—this was music that promised to cure your soul but was little more than a bottled lie. Deceit runs deep in American culture and both he and Little Richard knew it; the medicine show simply turned this deceit into theater.

For when the Beatles decided to rename themselves "Sgt. Pepper's Lonely Hearts Club Band," they took the spirit of the medicine show and remade it into a psychedelic happening. By choosing a "long rambling" name that sounded like Dr. Hudson's Medicine Show on acid, the Beatles—or rather, Sgt. Pepper's Lonely Hearts Club Band—beat the competition by joining it, embracing any deceit implicit in the American music scene by reinventing themselves with a false name.

The premise of the medicine show was simple: You go to the show ("and hope she goes"), take the medicine ("get high with a little bit of help"), and feel better ("a little better, all the time"). For with their new work, the album *was* the show. In this regard, *Sgt. Pepper's Lonely Hearts Club Band* was a reaction to the Beatles' recent retirement from playing real-life shows. "It came at a time when they wanted to concentrate on the studio," explained Martin, "and that probably fomented the idea of the alter-ego group: 'Let Sgt. Pepper do the touring.'"[7] And so, the Beatles' project took the central notion of escape in rock and roll and used it to escape themselves. This allowed them to do the impossible: They took all of the promises hawked at the medicine show and actually kept them.

A crowd rustles. An orchestra tunes their instruments in preparation for the show. A hush falls over the audience as a searing guitar pierces the air. One hears Paul McCartney's voice as the mystical bandleader, establishing who they are with the gruffness of Little Richard hawking snake oil: *IT'S SGT. PEPPER'S LONELY HEARTS CLUB BAND!* The orchestra chimes in with a bouncy tune as the crowd laughs and applauds. The Beatles have broken free from themselves, triggering the album's conceptual journey in one fell swoop: "We're Sgt. Pepper's Lonely Hearts Club Band," they sing, and hope we enjoy the show. Nothing remains hidden or elusive; instead, it all feels like a grand carnival of dress-up. And, keeping with the theme, Sgt. Pepper's Lonely Hearts Club Band calls on one of its own, "Billy Shears," to sing the next number over the roaring crowd.

"With a Little Help from My Friends" serves as a rollicking call to arms that invites everyone *and* their friends, while establishing the importance of drugs in this experience. But this comes as no surprise once the album's main influence is considered. "In one word ... Pot," McCartney stated years later, "*Sgt. Pepper* was a drug album."[8] Yet there was also a more profound drug, LSD, which fundamentally shaped *Sgt. Pepper*. Beatles historian Ian McDonald has declared that "The album's sound—in particular its use of various forms of echo and reverb—remains the most authentic aural simulation of the psychedelic experience."[9] If "With a Little Help from My Friends" raised the implications of drugs, the album's third song, Lennon's "Lucy in the Sky with Diamonds," is *the* drug song on the album—it put you into a psychedelic state if you weren't already in one. Surprisingly, Lennon denied that "Lucy in the Sky with Diamonds" was about LSD or any other drug. "I swear to God, or swear to Mao, or to anybody you like, I had no idea it spelt LSD ..." Lennon later proclaimed. "*This* is the *truth*: my son came home with a drawing and showed me this strange-looking woman flying around. I said, 'What is it?' and he said, 'It's Lucy in the sky with diamonds,' and I thought, 'That's beautiful.' I immediately wrote a song about it ... The images were from *Alice in Wonderland* ... It's *not* an acid song."[10] Yet its psychedelic sound and surreal lyrics remain a quintessential acid rock experience for countless listeners. And, once "Lucy in the Sky with Diamonds" lets the influence of drugs out of the box, the album's journey becomes obscure—a free-association state of whatever you make of it.

Even the song's author recognized that. "*Sgt. Pepper* is called the first concept album, but it doesn't really go anywhere," admitted Lennon, "All my contributions to the album have absolutely nothing to do with this idea of Sgt. Pepper and his band; but it works, because we *said* it worked, and that's how the album appeared."[11] Ringo Starr agreed: "It had started out with a feeling that it was going to be something totally different, but we only got as far as Sgt. Pepper and Billy Shears (singing 'With a Little Help From My Friends'), and then we thought: 'Sod it! It's just two tracks.' It still kept the title and the feel that it's all connected, although in the end we didn't actually connect all the songs up."[12] Both Lennon and Starr are correct in their assessments, and in this way, *Sgt. Pepper*'s medicine show is the most deceitful one of them all. When you break it down song by song, *Sgt. Pepper* doesn't hold together, but as a singular listening experience, it works masterfully. And much of this experience belongs to McCartney. His songs comprise the majority of *Sgt. Pepper*, upholding its cheery mood. "Getting Better" is pure bouncy pop about things looking up, while "Fixing a Hole" finds its singer ruminating over household repairs. And in "She's Leaving Home," a wistful ballad about a teenage runaway, McCartney uses his keen sense of melody to reach a bittersweet conclusion through the ghostlike chiding of her parents.

As Lennon's "Being for the Benefit of Mr. Kite!" follows McCartney's "She's Leaving Home" at the end of the album's first side, it gives the effect that the girl is running away from home to join the circus. For despite Lennon's claim that his songs have nothing to do with Sgt. Pepper, "Being for the Benefit of Mr. Kite!" is the thematic centerpiece of the album, as well as its most vibrant song. Here is where all of the notions of an escape into the medicine show world are fully realized. The song's inspiration came from an antique 1843 circus poster that Lennon put up over his piano, rolling its words around until he had a song. "Messrs. Kite & Henderson . . ." read the advertising bill, "assure the Public that this Night's Production will be one of the most Splendid ever produced in this Town, having been some days in preparation."[13] The singer becomes a deadpan circus barker, weaving surreal imagery like "Henry the Horse dancing the waltz" almost straight from the poster's text. Meanwhile, Martin's production brings these words to life, filled by gothic organs swirling with excitement and hauntingly seductive interludes. It was as though Sgt. Pepper's Lonely Hearts Club Band had disappeared back into the traveling show tradition from which it had emerged.

George Harrison's sole contribution to the album, the second-side opener "Within You Without You," was the perfect contrast to the archaic psychedelia of

"Mr. Kite!"—its India raga represented the most modern of psychedelic experiences. Countless uncredited Indian musicians illuminate the song with their trance-like playing while Harrison's relaxed but passionate delivery infuses it with a revelatory, drug-induced calm. If "Mr. Kite!" offered where the Sgt. Pepper creation had come from, "Within You Without You" suggested where it was going; where Lennon sought to conquer the world, Harrison wanted to save it.

McCartney's "When I'm Sixty-Four" centered these songs by supplying a charming music hall two-step that actually sounded like the kind of music one could expect from a lonely hearts club band. The following psychedelic echoed wash of "Lovely Rita" provides a pop present for the previous song's pop past, with a touch of modern irreverence (it is, after all, an ode to a parking attendant). Lennon's hard-rocking (and equally irreverent) "Good Morning, Good Morning" showed that what the composer was lacking in numbers, he made up for in sound. And, in presenting us with the break of morning at the end of the band's performance, the song jars its listener like the rising sun at the end of a long night's party. For this morning is a new morning, signaling the end of the medicine show's main act.

"One, two, three, four," Sgt. Pepper counts off neatly, as pulsing drums meet his tempo and his band magically re-appears. This time their song is sprightlier, but for good reason—it holds the most revolutionary part of the album: Sgt. Pepper's Lonely Hearts Club Band reprise their opening song to say goodbye. By tapping into a classical feel that has been present all along, *Sgt. Pepper* comes full-circle and feels more unified than it really is, a sum that's greater than its parts. All themes tie back to the main one by way of the reprise, transcending a mere rock album to imply a sophisticated song cycle.

Once Sgt. Pepper's Lonely Hearts Club Band's show is over, the Beatles themselves return for the show's finale, "A Day in the Life." It is an unmistakably state-of-the-art Beatles song in which the Lennon and McCartney parts that were woven together seamlessly elsewhere on the album are now sectionalized, with one part leading into the other. Lennon's contribution begins as a bleak folksong, relaying a newspaper story about a car wreck and then watching a war film. The singer's mind drifts. "I'd love to turn you on," he sings in a slow, lingering falsetto, launching an orchestral storm builds upwards, climbing stairs of strings and noise until it reaches the top-floor bedroom of a house. An alarm clock rings, signaling McCartney's singer to get out of bed and ready for work as fast as he can, until he goes into a dream.

The music picks up the singer and carries him along at an easy and relaxed tempo, shifting altitude with each new extended note, before finally depositing him into the dream he has just left—Lennon's segment—now hurrying along at a choppier pace. The singer looks through the newspaper once again, only this time he finds an article about how there are 4,000 holes in Blackburn, Lancashire. He pictures the men counting the holes and then the men becoming the holes as the holes become the seats at the Royal Albert Hall. They are empty seats that watch an empty show—as false and unreal as the one just completed by Sgt. Pepper's Lonely Hearts Club Band.

As the singer sings the "I'd love to turn you on" refrain for a second time, he is answered by a rising storm that was recorded by studio musicians dressed in formal attire wearing carnival masks. The music takes the grotesque excesses of the carnival midway and pushes it into a crashing, terrifying crescendo that builds up into dead silence before bursting with one final, fatal chord. And then everything—the musicians, the Beatles, Sgt. Pepper's Lonely Hearts Club Band—is gone.

That is, until the Beatles deceive us once again. *Sgt. Pepper* ends with a high-pitched noise that triggers dogs to bark, followed by a secret inner groove of gibberish that springs up out of nowhere right after it, catching the needle so that it continues endlessly in a loop until the listener gets up to turn off the record player. With this parting shot, the Beatles' fantasy world that went on forever metaphorically ends so literally, making a final escape out of the confines of the black vinyl that contained it.

Sgt. Pepper's revolutionary approach went even beyond the sounds in its grooves. The presentation of the album itself was fully considered in a way that was unprecedented in rock. A glossy gatefold with a portrait of the Beatles in their Sgt. Pepper suits adorned its center and printed lyrics appeared on the back. But most important was *Sgt. Pepper*'s cover. Pop artist Peter Blake designed it; he later explained the Beatles wanted to look like they "had just finished the concert, perhaps in a park. I then thought that we should have a crowd standing behind them, and this developed into the collage idea." The "collage idea" became the most iconic album cover of all-time, as well as the clearest example of McCartney's intent to "make up all the culture" around the group and "collect our heroes in one place." And so, flanked by glamorous Hollywood stars, historical figures, mystical gurus, and Bob Dylan, the Beatles created the visual counterpart for their music by appearing in their bright psychedelic uniforms as Sgt. Pepper's Lonely Hearts Club Band.

For as the drum clearly tells us, this is not the Beatles' show—this one belongs to Sgt. Pepper. "Beatles" is only written in the flowers on the ground as wax sculptures of the Beatlemania-era Beatles sadly watch on. They are the "real" Beatles, the ones who could bang out an album in a day, but now have been sacrificed for the make-believe community of *Sgt. Pepper's Lonely Hearts Club Band*. It is in the younger Beatles' sullen eyes that the album's cover goes from a concert to a funeral—and, in turn, from the most communal experience to the most isolated one—as *Sgt. Pepper* makes the journey beyond death.

I left and joined up with Dr. Hudson's Medicine Show. I didn't tell anybody I was going. I just went. What Little Richard did literally, the Beatles did figuratively—they disappeared from the world to join the traveling show and re-emerged from the other side like a carnival coming to town. They met the fantasy world on its own terms, only to escape it through the gesture of their action. The result was *Sgt. Pepper's Lonely Hearts Club Band*'s final trick: turning rock and roll music into art—and *the* artistic achievement of the modern rock and roll era. *Sgt. Pepper's Lonely Hearts Club Band* became the largest-selling rock album up to that time, staying at Number 1 in America through the Summer of Love and landing the Beatles on the cover of *TIME*.[14] With no singles culled from the album, many radio stations initially played it in its entirety, while the Grammys crowned it as the first rock LP to receive Album of the Year.

To listen to the albums recorded just before *Sgt. Pepper's Lonely Hearts Club Band*—the Beach Boys' *Pet Sounds*, the Rolling Stones' *Aftermath*, and even the Beatles' own *Revolver*—is to listen to a community collectively closing in on an artistic space without quite capturing it. With *Sgt. Pepper*, the Beatles not only found that artistic space and grasped it, but they also turned it into an all-inclusive community that anyone could join, a rock concert that never ran out of seats (because the seats were made of holes). *Sgt. Pepper* united an entire generation of rock and roll in one stagnant place by creating an abstract journey that everyone could follow together. It marked a watershed for rock and roll's artistic development; here was an album that was conceived of as high art and was treated as such. One critic, Kenneth Tynan of *The London Times*, famously called *Sgt. Pepper* "a decisive moment in the history of Western civilization,"[15] but at its heart, it was just another journey. By bringing the concept album into the rock mainstream, *Sgt. Pepper* provided a turning point for the art of popular music.

Notes

1. Miller, 256.
2. MacDonald, 171–2.
3. Ibid., 184.
4. The Beatles, 241.
5. Ibid.
6. White, 21–2.
7. The Beatles, 241.
8. Miller, 253.
9. MacDonald, 199.
10. The Beatles, 242.
11. Ibid., 241.
12. Ibid.
13. MacDonald, 188n.
14. Miller, 259.
15. MacDonald, 198.

2

This Day Will Last a Thousand Years:
Days of Future Passed

The original concept album was the classical symphony. Centuries before recording technology cut music into three-and-a-half-minute clips, it could stretch out for hours. The music had freedom—it was a fleeting thing that could only be captured by the notes on the page, or in the ear of the listener. Since the dawn of recorded sound, people have sought to capture the symphony orchestra in a way that does it justice; the length of the original compact disc was initially set at seventy-four minutes so that it could fit Beethoven's Symphony No. 9. "We're as good as Beethoven," John Lennon told a biographer not long after *Sgt. Pepper* was released.[1] While that statement may be up for debate, more than any other rock album up to that time, *Sgt. Pepper* suggested a sophisticated song cycle. In his review of *Sgt. Pepper* in *The New York Times*, Richard Goldstein noted how "the structure of the album itself" is noteworthy, in that "one song seems to run into the next. This produces the possibility of a Pop symphony or oratorio, with distinct but related movements."[2] This was a quantum leap from covering Chuck Berry's "Roll Over Beethoven."

The Beatles spent years cutting their teeth on African American R&B hits; the British groups that emerged in their wake tried to prove their worth by also remaking this music into their own style. One group was the Moody Blues, who hit big with "Go Now," an obscure R&B song first recorded by Bessie Banks in 1964. As the Moodies struggled to produce another hit, their membership frayed until settling on its classic lineup in late 1966: keyboardist Mike Pinder, multi-instrumentalist Ray Thomas, drummer Graeme Edge, bassist John Lodge, and lead singer and guitarist Justin Hayward, with the latter two members as recent additions. It was a transitional period for the band. "We had been playing music that wasn't suited to our characters," remembered Hayward. "We were lower middle-class English boys singing about life in the Deep South of the USA and it just wasn't honest. As soon as we began to express our own feelings and created our own music, our fortunes changed."[3]

Helping them find their sound was the Mellotron, a new instrument discovered by Pinder. "The Mellotron enabled me to create my own variations of string movements," he explained. "I could play any instrument that I wanted to hear in the music. If I heard strings, I could play them with the Mellotron. If I heard cello, brass, trumpets or piano, I could play them ... I could create the backdrops and the landscape for the melodies that the guys were writing."[4] The Mellotron was a complex keyboard in which the keys were connected to tape strips of pre-recorded sounds such as violins or flutes. One could pre-program the instrument with the desired sounds, making it a great-grandparent to modern digital sampling. "Mike had been working with Mellotrons," Thomas later explained, "so instead of just going on stage and doing one number after another ... we thought it would be a nice idea to do, not a medley of songs, but something like a rock symphony."[5] With *Sgt. Pepper*'s stately song cycle on everyone's minds and major hits like Procol Harum's Bach-inspired "A Whiter Shade of Pale" blurring the line between rock and classical music, mid-1967 was just the right time for such experimentation.

The Moody Blues were approached by their label, Decca Records, to record an album for their new subdivision, "Deram" (short for "Decca Panoramic Sound"), which was introducing a new kind of high fidelity. Although two-channel stereo had been around for years, the rock music industry was built on monaural—or "mono"—sound, in which all the sound comes through one channel at once. Deram was using a more sophisticated technique, where the instruments and vocals were placed in a manner that surrounded the listener across a spectrum, akin to images on a panoramic screen. The label already released a line of highbrow albums to show off this technology, but they now sought to bring it to rock and roll.

"They wanted a record that would demonstrate that rock and roll could be just as interesting in stereo as classical music, because there weren't many rock and roll stereo records ..." Hayward explained in 1996. "They wanted us to play Dvořák—work out baroque arrangements of the main themes—and then the orchestra conducted by a 50-year-old classical composer and arranger named Peter Knight would play real Dvořák in between. That wasn't what we wanted to do, but we agreed because it was our only opportunity to spend more than three hours in the studio."[6] While previous sessions had been focused on producing hit singles, the Moodies were now thinking in larger terms.

They found a strong ally in producer Tony Clarke. Pinder remembers that Clarke "was always full of ideas. We called him the sixth Moody. He played bass and had a musical background, which allowed him to soar with us in the studio."⁷ Also key was Hugh Mendl, the head of Decca A&R. Despite the Dvořák plan they signed up for, Mendl told the group, "Do what you want to do." Empowered, they now had to get composer/arranger Peter Knight on board. Edge remembered the stakes of "talking Peter into becoming an accessory before the fact. Naturally, he was very apprehensive, but he listened to what we had to offer and finally agreed to stick his neck out. I salute his tremendous guts."⁸ Now the project was inverted. Instead of the Moodies writing songs to match with Knight conducting Dvořák, Knight was now writing music to match with the Moodies. Their song cycle was connected by a simple theme: The phases of the day. The result was the first major rock album to have a single unified narrative. As the Moodies cobbled together their parts, Knight wrote arrangements for the group that received co-credit on the album alongside the Moody Blues, the London Festival Orchestra.

Only there is no London Festival Orchestra. It was just a name for the classical musicians Knight knew who could knock out his arrangements in one take, a fake group to give the project an air of sophistication. The Moodies recorded their parts separately before the orchestra came in, leaving Clarke to stitch the two elements together into one grand design.

Days of Future Passed begins with the sound of a gong played backwards, which will mirror the same gong sound played forward at the close of the record. The opening sound is a slow fade-in that conjures the emptiness of space. It grows in velocity and volume, before abruptly being cut off by a tense note held by a symphony, wavering in intensity like a suspenseful moment in a film noir. The music stretches out, twirling and swirling around like cartoon butterflies and birds; the Moody Blues have traded in their deep-south rhythm and blues style for an idyllic pastoral scene. Titled "The Day Begins," this orchestral piece stretches out across four minutes, until it's joined by Graeme Edge's ominously spoken poem about morning as the music twinkles behind him. The orchestra swirls up like mighty waves; if the opening overture sounded like Disney's *Song of the South*, then the overture's ending sounds like Disney's *Sleeping Beauty*. Either way, it doesn't rock.

Mike Pinder's "Dawn: Is a Feeling" is the first non-orchestra song to come in after over six minutes of prelude and it brings relief. The album suddenly becomes solid and sure-footed, as the orchestra is sacrificed for the sounds of Pinder's Mellotron. For a song about the first rays of morning light, "Dawn is a Feeling" is oddly brooding, its soulful melody winding down into a haunting refrain: "This day will last ... a thousand years," Pinder intones, before adding slowly, "If ... you ... want ... it ... to ..." There is no joy or redemption in this morning, only a self-inflicted prison sentence. The Moodies' portion of the song doesn't resolve so much as it ends, with the orchestra seamlessly picking up the melody and seeing it out; it's like hearing a song on the radio and then stepping onto an elevator and hearing the same song continue as Muzak.

The idea that morning equates with youthfulness is not lost on the band. Ray Thomas's "The Morning: Another Morning" finds the bouncy, lilting tune of the melody matched with the children prancing in its lyric. Rhymes and images are stacked up like blocks in a kaleidoscopic tour of toys and games. The singer notes how time stands still for a child, which is another way of saying that the day can last a thousand years. Childhood becomes its own lost world, locked away forever yet ever-present while it was there, like a dream.

The following song, John Lodge's "Lunch Break: Peak Hour," is the hardest rocking song on the album. But before we reach this song, we have to make our way through what sounds like music for a choreographed water ballet from an old television special. When "Peak Hour" comes in, it kicks like little else on the album, employing an explosive guitar riff powered by Edge's rumbling drums. It only lets up during a pensive psychedelic bridge, in which the singer wants to run out and tell the crowds of people that "I've got time." Again, we have the idea of time standing still—this time, sung by one person to a faceless crowd. The album's first side ends with the Moodies' crashing close on "Peak Hour," with no orchestral music following it. For a moment, it feels like a normal rock album.

Perhaps even more surprisingly, the album's second side also begins with no orchestra. The album's first true classic, Justin Hayward's "The Afternoon: Forever Afternoon (Tuesday?)" begins with Pinder's suspended Mellotron leading the way into the song's central Eastern-tinged spinning riff. Hayward remembered that "Tuesday Afternoon" "was just about searching for some kind of enlightenment ... I didn't really mean it to be taken too seriously, but six months later, there it was: Our first single in America."[9] Hayward's song takes its cue from the Beatles' "A Day in the Life," as its mystic opening section coasts into a jaunty bridge that deftly shifts the mood from a daydream into a clock factory. "It's just the kind of day to leave myself behind," the singer announces, using the day to inspire his own psychological journey.

This segues into John Lodge's haunting "Time to Get Away." The power of the acoustic guitar is surprising and finds a willing partner with the piano. "Evening has earned its place today," the singer laments, as though the misery of the workday has willed the evening into being. The song finds escape in its psychedelic refrain, with Edge tumbling away on the drums. The swelling falsetto bridge only adds to the feel, until the whole thing abruptly fades out on one last refrain, killed off by the swooning sparkle of the London Festival Orchestra.

Pinder's "The Sunset" leads us through the transition from light to dark in an almost raga-like tempo, with what sounds like Eastern Indian percussion accenting the decidedly psychedelic sound. "The Sunset" takes itself so seriously that it comes close to being a parody of hippie music. The London Festival Orchestra rescues the song with swooning passages that add new layers of depth. Ray Thomas's following "Twilight Time" picks up the narrative with a driving feel that is at once comforting and disorienting. For once, a song on *Days of Future Passed* fails to reach the album's grasp. Ironically, the album's weakest song in turn unleashes its most effective use of the orchestra. The strings turn the clunky refrain into a piece of sublime beauty, which itself spins into a bittersweet, haunting passage where the melody is suspended like ghosts across the plucked strings of cold pines.

The orchestra plays a brief introduction before the music lands on the slow, churning drum pattern of the album's final, finest, and most famous song, Hayward's "Nights in White Satin." For all of the song's supposed symbolism, its origin was quite literal. Hayward later explained how "a previous girlfriend had bought me some white satin sheets. I was at the end of one big love affair and was at the beginning of another, and there were a lot of random thoughts by a nineteen-year-old boy. There's quite a lot of truth in it. I did write letters, never meaning to send."[10] For an album about the passage of time, "Nights in White Satin" has an oddly lingering feel, a moment of suspended animation with no beginning or end. Despite its relatively simple melody and arrangement, the song wields an unseemly power, especially in the crescendo refrains that turn a plaintive ballad into an avalanche. For the first and only time on the album, the London Festival Orchestra and the Moodies play in unison, and the album's formal concept of blending rock and classical is fully realized.

"Nights in White Satin" is such a complete and powerful statement that the final three minutes of the album that follow feel arbitrary. The orchestra steps in and brings the song to a close by repeating its themes before delivering an over-the-top crescendo like the end scene of a 1950s psychological thriller. The music parts way for a closing poem by Graeme Edge, ruing the orb that obscures the colors and leaves us to "decide which is right, and which is an illusion." The orchestra then delivers a second over-the-top crescendo, which closes the album like a late-night B-movie, smugly writing over the last shot: "The End?" And then the album ends with the opening gong sound played forwards, bringing the cycle of the day to a close.

The label was less than impressed. According to the band members, the Decca brass hated the album. Some speculate they were expecting Dvořák-'n'-roll and felt swindled by the final product; others claim that they were baffled by a rock record that you couldn't dance to. According to Edge, they only entertained releasing it when someone pointed out they already sunk £25,000 into it. Luckily for the Moodies, Decca A&R head Hugh Mendl and Walt McGuire, the vice-president of Decca's American branch, understood what they were trying to do and saved the record from neglect. Mendl contributed liner notes that were pitched between self-congratulatory praise and a commercial for the Deramic Sound System technology: "In *Days of Future Passed* the Moody Blues have at last done what many others have dream of and talked about: they have extended the range of pop music and found the point where it becomes one with the world of classics." If *Sgt. Pepper* suggested high art, *Days of Future Passed* literally declared it. The notes brag about how DSS sound allows the listener to become "totally submerged—and hence totally committed to such a deeply emotional statement of the human condition today."

Above these words was a photo of the Moody Blues hunched around a table along with producer Tony Clarke and engineer Derek Varnals. On the table are various books and notepads—along with an open volume showing the phases of the moon. They look less like a rock band making a record than a board meeting huddling over marketing strategy. One reason for the unusual candid photograph was that everything was happening very quickly. The Moodies recorded the album over nine days in late October, followed by Knight and the London Festival Orchestra, who recorded all of their parts in a single day. Eight days after that, the album was mixed, given its hideous abstract cover (Hayward: "I find that artwork quite difficult to look at, to be honest . . ."), and was in stores by Armistice Day.[11]

For all the ink spilled about *Days of Future Passed* being a collaboration between rock and classical music, the two genres largely sit side-by-side of each other, as opposed to fully immersed. "The Moody Blues' *Days of Future Passed* (1967) has perennially been lauded as an early fusion of classical and rock music, but it was nothing of the sort," explains Mike Barnes in *A New Day Yesterday: UK Progressive Rock & The 1970s*. "Indeed, the most noticeable aspect of the album is the almost complete lack of fusion of rock and classical music, except on brief sections of 'Nights in White Satin.' The group were never in the same room as the orchestra, and Peter Knight's orchestral interludes, composed and recorded separately, have the punch and gloss of TV and film soundtrack music at odds with the group's songs."[12] Others heard soundtrack music in the album, too. A rare contemporary American review called it a "'total album' concept, employing serious forms..."[13] The reviewer held that the Moodies had come off fine, but the orchestra sounded like a film soundtrack playing Moody Blues covers.

For many people today, *Days of Future Passed* is best remembered for "Nights in White Satin." The song eventually became a major hit, and for many, the defining song of the Moodies' long career. *Days of Future Passed* entered the US charts in May 1968 and stayed for the next five years, eventually peaking at #3 in 1972. Although "Nights in White Satin" was first released as a single when the album first came out, it was now re-released as a single five years later, peaking at #2 *Billboard*'s Hot 100 and #9 in the UK. For all of the song's success, Hayward feigns indifference: "I sometimes hear it on the radio, and I think, 'Nothing's happening!' I never really got why it was a hit."[14]

Yet the album it appeared on was arguably the first concept album to be conceived as focused on one singular story, and by extension, a clear journey on which it took the listener. This was the promise of the LSD experience realized by music in a new and influential way. If *Sgt. Pepper* remains locked in its time, then *Days of Future Passed* remained ahead of it, fitting in much better commercially in the early 1970s than in the heady days of the 1960s. It is a vital touchstone for stereo production, proto-progressive rock, and, in time, the concept album itself.

Notes

1 Davies, 291.
2 Goldstein, 104.
3 Powell, 4.
4 Runtagh.
5 Cushman, 135.
6 Ibid., 147.
7 Runtagh.
8 Cushman, 148.
9 Beard.

10 *Uncut.*
11 Beard.
12 Barnes, 87.
13 Donnelly, B-3.
14 *Uncut.*

3

We Are the Other People:
We're Only in It for the Money

Frank Zappa was one of the most iconoclastic voices in rock and roll. Disgusted by contemporary American normalcy, Zappa and his band, the Mothers of Invention, sought refuge with the freaks. At the dawn of the psychedelic era, "freak" was originally the term for any kind of hippie in southern California (or it was often used as a modifier, such as a "hippie freak" or "Jesus freak"), but by the time Zappa moved to Los Angeles in the mid-'60s, freaks were forming their own subset. With his long black hair, bushy black mustache, thick soul patch, deadpan voice, and uncompromising music, he fit in with the freaks if only because he fit in nowhere else. The freaks were a counter to the counterculture, a sort of counter-counterculture. For Zappa, the so-called hippie counterculture was already "a commercial joke" because by the time it "was recognized by the US media, it had already been absorbed by corporations. I think if there's a real counter-culture it should exist … I'm not against counter-culture, I'm against things that are *fake*."[1] Meanwhile, the Mothers of Invention became *the* freak band in Los Angeles, and Zappa used his music as a vehicle for his freak vision.

In the fall of 1967, the Mothers made their British debut at the Royal Albert Hall to rave reviews. In *Melody Maker*, Nick Jones noted that "very few people can have avoided Zappa's verbal or musical axe. The Supremes and 'Baby Love' was the subject of much hilarity, so too the Doors, so too most of American society, flower power, and finally the Mothers quite happily send up both themselves and their audience."[2] Unbeknownst to Jones, his words not only described the show he had witnessed, but also the album that the Mothers were recording on either side of their trip to England. It would be Zappa's masterpiece, a scathing satire of hippie and American culture that tore them both apart.

By this point, the Beatles' *Sgt. Pepper's Lonely Hearts Club Band* towered over the rock scene, but Zappa wasn't impressed. "*Sgt. Pepper* was okay," he later said, "but just the whole aroma of what the Beatles were was something that never really caught my fancy. I got the impression from what was going on at the time that they were only in it for the money—and that was a pretty unpopular view to hold."[3] Zappa's cynicism was reflective of a fundamental difference between the mood of American and British mid-1960s culture. By the time George Harrison traveled to Haight-Ashbury in August 1967, he was expecting the hippies "all to be nice and clean and friendly and happy." Instead, he found "hideous, spotty little teenagers"; he further described the afternoon as "living in a Hieronymus Bosch painting."[4] Indeed, had *Sgt. Pepper* "been created in America," mused Beatles historian Ian MacDonald, "where the clash between and counterculture was violent, Sergeant Pepper would have been a reactionary pig, Lovely Rita an uptight bureaucrat. The Beatles, their age-prejudice dissolved by LSD, were having none of this. Theirs was an optimistic, *holistic* view."[5]

The Mothers of Invention's *We're Only in It for the Money* was the American *Sgt. Pepper's Lonely Hearts Club Band*. Released on March 4, 1968, while *Sgt. Pepper* was still lodged in the American Top 20, it was a rock and roll *Bride of Frankenstein*—a sequel that, in sending up its source material, actually improved it. The album's artwork was the giveaway. Its original cover was supposed to be a direct parody of the Beatles' already-iconic album cover, only with all of *Sgt. Pepper*'s glamorous Hollywood stars and spiritual gurus replaced by a freak show of controversial political figures (President Lyndon Johnson—twice!), pop culture celebrities (Jimi Hendrix—in the flesh!), infamous media icons (Lee Harvey Oswald being shot!), and of course, freaks (Max Schreck as Nosferatu—twice!), many with black bars over their eyes. Unlike the artistic collage that had been done for *Sgt. Pepper*'s surreal crowd, this version felt far more crude, a child's cut-and-paste job of the of the polished original. At the center was the Mothers of Invention, cross-dressed and stunned, holding the whole thing together.

But this image wasn't allowed to be on the cover, Zappa always maintained, because Paul McCartney refused to grant him permission to do it. Years later, McCartney claimed otherwise: "I never understood why Zappa blamed me for not being able to use the *Sgt. Pepper* sleeve ... I don't think EMI would have stopped them, or even could have stopped them."[6] Zappa's artistic loss was his album's conceptual gain—instead of using his faux-*Pepper* cover photo on the outside, he hid it on the inside, inverting *Sgt. Pepper*'s artwork. Now, the inside gatefold of the Beatles album—the Beatles dressed in Sgt. Pepper suits against a bright yellow background—became Zappa's outer front and back cover, only with the Mothers wearing dresses against the same bright yellow background. Like the music it held, the artwork of *We're Only in It for the Money* literally turned *Sgt. Pepper* inside-out.

Just as *Sgt. Pepper*'s cover seemingly united the international, countercultural hippie community, the hidden inside cover of *We're Only in It for the Money* brought together a secret community, a community that, like the traveling freak shows that had all but died out by the time of *Money*'s release, spoke to a periphery world that existed on the cusp of something far more celebrated. All put together, *We're Only in It for the Money* was as much a call-to-arms to the freaks as *Sgt. Pepper* was to the hippies. Freaks can be heard everywhere in the music, as Zappa sped up and overdubbed his own voice to create a chorus of freaks to sing the songs, which gave the effect of weird voices singing his childlike ditties with him. The closest parallel was the famous banquet scene of Tod Browning's 1932 film *Freaks*. "We will make you one of us!" the freaks chant to initiate the "normal" trapeze artist Cleopatra into their clan upon her wedding to their fellow freak, a dwarf named Hanz, but Cleopatra rejects their fraternity outright. When the freaks later learn she has married Hanz to poison him and steal his money, their "offend one, offend all" code is broken. They band against Cleopatra, turning her into a wretched bird-woman, which made her into what she had been all along—*the ugliest freak of them all*.

Part of what makes *Freaks* so fascinating is that Browning went against the wishes of the studio that funded it—MGM, the most glamorous studio of them all, which was also the parent company that released *We're Only in It for the Money* thirty-six years later—and made a film that was sympathetic to the freaks' point of view. Initially, this killed all commercial potential for the film as well as Browning's Hollywood career. But by the 1960s, the film was reclaimed by radical young agitators like Zappa (who ranked *Freaks* among his favorite films), while its stars became cult legends. But one freak, the legless "Living Half-Boy" Johnny Eck, wanted nothing to do with such newfound acclaim after his house was robbed by two men in the late 1980s, one of whom took his belongings while the other reportedly pinned him down by sitting on him. "If I want to see freaks," he said shortly before he died in early 1991, "all I have to do is look out the window."[7]

The first side of *We're Only in It for the Money* looks out the window onto the country's ugly landscape. The album begins with the sound collage "Are You Hung Up?" in which the voice of God (or, as he liked to be called, Eric Clapton) tries to come on to a girl by speaking hippie gibberish over random electric noises until the tape gets eaten up and the voice of the album's recording engineer Gary Kellgren whispers like a mad scientist in an echo chamber:

> *One of these days I am going to erase every tape in the world ... All the Frank Zappa masters ... nothing ... blank, empty space ...*
>
> *Hello, Frank Zappa!*

A loud, sputtering motor sounds, spinning out an electric guitar flourish that turns into a gurgling B-movie monster's laugh, itself broken by the Mothers' drummer saying—

"Hi boys and girls, I'm Jimmy Carl Black and I'm the Indian of the group!"

—and then, someone's low, nervous laughter.

The bright shining music of "Who Needs the Peace Corps?" appears, which, like much of the music on this album, seems more straightforward than it is. The churning rock music doubles upon itself and forms a dense network of interconnected guitars, horns, and percussion, sort of a freak incarnation of Phil Spector's Wall of Sound. Every instrument seems to be playing a melody or countermelody interwoven with every other instrument, all knit together and progressing at a stuttering, off-kilter time signature. When Zappa's detached and mocking sing-song vocals appear, they skewer the hippie scene. The singer goes to San Francisco, walks past the wig store, dances at the Filmore, and announces he's really just a phony who is stoned. Over the extended coda, Zappa interjects some of his own hippie patter: "First I'll buy some beads, and then perhaps a leather band to around my head ... I will love everyone. I will love the police as they kick the shit out of me on the street ..."

The hippie utopia-turned-nightmare of "Concentration Moon" features the police, too, as it likens California's counterculture scene to that of a Nazi-like police state. The music plays up the irony by taking the form of a lilting, psychedelic waltz before switching time into a militant march, culminating with:

COP KILL A CREEP!
POW! POW! POW!

And then, the whispery voice returns:

> *Tomorrow I get to do another Frank Zappa creation ... And the day after that ... And the day after that ...*

A record scratch cuts in and then—

"Hi boys and girls, I'm Jimmy Carl Black and I'm the Indian of the group!"

—before the music cascades back to the main faux-psychedelic "Concentration Moon" theme and the whole thing starts again. The whole album is like this, bizarre little ditties that are built upon or abandoned at random by any number of things—a song in a different time signature, an abstract sound collage, a recording of someone talking. It's a restless and relentless assault that is often messy and unpredictable, but no more than America itself in the late 1960s.

"Concentration Moon" shifts gears into "Mom & Dad," as the kids killed by the cops in the former song are enclosed upon a television in the latter. "They looked to weird," the Mom & Dad reassure each other, "It served them right." The end of the song brings things full-circle by Mom & Dad being told that their daughter was among the kids shot in the park. A phone rings, initiating "Telephone Conversation," a cryptic phone dialog. In its fifty-second running time, everything feels wrong—one woman warns another about being bumped off by a man with a gun, a second woman tries to relay a message from the first woman's father, the line is tapped, but no one seems to care. "Alright, your father called me up this morning . . ." begins the second woman; the first one interrupts: "Just a sec—" A tapping snare drum initiates the thirty-second vaudevillian ditty "Bowtie Daddy," which advises its subject not to stop thinkin', keep on drinkin', and then "drive home in your Lincoln." The song ends with a stop-time ending that plays like such an anachronism, you can practically see the singer get pulled off the stage by a long wooden cane around his neck; instantly piano flourishes signal "Harry, You're a Beast," a taunting assault on the female gender. And then, in a characteristic Zappa twist, the song that is cruelest to American women ends with a skit that makes the American man look even worse. The repeated line "Don't come in me," was too controversial to leave in the album, so it was played backwards, adding another hidden layer to this project.

It is here at the album's ugliest moment that it descends into its central theme, the one-minute doo-wop of "What's the Ugliest Part of Your Body?" over the standard "Earth Angel" chord changes. The singer playfully throws out options—could it be your toes, or maybe your nose?—bringing the song to the edge of a dirty joke before providing his own punch-line: *"But I think it's your mind . . ."* A huge Orwellian voice appears over a militant beat, barking information that can no longer be contained in lyrical form:

ALL YOUR CHILDREN ARE POOR UNFORTUNATE VICTIMS OF SYSTEMS BEYOND THEIR CONTROL

"What's the Ugliest Part of Your Body?" then segues into the psychedelic send-up "Absolutely Free." "The first word in this song is discorporate," Zappa's voice announces at the top, "It means to leave your body." The lyrics invite the listener to "Unbind your mind" into a world of freedom and love where one can "be absolutely free!"—all except for the telling last line: " . . . *only if you want to be.*" Foreshadowing John Lennon and Yoko Ono's iconic "WAR IS OVER! (IF YOU WANT IT)" international billboard campaign of 1969, Zappa's lyric reveals the key to his America, the source of its power and its ugliness: You are free to do whatever you want to do, but only if you let yourself.

The unhinged, spiraling ending of "Absolutely Free" falls into "Flower Punk," which takes the hippie anthem "Hey Joe" and drives it back into its garage-punk roots with searing lyrics against the hippie scene. The voices chatter on top of one another, in strange pitches and speeds, mocking hippie chatter about forming a band, making it big, and cashing in on the material successes. The whispery voice interrupts, wondering in part *"what everyone else is whispering about . . ."* A backwards tape plays the second side's "Mother People" in reverse for a few seconds before getting swallowed by a gurgling movie monster, and with that, the first side is over.

In less than twenty minutes, Zappa has taken us on a stream-of-conscious whirlwind tour of everything ugly in his contemporary American society: from the hippies to the cops to the parents to the man to the woman to the ugliest place of all—your mind—only to then "discorporate" from your mind to where you are absolutely free (but only if you want to be), and then deliver us back to the petty banality of the hippie punks. Throw in some television violence, a wiretapped telephone conversation, and a few dead kids on the street, and you've got yourself a country.

And that's just side one. If the first side of *We're Only in It for the Money* shows the freaks assessing the problems of the country-at-large, the second side finds them providing solutions from their outsider perspective. It begins with the sound electric sound collage "Nasal Retentive Calliope Music," once again featuring the voice of Eric Clapton—this time exclaiming, "Beautiful! God, it's God, I see God!"—cashing in on the famous "Clapton is God" graffiti he hated so much, while adding yet another in-joke to Zappa's record.

The wheels of time speed up, slow down, and double back on themselves, eventually morphing into a surf rock song on a transistor radio dial. The dial then interrupts the song to flip around, eventually landing on "Let's Make the Water Turn Black," a song inspired by two boys who Zappa knew in his youth who liked to preserve their bodily functions in jars. One day the boys were shocked to find that a container that had held their urine had turned black with small white creatures swimming in it, leading the kids to believe that they had created life. It's pure juvenilia, but Zappa crammed all of it and more into a tight, two-minute pop song overflowing with internal rhymes. Keeping with the radio motif, an obnoxious radio DJ interrupts the end of the song with some nonsense patter, which itself is cut off by the babbling roar of a movie monster.

Next up is the mock-raga "The Idiot Bastard Son," telling the saga of the illegitimate son of a Nazi congressman and L.A. hooker who was left abandoned in a car. "You think you know everything, maybe so," goes the bridge, with the singer stepping out to point his finger at the listener, "The song we sing: do you know?" From "The Idiot Bastard Son" we go to the "Lonely Little Girl," who is neglected by parents who don't care for her, which then gives way to the "*ALL YOUR CHILDREN ARE POOR UNFORTUNATE VICTIMS*" Orwellian section last heard in "What's the Ugliest Part of Your Body."

The words echo around and around and back over themselves, creating a swell that climaxes with rapid, almost Eastern-style string picking that erupts with a belch. Peppy go-go music falls into its place with "Take Your Clothes Off When You Dance." The song is the ultimate statement American freak utopia—not just *of* speech or action, but *from* judgment and fear. So, what's the only thing preventing this from happening? "I think it's your mind," taunts Zappa in a reprise of "What's the Ugliest Part of Your Body?" a move that both mirrors and mocks the reprise of "Sgt. Pepper's Lonely Hearts Club Band." But like the freaks in *Freaks*, Zappa gets the last laugh. Sped up, chiming music plays to begin "Mother People" with the Mothers singing in a weird pitch, declaring that "We are the other people," but also that "You're the other people too!" And they're right—if the pure and free ugliness of one's mind is all one needs to join Frank Zappa's Freak Nation, then every citizen has already joined.

The final song was this ultimate test of freedom put into practice, a challenging piece called "The Chrome-Plated Megaphone of Destiny," largely consisting of random struck piano keys and electronic whirring noises. Zappa printed full instructions of what must be done once one read Kafka's *In the Penal Colony*, such as the fifth instruction, which read: "As you listen, think of the concentration camps in California constructed during the Second World War to house potentially dangerous oriental citizens … the same camps which many say [are now] readied for use as part of the FINAL SOLUTION to the NON-CONFORMIST (hippy) PROBLEM today."[8] It is a decidedly messy conclusion to a messy album—a song that suggests that the only thing uglier than the actual act of freedom is the act of restricting people from experiencing it.

And, just to throw you off one final time, in the middle of the song, sped-up cartoon voices laugh at the listener like the characters in *Freaks* chanting their way through the "one of us" initiation ritual.

We're Only in It for the Money was Frank Zappa's greatest hit up to that point, reaching #30 on the *Billboard* album charts and becoming his best-selling album until the mid-1970s. What gave the album its unique power was the way in which the hippie counterculture provided the perfect target for Zappa's already-formed ideas about rock and roll music and American culture. Zappa would spend the rest of career testing the limits of musical and political freedom, but never again would the two merge in such a way that made his music both so relevant and accessible to a mass audience.

But characteristically for Zappa, *We're Only in It for the Money* was only one of many music and film projects he had ongoing at the time, and the production delay caused by the album's artwork only slowed things down further. By the time that *We're Only in It for the Money* came out, Zappa was already off to the next thing. He moved into the sprawling estate built by the silent cowboy movie star Tom Mix, turning it into a home for all of his artistic endeavors. It was a rustic landscape that contained endless trees, a lake, and the biggest freedom of all: blank, empty space.

Notes

1 Miles, 116.
2 Gray, 83–4.
3 *Rolling Stone*.
4 Giuliano, 80.
5 MacDonald, 185.
6 Miles, 151.
7 Lammle.
8 Walley, 91.

4

The One That Rambles on for a Million Miles: *Electric Ladyland*

"I'm American," Jimi Hendrix told a British reporter in the summer of 1968. "I want people there to see me. I also wanted to see whether we could make it back in the States. I dig Britain, but I haven't really got a home anywhere." He continued in the words of a rambler: "The earth's my home. I've never had a house here. I don't want to put down roots in case I get restless and want to move on. I'll only get into the house thing when I'm certain I won't want to move again."[1] He was, as he sang in the B-side of his first single, stone free until he died. For Hendrix, his music was his home.

Generally considered the greatest guitarist in rock and roll, Hendrix founded the Jimi Hendrix Experience in England with bassist Noel Redding and drummer Mitch Mitchell—both British—and together they created a psychedelic sound that catapulted Hendrix to the forefront of rock and roll. Their songs were like dispatches from outer space, alien in sound and bottomless in depth, whether the effect was ominous ("Hey Joe"), explosive ("Purple Haze"), or contemplative ("The Wind Cries Mary"). This was true acid rock—each song was its own trip. Hendrix's first two albums, *Are You Experienced* and *Axis: Bold as Love*, both from 1967, reimagined the limits of rock and roll's sonic depth and texture, while showing he could craft a masterful album. In 1968, Hendrix received unlimited studio time and acted as his own producer for the first time. Whenever Hendrix wasn't on the road, he spent hours buried in the studio, crafting his transcendent music. Released in October as the double-album *Electric Ladyland*, Hendrix put out the most uncompromised and sophisticated album of his career.

"Yeah, that whole LP means so much, you know," Hendrix told an interviewer in early 1969. "It wasn't just slopped together. Every little thing that you hear on there means something, you know. It's no game that we're playing trying to blow the public's mind or so forth, it's a thing that we really, really mean, you know, it's a part of us, another part of us."[2] Hendrix also said that he only got half of what he wanted to say on it—and would need two more records to include everything he wanted to.

Like many other double albums of this era, such as the Beatles' self-titled "White Album" (released one month later), *Electric Ladyland* was a sprawling, messy affair that many found too long and unfocused. To some, it implied a concept album without quite getting there. "Hendrix is a good musician, and his science fiction concepts surmount noise," Tony Glover wrote in his review for *Rolling Stone*. "There isn't really a concept (no *Sgt. Pepper* trips here)—instead there's a unity, an energy flow."[3] Barret Hansen grasped at the same issue in *Hit Parader*: "The four sides are lettered A, B, C and D; it seems obvious that Jimi meant them to be played in that order. Though this is not exactly a 'concept' album, the order of the cuts makes more sense, emotionally and musically, than that of any other album I know."[4] Yet Glover's "unity" and "energy flow" and Hansen's "order" making sense "emotionally and musically" are key to what indeed makes this a concept album. *Electric Ladyland* comprises of four mini-suites, which make four different listening experiences, four different journeys that Hendrix takes the listener on. I hear each album side corresponding to an ancient element, with each side representing "Earth," "Wind," "Water," and "Fire." This helps give the album order and shape, which allows each song to jump out individually, while reinforced by the album's greater context; all four sides combine to make a new world.

Beginning with a cryptic, experimental track of thundering drums, delayed voices, and spiraling supernatural effects, the album began by instantly challenging the listener; never one for understatement, Hendrix titled the brief sound collage "...And the Gods Made Love." Hendrix told *Melody Maker* that it was "an attempt to give a sound picture of the heavens," before noting: "I know it's the thing people will jump on to criticize so we're putting it right at the beginning to get it over with."[5] The song is both a holy incantation and a throwing down of the gauntlet.

After hearing the sounds of the gods making love (Hendrix: "or whatever they spend their time on"), the album's first side ("Earth") finds Hendrix mapping out his terrain, beginning with its national anthem "Have You Ever Been (to Electric Ladyland)?"[6] Hendrix often used the term "electric ladies" for his female groupies after a gig, turning the album from the sacred to the profane.[7] We then go from the lush countryside of the title track to the crowded city streets of "Crosstown Traffic." The song finds Hendrix joining the great American tradition of sexualized car songs—which at least begins with Robert Johnson's 1936 recording of "Terraplane Blues"—and reclaims it for the blues, taking the spirit of early rock and R&B and filtering it through his own acid rock. As with his best moments on record, Hendrix creates an enormous sound for "Crosstown Traffic," the sonic equivalent of lying down in the middle of an interstate highway.

A smattering of applause links "Crosstown Traffic" to the next song, "Voodoo Chile." Clocking in at fifteen minutes, "Voodoo Chile" is the longest song on the album, a slow and simmering blues featuring Traffic's Steve Winwood on organ and Jefferson Airplane's Jack Cassady on bass, along with Mitch Mitchell taking his usual seat behind the drums. Hendrix uses his guitar to become a superhuman of the earth, stomping across the land wherever and however he sees fit. Unlike most modern blues, Hendrix's song doesn't cycle through the usual chord changes, but instead stays on the one tonic chord, harkening back to the earliest blues singers around the turn of the twentieth century. The subject matter reaches back even further.

According to Eugene D. Genovese's *Roll, Jordan, Roll: The World the Slaves Made*, voodoo peaked as a religion in the mid-nineteenth century and never caught on much outside of New Orleans, despite its saturation into the popular vernacular: "Voodoo remained peripheral to the slave experience, but as its reputation and fragments of its practice spread, they strengthened the slaves' commitment to the folk aspect of their religion and their sense of being in the hands of powers other than those of the whites."[8] By declaring himself a "Voodoo Chile," Hendrix taps into the greater mystique of slave folk culture—just around when "rock" increasingly was seen as white music while Black music was syphoned off as "R&B" or "soul." As someone who cut his teeth in Little Richard's backing band, Hendrix knew that race had nothing to do with genre. Hendrix was a rare Black singer who couldn't be called soul or R&B—he played straight-up hard rock. His "Voodoo Chile" fluctuates sonically while varying in tempo, at one point spinning into a freeform jam that finally recedes until Hendrix picks it back up again and brings it home to his hulking blues lick. The Voodoo Chile has been reborn, and not for the last time on the album.

The second side of the album ("Wind") is both the album's most conventional part—five three-and-a-half minute pop songs—and its least successful. Hendrix chose to start the side with "Little Miss Strange," the album's token track by Experience bassist Noel Redding, whom Hendrix allowed to compose and sing lead on one song per album. While "Little Miss Strange" allows us the rare chance to hear Hendrix's talent as a sideman ("But what a sideman!" declares John Perry in his 33⅓ series volume about the album), it kicks off an unmemorable set of songs: the solid but unexceptional "Long Hot Summer Night" and Hendrix's psychedelic reworking of the R&B chestnut "Come on (And Let the Good Times Roll)."[9]

Things pick up with the driving "Gypsy Eyes," which, building on a two-headed ambush on drums and guitar, has a distinctly airy feel. It is also the most explicit track about rambling, with the singer going down the girl's "rebel roadside," which "rambles a million miles." The endless road is a motif often heard in blues songs, most notably in Tommy Johnson's "Big Road Blues" from 1928, Charley Patton's "Down the Dirt Road Blues" from 1929, Robert Johnson's "Stones in My Passway" from 1937, and Floyd Jones' "Dark Road" from 1952. All are songs by Black men who stare down a road that is insurmountable, unknowable. In "Gypsy Eyes," the road does not feel as daunting—it's where he'll find his girl's love and his own soul—and rambling a million miles is nothing if you're already heading to space.

The second side peaks with "Burning of the Midnight Lamp," an epic, searing song that builds endlessly on itself, reaching higher and higher into the atmosphere of its own momentum. It was first released as a UK single between Hendrix's first two albums but was unknown to American audiences. At the time, it was Hendrix's most sophisticated production yet, and it more than holds its own on *Electric Ladyland*. But its previous incarnation as a single (as well as the subsequent disappearance of its master tape) explains why it doesn't sound like anything else on the record—in an album filled with expansive, swaying tracks, "Burning of the Midnight Lamp" sounds uncharacteristically dense and compact. But the song's kinetic energy rises like a mountain coming out of the sea, encouraged by the swirling angelic choir of female backing vocals, reaching a crescendo each time the singer reaches his midnight lamp. He guards the light like it was a newborn, ruminating on the isolation of his task. "*Loneliness,*" the singer announces midway through the song, "*is such a . . . drag.*"

Electric Ladyland's third side ("Water") is its most ambitious. Water is everywhere, flowing through the songs like interconnected rivers. Beginning the suite is "Rainy Day, Dream Away," built around a laid-back jazz groove. Hendrix hired the Serfs, a late-night jazz club band, to back him on the recording. Freed up from having to record most of the instruments himself, Hendrix flashes a rare comic side on the album, overdubbing himself in a stoned dialog.

"Rainy Day, Dream Away" recedes into the album's centerpiece, the thirteen-minute-plus "1983 (A Merman I Should Turn to Be)." Sounds suggest the gray haze of a foggy beach. Out of this emerges the song's main guitar riff—an elegant, stately melody that reaches out and pulls back into itself like the waves breaking on the shore, controlled by the rolling tide of a marching drum. The singer wakes up with his lover to take their final walk from the land to the sea, "not to die," he tells us, "but to be reborn" into an underwater world. And then something remarkable happens. When the song's protagonists go into the water, they take the album with them, and for a few minutes, everything disappears into a suspended aural seascape. The swishing patter of the high-hat cymbals sway from one side to the other, as Hendrix turns his guitar into an oceanfront, filled with swirling sea mist, clanging boats, and cawing seagulls—a seascape so vivid that you can smell the salt air. Hendrix's oceanfront feels that much more unified because it relies entirely on electric guitar wizardry to make the most elusive natural sounds; this is a song about becoming one with the ocean that becomes one with the ocean itself.

The music builds into a thrashing sea storm, but not before the singer is swimming safely underneath. They make their way into a world of Neptune's games, ushered in by a smiling mermaid; the music takes over and turns into a wild underwater freakout over the song's main guitar theme, before receding back into the clanging boats and cawing seagulls on the water's shore. "Moon, Turn the Tides ... Gently, Gently" provides a brief conclusion to the suite, a sound collage of otherworldly, wispy sounds that go from the rolling waves up into the outer reaches of space, where all water is pulled by the gentle tides of a heavenly moon.

Once you flip the record to its final side, "Rainy Day, Dream Away" is reprised as "Still Raining, Still Dreaming." It's largely the same groove and words, only this time played by a rock and roll band, as though Hendrix followed a lighter jazz sound into his rainy dream, but now awakes in his fully formed hard rock world. The song gets a bucket of water ready for the album's final three tracks ("Fire"), which forsake the side three's underwater dreamland for a world doused in flames.

Hendrix clears the ground with the blistering hard rock guitar intro for "House Burning Down," which coalesces into a strutting, relentless groove that marches ahead like a military regime. "Look at the sky turn a hellfire red!" the singer cries out, like he's witnessing a biblical punishment. "House Burning Down" is the closest thing to a protest song that Hendrix ever wrote, reportedly under pressure from both his African American fans and his record company. The result is a song that shows Hendrix acquiescing to their demands, but only to an extent. For every line of token liberal wisdom—"Try to learn instead of burn, hear what I say"—Hendrix throws in another psychedelic riddle, epitomized by the song's bizarre coda in which a giant boat from space comes down and takes away all of the dead people.

As strong as "House Burning Down" is, it's merely the warm-up for "All Along the Watchtower," Hendrix's finest moment on record. The song was first written and recorded by Bob Dylan, who included it on his mystical acoustic album *John Wesley Harding*. Hendrix took a stirring folk song and re-imagined it as a psychedelic explosion of Old Testament wrath. Taking its origin from a passage in the Bible (Isaiah 21:7-9), the song spins a parable about a joker and a thief riding to a princess in the watchtower. Hendrix sings Dylan's lyrics coolly, relaying the mysterious dialogue between the joker and the thief, with guitar playing that was just as mysterious, rich, and expressive as the words surrounding it. In an extended solo between verses, Hendrix fluctuates between different guitar sounds, at one point pulling the song down with electric slide guitar, before picking it up again with a scribbly, funky part that throws the song back up to an even higher level. By the time that Hendrix gets to the closing lyric of the wind beginning to howl, he's screaming, and then unleashes a searing guitar solo that burns anything not already reduced to ashes.

For the final song on *Electric Ladyland*, Hendrix reprises the first side's extended blues jam, renaming it "Voodoo Child (Slight Return)." This time, the song is pure hard rock with Hendrix's guitar setting off fireworks every which way. In an economy of lyrics, Hendrix evokes a man with otherworldly voodoo power. He gives us the most vivid words he would ever write, declaring he can "stand up next to a mountain" and chop "it down with the edge of my hand." What helps to make the line so powerful is Hendrix's conviction when he sings it. Unlike many of his other vocals where Hendrix employs an offhanded detachment, in "Voodoo Child (Slight Return)," he doesn't so much sing the lyrics as he conquers them; when the song explodes into the transcendent refrain where the singer proclaims himself a voodoo child, you already believe him.

The only element of *Electric Ladyland* that Hendrix didn't maintain full artistic control over was its cover. His UK label took it upon themselves to interpret the title as sophomorically as possible and rounded up nineteen women to pose nude for a wrap-around front cover. The result was a poorly lit photograph that made the women look weird and disfigured. As one of the women told *Melody Maker*, "It makes us look like a load of old prostitutes. It's rotten. Everyone looked great but the pictures makes [sic] us look old and tired."[10] It was a cheap grab for publicity for an album that didn't need one. Hendrix distanced himself from the cover and reached out to his American label, giving them strict instructions on the album layout and art, including a cover photograph of his group surrounded by kids on Central Park's Alice in Wonderland statue. While the label followed some of Hendrix's ideas about the layout, they completely ignored his front cover request and instead used an evocative red and yellow close-up of Hendrix's face on stage. While still not what Hendrix wanted, it was far better than the UK cover. It was larger-than-life and he looked like just emerged from the fiery landscape of *Electric Ladyland*'s final side.

Initial reviews of the album were mixed. Some critics loved it, but many more found it baffling, meandering, or putting psychedelic wizardry over musical quality. Perhaps the most telling review came from Geffrey Cannon in *The Guardian*. "[Hendrix] has lost interest in the news, in the time-dimension," Cannon writes. "Now, he has put himself in a capsule. *Electric Ladyland* is the diary of a traveller [sic] far out in space."[11] In this way, *Electric Ladyland* catches Hendrix as both an inheritor of his rambling blues influences like Robert Johnson and Muddy Waters, as well as a pioneer of the Afrofuturism movement that was yet to come, which mixed Black music with futuristic science fiction narratives. But more on that later. Suffice to say now that Hendrix claimed he didn't have a home anywhere, took the form of a voodoo child, and used *Electric Ladyland* as his travelogue into realms unknown, where there was no distinction between outer space and his own inner space.

Notes

1 Potash, 16–17.
2 Fairchild, 6.
3 Glover.
4 Hansen, 53.
5 Fairchild, 8.
6 Potash, 16.
7 Cross, 238.
8 Genovese, 220.
9 Perry, 82.
10 *Melody Maker*, 6.
11 Cannon.

5

Amazing Journey: *Tommy*

For many in the 1960s, the Woodstock Festival was the defining moment of its era. Opening with Richie Havens and closing three days later with Jimi Hendrix, a who's who of late-1960s rock played in between, including Janis Joplin, Sly and the Family Stone, Grateful Dead, Creedence Clearwater Revival, and Jefferson Airplane, among many others. It was the ultimate destination for a generation of journeyers, but not everyone was impressed. Pete Townshend, the leader of the Who, had be coaxed into playing the festival; nearly two decades later, he still felt the burn. "When you look back at the flower-power era, it all looks daft," he told *Rolling Stone* in 1987, "I feel particularly cynical, because I thought it was daft at the time. I didn't like Haight-Ashbury. I didn't like Abbie Hoffman. I didn't like Timothy Leary, and I didn't like Woodstock."[1]

The Who built their set around a three-month-old "rock opera" called *Tommy*, which told the rise and fall of a pinball-playing blind, deaf, and dumb boy who becomes a spiritual martyr. The Who was at the height of their powers—Pete Townshend slashing chords on his guitar like a windmill, singer Roger Daltrey whipping his microphone cord like a lasso, Keith Moon attacking his drums with restless fervor, and bassist John Entwistle standing like a statue in the eye of the storm. But as something more than just a rock performance, album, or opera, *Tommy* positioned the Who at the forefront of rock's artistic elite.

After establishing themselves as a great singles band with "My Generation," "Substitute," and 'The Kids Are Alright," the Who made their first bid for rock artistry in late 1966. They released a nine-minute "mini-rock opera" called "A Quick One, While He's Away," an extended medley of songs into a tale of earthly infidelity and heavenly forgiveness that freely mixed British music hall and the American West. For the Who's next album, *The Who Sell Out*, Townshend crafted a loving tribute to British pirate radio—complete with fake advertising jingles in between the songs. Although the concept fizzles out halfway through the second side, it was one of the first major concept albums when it came out in December 1967. Townshend later wrote: "Despite its ambition, some poor material . . . was included in the half-cooked package ... our album seemed potentially brilliant but ultimately inconclusive."² He was sure never to go halfway again.

Townshend threw himself into the Who's next project, spending much of the next year in the studio and working out his ideas in interviews like they were therapy sessions. "We've been talking about doing an opera, we've been talking about doing albums, we've been talking about a whole lot of things," he explained to *Rolling Stone* in mid-1968. "We've condensed all of these ideas, all this energy and all these gimmicks, and whatever we've decided on for future albums, into one juicy package. The package I hope is going to be called *Deaf, Dumb and Blind Boy*. It's a story about a kid who's born deaf, dumb and blind and what happens to him throughout his life."³

When the Who finally released *Tommy* in May 1969, the album was a major breakthrough. If not the first proper album-length rock opera (that distinction usually goes to the Pretty Things' 1968 rock opera *S.F. Sorrow*), then it was the first major one, as well as the first rock and roll album to be executed as a self-contained narrative story. Unlike *Days of Future Passed*, where the songs were linked by the times of day, *Tommy* found the story driving the structure, as opposed to the other way around. Furthermore, the album was a smash on both sides of the Atlantic—#2 in the UK and #4 in the US—and was the most ambitious concept album up to its time.

Over the course of two vinyl records, *Tommy* tells a rock and roll version of the Greatest Story Ever Told. Beginning with the "Overture," the Who create the story's landscape as they play it, separating the highs from the lows, tearing the sky from the ground, building soaring mountains with one melody, providing low valleys with another. Several key musical motifs are introduced, highlighted by John Entwistle's French horn, a blaring Hammond organ, and Pete Townshend's defiant guitar chords. Into this landscape they bring Tommy, a small boy who accidentally witnesses his father murdering his mother's wartime lover. In frantic shock, Tommy's mother tells him that he didn't see it, he didn't hear it, and he can never speak of it. This makes him blind, deaf, and dumb, as the trauma cuts him off from the rest of the world and seals him into his own.

"Tommy was deaf, dumb, and blind, and he experienced life completely through vibration," singer Roger Daltrey wrote in his autobiography. "I just loved that. Music is vibration. That's the whole point. It was an abstract idea, but I knew there was something in it and I just went with it." Daltrey remembers it being a group effort. "People tend to forget that Pete didn't write the whole of *Tommy*. It was his inspiration, but it was about as collaborative as anything we ever did. It wasn't all formed at the start ... The story kept changing. Fragments of songs grew into whole plot lines. It was like putting a jigsaw together with no picture, no straight edges, and half the pieces missing, but it was completely absorbing."[4]

If we close our eyes and listen to *Tommy*, we can internally create Tommy's inner body with our own inner body, turning ourselves into a shell filled with Tommy's strange, winding music. This concept is introduced through the song "Amazing Journey," in which sickness takes the mind to "learn all you should know." The creation of Tommy's internal world is described as sensations causing notes in his symphony, with Tommy becoming the leader and guide. The following instrumental "Sparks" establishes Tommy's internal world much like the "Overture" established his world's outside landscape, only with light, color, and sensation in the place of natural formations. The song engulfs us, roaring with authority, tensing up like a roller coaster, and then stretching out as John Entwistle's bass swirls around Pete Townshend's guitar chords like a double helix.

Once Tommy's mystic inner world is established, the album returns to the harsh outer world. "The Hawker" rewrites the old Sonny Boy Williamson blues "Eyesight for the Blind" to demonstrate how the hawker's claim about a woman's loving can't save Tommy. However, *Tommy*'s finest moments are when Tommy's inner-world meets the outer-world. This first occurs in "Christmas," comprised of breathless verses sung by Tommy's father and a refrain sung with cruel exasperation: "Tommy doesn't know what day it is!" His father sees no way for Tommy to be saved. But unbeknownst to his father, Tommy already has the answer, which he sings in a high, melancholy refrain:

> See me, feel me
> Touch me, heal me

But Tommy's message is lost on the outside world, as "Christmas" closes with his father still wondering how the boy will be saved.

We then return to the outside world: there's the dreadful song "Cousin Kevin" (since when do tough bullies sing drawn-out, cloying melodies in multi-part falsetto harmonies?), who physically abuses his young cousin, and "The Acid Queen," another sham healer who offers hallucinogenic drugs. The Gypsy Queen's journey leaves Tommy with his hands clinching and his body writhing—and still blind, deaf, and dumb. Then it's onto Tommy's acid trip through the dark and brooding sea of "Underture," which is little more than an endless rehash of the musical theme of "Rael," an album track from *The Who Sell Out*, which the Who had already explored in the instrumental "Sparks." The nine minutes of "Underture" makes for an underwhelming close to *Tommy*'s first record.

At first, the second record of *Tommy* is more of the same—in "Do You Think It's Alright?" his parents ask each other if they should leave Tommy alone with his Uncle Ernie; they do, and in "Fiddle About," Uncle Ernie sexually molests him in a tasteless moment played broadly as a joke that hasn't aged well. But if this is the album's lowest point, it's followed by its most exciting one. Townshend's windmill-in-a-hurricane strumming initiates *Tommy*'s signature song, "Pinball Wizard," which reveals "that deaf, dumb, and blind kid" can "sure play a mean pinball." Because "Pinball Wizard" is *Tommy*'s best-known song, most people remember the whole album as being all about a deaf, dumb, and blind boy playing pinball. However, except for one minor reference to pinball before this song ("poxy pinball" in "Christmas"), this is the first time pinball is mentioned in the opera, and, with the exception of two other relatively minor references (he's called the "Pinball Wizard" in "Miracle Cure" and the crowds playing pinball in "We're Not Gonna Take It"), it will be the last. If pinball serves as more of an afterthought than a central theme, that's because it was. It was supposedly worked in to impress rock critic (and pinball freak) Nik Cohn, who found an early version of *Tommy* lackluster. But pinball is still essential to the album's story. Not only does it lighten the story, but it also solidifies *Tommy* as an opera by giving it something mystical to ground it—a rock and roll Magic Flute. Just as *Tommy* is saved by pinball, so too does pinball save *Tommy* from its dark themes and pretensions.

Right away we see the improvement. After Tommy is hailed as the "Pinball Wizard," there's a brief interlude, "There's a Doctor," in which Tommy's father announces he's found a physician who can cure him. He arrives in the storming garage rock of "Go to the Mirror, Boy!" in which the outer world meets the inner world once again. The doctor is baffled at first by his new patient, declaring him "completely unreceptive"—his eyes and ears react to his instruments, but Tommy gives no response. (Meanwhile, from his inner world, Tommy does in fact reply with the "see me, feel me" refrain of "Christmas," but it again goes unheard.) Faced with a patient with a symbolic sickness, the doctor prescribes a symbolic treatment: Go to the mirror, boy!

The father replies that he has often observed Tommy looking in the mirror dreaming, wondering "what is happening in his head"; Tommy answers him by singing a new refrain from his inner world: "Listening to you, I get the music," he can climb a mountain, and get excitement at your feet. For the first time, Tommy is established as a mystic, although the outside world doesn't realize it yet. Despite its cumbersome title, "Go to the Mirror, Boy!" is perhaps the finest song on *Tommy*, featuring a galloping riff, bold melody, and both of Tommy's main themes ("See Me" and "Listening to You"); with the exception of the "Pinball Wizard" strumming, the majestic "Overture" gets nearly all of its music from this one song.

Things start happening fast. Frustrated by Tommy's endless hours staring at himself the mirror, his mother breaks the glass in the storming "Smash the Mirror," which shatters the boundary between Tommy's two worlds. He leaves his inner world to emerge in the outside one as a "Sensation." Newsboys shout of Tommy's awakening in the interlude "Miracle Cure," and we see Tommy emerge as a spiritual icon through the eyes of "Sally Simpson," a young girl who ignites a riot the night she tries to touch him. In "I'm Free," Tommy explains his philosophy—it's simple "to reach the highest high," because "freedom tastes of reality"—but the masses all want to know how exactly they can follow. Tommy answers them with the dreary ballad "Welcome," which lifts the motto of the freaks by inviting everyone to "be one of us" in a commune utopia. When it becomes too full, Uncle Ernie announces the opening of "Tommy's Holiday Camp," with a sinister whisper of "Welcome..."

In the album's finale, "We're Not Gonna Take It," Tommy welcomes his followers to the camp, where people can experience their own Tommy-like awakening by putting on eyeshades, earplugs, mouth-corks, and play pinball. Now it's Tommy who is the charlatan healer and the masses turn on him with the rallying cry of the song's title, as they reject their fallen leader. Once again, the wall between the outside world and Tommy's inner world is raised, and the album closes with Tommy singing the "see me, feel me" refrain of "Christmas" followed by the "Listening to you, I get the music" refrain of "Go to the Mirror, Boy!" as his music serving as his own resurrection.

Upon release, *Tommy* was hailed almost as much of a sensation as its title character in the album's story. Adding the pinball factor to impress Nik Cohn certainly didn't hurt. In *The New York Times*, Cohn wrote that "the individual songs aren't really the point; it's the sum effect that's the clincher. So much stamina, such range and musical invention—this might just be the first pop masterpiece."[5] Barry Miles (using his pen name "Miles") wrote in the *International Times* that "It is impossible to praise this album too highly," seeing it as "the final step" in rock "becoming more and more of a 'fine art' in its own terms." He sees

Sgt. Pepper as only containing a "binding device," whereas "the Who have done the opposite and used the operatic form as stepping-off point for musical development, knowing that the bond is so strong that no deviations can ever weaken its cohesion . . . The Who are ahead of everyone!"[6] A rare scathing review by Richard Green for the *New Musical Express* was titled "Who's Sick Opera": "Pretentious is too strong a word; maybe over-ambitious is the right term but sick certainly does apply. One line goes 'Sickness will surely take the mind.' It does."[7] Green's review is a reminder for those who forget that this album attempts to make light of subjects such as physical abuse and sexual molestation.

So where does that leave us? At its best—songs like "Pinball Wizard," "Christmas," "Go to the Mirror, Boy!" and "We're Not Gonna Take It"—*Tommy* represents some of the finest rock and roll ever conceived, but at its worst—the awful "Cousin Kevin," the needless "Underture," and the tedious "Welcome," which together form over a fifth of the album's running time—it remains helplessly weighed down by pretension. Ultimately, *Tommy* is a bit of a wash—a two-record set which could have been easily cut down to one, leaving the remaining half tremendously improved. And in time, that's essentially what happened.

Unlike albums such as *Sgt. Pepper*, which remained locked in the studios where they were recorded, too precious to play out, *Tommy* was different. Townshend personally fought against overdubbing orchestras and choruses on the album primarily so that they could play it live upon its release.[8] The Who were first and foremost at the peak of their creative powers as a live act and it was through this setting that *Tommy* became the high art it had the potential to be. A work of equal parts inspiration and pretension, the live performances of *Tommy* from this era kept the piece what it was at its best: raw rock and roll.

For an album often misunderstood as a monument to psychedelic ideals, *Tommy* in fact is a warning *against* the use of psychedelic drugs, sex, or alcohol to find true meaning. "There was a parallel within the shape of the autistic child," Townshend once explained, "so the hero had to be deaf, dumb, and blind so that seen from our already limited point of view, his limitations would be symbolic of our own."[9] The irony of playing *Tommy* as the centerpiece of their performance at the three-day festival of peace, love, and understanding was clearly not lost on Townshend.

What the overwhelming crowd at Woodstock witnessed was a tighter, better *Tommy* than the one sold in record stores. In terms of the narrative, "The Acid Queen" went right into "Pinball Wizard," which in turn yielded the "Do You

Think It's Alright?"/"Fiddle About" part. This meant that Tommy's first appearance as a mystic comes earlier in the story, while the album's two worst songs—"Cousin Kevin" and "Underture"—were dropped entirely. Also jettisoned were "Overture," "Tommy Can You Hear Me?" "Sensation," "Miracle Cure," "Sally Simpson," and "Welcome." Now "Go to the Mirror, Boy!" slammed right into "Smash the Mirror," without "Tommy Can You Hear Me?" popping up in between; likewise, after the mirror is smashed, we go straight to "I'm Free," without "Sensation," "Miracle Cure," and "Sally Simpson" clogging up the narrative. And, perhaps most rewarding of all, right after Tommy declares he's free, we hear the "Tommy Holiday's Camp"/"We're Not Gonna Take It" finale, without the let-down of "Welcome" getting in the way. Roughly a third of the album was left out, allowing for a work that came come alive through the reality of its own sound.

The Who's Woodstock set was redeemed when, at the end of *Tommy*, the morning sun broke across the horizon as the Who went into the final "See me, feel me" refrain. The crowd was blown away—and so was the usually cynical Townshend. "It was just incredible," he remembered, "I really felt we didn't deserve it, in a way."[10] Deserved or not, it happened, and everything came together during that finale. While the film footage that survives doesn't catch the famous sunrise, what it does catch is the Who in the midst of an intense and awesomely powerful performance of the main theme of their rock opera, playing their spiritual music at the epicenter of the rock and roll world. For that moment, everyone gets the music, and everyone gets the story.

Notes

1 Fricke, 179.
2 Townshend, 136.
3 Wenner.
4 Daltrey, 111.
5 Cohn.
6 Miles.
7 Green.
8 Marsh, 325.
9 Barnes, 3.
10 Marsh, 350.

Part Two

The Golden Era (1970–4)

6

God Knows Where We're Heading: *What's Going On*

On May 23, 1977, Marvin Gaye appeared on Dinah Shore's television show, where she asked about her favorite album of his, *What's Going On*. "I learned today that you consider that a concept album, as did I," she tells him in her soft and lilting Southern drawl. "Would you explain what you meant by that?"

Gaye thoughtfully stumbles over his words as he attempts to set the scope of the project. "Well, when the world and—well, the state of the union was and—well, the Vietnamese War was raging hot and heavy during that period that we conceived it and there was a lot of unrest in America. There were college kids being shot in campuses. My brother was at war and I prayed a lot that he would come through safely. It was a very, a very trying period for me at Motown, even…"

Shore redirects her questioning to be more about the album's universal themes, as *Charlie's Angels* star Kate Jackson looks on starstruck, mesmerized by Gaye's words.

"I tried to write a general kind of broad statement," Gaye responded. "I didn't want to step on any toes particularly and I still don't, but it was quite an experience … I don't recall much about the album, I feel that it was very divine and … Well, very personal, very divine. I don't hardly remember writing these songs. I mean, it was like, I was in a, kind of a, some sort of other dimension or something when we did it…"[1]

Although Gaye is only thirty-eight years old and nearly as many years away from making *What's Going On* in 1971 as he was from getting killed in 1984, he speaks about his masterpiece with a bemused detachment. If, as Shore implied, Gaye had just declared his masterpiece as a concept album earlier, he now hovers around the term like a pilgrim looking back and trying to figure out how he got to where he is.

By the end of the 1960s, Marvin Gaye was the biggest star of Motown Records, a Detroit-based, Black-owned R&B label founded and operated by Berry Gordy.

The previous year, Gaye provided his label with "I Heard It Through the Grapevine," its biggest hit up to that point, which topped the *Billboard* Hot 100 for seven weeks straight across late 1968 and early 1969. Despite this success, Gaye felt artistically frustrated and adrift in a rapidly changing world. He watched Woodstock from afar, but it remained on his mind when he read Carlos Castaneda's *The Teachings of Don Juan*, a mystical book about the author's supposed training under a Yaqui Mexican shaman.

Gaye recalled: "I opened it up and saw this quote on the first page from Don Juan that said, 'For me there is only the traveling on paths that have heart . . . the only worthwhile challenge is to traverse its full length.' I studied that book and treasured its wisdom. I looked at what was happening at Woodstock and thought to myself, Here's a whole generation of people about to travel a new path. I understood musically I'd have to go on a path of my own. The Motown corporate attitude didn't give me much room to breathe, but I was starting to feel strong enough to start my own path."[2] Gaye found the impetus he needed to embark on his own creative journey that led him out of his jadedness: "What's Going On," a jazzy song driven by a funk groove with lyrics that served as a sobering tour of a modern-day America in crisis. All put together, this was state-of-the-art soul—new, ambitious, and uncompromised.

And Berry Gordy hated it. Gaye held his ground and refused to release anything in its place. Finally, in January 1971, two Motown executives authorized the release of "What's Going On" without Gordy's knowledge. By the time they told him, the first-day sales had come back at 100,000 copies, giving Gordy an instant change of heart. In fact, he now wanted an album to go with it, to be finished by April. This gave Gaye one month to record it—March 1971—the better part of which Gaye stayed away from the studio. When he finally got to work in late March, Gaye recorded the album in ten days. It appears the songs were recorded in order, reinforcing the album's stream-of-conscious flow. He saw it as a divine work being created through him. "God is writing this album," Gaye told fellow Motown legend Smokey Robinson. "God is working through me."[3]

What's Going On is more than just a concept album. It reaches back over three centuries into America's past—nearly 150 years before America even existed—invoking one of the earliest forms of American communication, the sermon. In 1630, Puritan leader John Winthrop delivered a sermon called *A Modell of Christian Charity* that shaped American identity before his boat even reached the New World. In the sermon, Winthrop wrote, "wee must Consider that wee shall be as a City upon a Hill, the eies of all people upon us . . ."[4] Winthrop's words were at once a prophecy and a millstone. On one hand, they remain a credo to aspire to, while on the other, they haunt us with every news story about police brutality, climate disaster, or poverty that we encounter. Marvin Gaye's *What's Going On* is an answer sermon to Winthrop's *A Modell of Christian Charity*, written by an African American man some 341 years later. His words too are prophetic, touching on issues with such timelessness and grace, in an album that could have been recorded tomorrow.

A party is stirring. Welcoming voices pull you in to its friendly ambiance. We're not even seven seconds in and there's already a sense of community. We hear a saxophone leading the sound, revealing itself to contain an array of piano, congas, backing vocals, drums, and James Jamerson's bass. His restless pulse keeps the song moving along its churning rhythm, walking a fine line between a soul ballad and a funky protest song. Meanwhile, the singer looks out the window and surveys the scene. Separated from the music, the lyrics may sound trite—too many mothers crying, too many brothers dying—but once the two are paired together, "What's Going On" plays with a singular beauty that belies its violent inspiration.

"What's Going On" was inspired by police brutality witnessed by Renaldo "Obie" Benson, the bass singer for Motown stalwarts the Four Tops: "I was in San Francisco, up in Haight-Asbury, and I saw these [young] people speaking in the park. And then I saw the police come in and start running them over and beating on them. And I thought, 'what's going on?'" Benson enlisted Motown songwriter Al Cleveland to help compose the song. They showed it to Gaye, who recorded "What's Going On" in June and July of 1970, as marijuana and good vibes filled the studio. "I conceived every bit of the music," Gaye told *Rolling Stone* in 1972. "I hate to brag and everything like this, but I had no musical knowledge, I can't write music, can't read music. But I was able to transmit my thoughts to another person, and David Van DePitte, through the graces of God, had enough talent to be able to receive it and put it on paper for me."[5] Indeed, Van DePitte was Gaye's musical translator for *What's Going On*, taking Gaye's sung strings and horn parts and shaping them into musical scores.

"To understand Marvin Gaye's majestic achievements," explains Michael Eric Dyson in *Mercy, Mercy Me: The Art, Loves and Demons of Marvin Gaye*, "one must grasp a seeming contradiction: he produced his best music in collaboration with others ... He reworked words to a song begun by a fellow lyricist. He completed vocal gestures hinted at by another singer. He tapped into the energy and extended the vibration of another musician. He mapped musical secrets locked in his own soul through the charts of a composer ... In all of these ways and more, Marvin's art thrived on communal cooperation."[6] On "What's Going On," Gaye employed all of these. With Benson and Cleveland working with Gaye to hammer out the vocal and lyric and Van DePitte's strings swirling all around, it plays like a singular symphony with Gaye as its mastermind.

After the title track of *What's Going On* fades away, "What's Happening Brother" suddenly appears. The song was about Gaye's younger brother Frankie, who had recently returned home from Vietnam. Frankie spent hours talking to his brother about his horrific experiences, sympathy fueling frustration, frustration fueling creativity. "I knew I had something," Gaye recalled, "an anger, an energy, an artistic point of view."[7] He poured this into "What's Happening Brother," capturing the confusion and frustration surrounding the soldiers returning from the trauma of Southeast Asia. The singer of "What's Happening Brother" sees newspapers promising things are getting better, but he still can't find a job or financial security. In a lovely turn of phrasing, he confesses: "I just don't understand what's going on across this land." To hear the album's title sung so naturally in the middle of a song allows us to hear the phrase in a new way. What was a protest rallying cry in the title track is a poignant lament here, an expression of the singer's genuine confusion.

The veteran of "What's Happening Brother" finds comfort in "Flying High (in the Friendly Sky)," as the wash of cymbals and the ever-climbing bass leads the singer into a heady haze of psychedelic escape. But really, the song is a trap. The singer describes drugs as "the place where danger awaits me," calling himself "stupid minded" at how he goes "crazy when I can't find it." "Flying High" marks a transition in the portrayal of drugs. Unlike 1960s classics like the Beatles' "Lucy in the Sky with Diamonds," the fantasy reality of marijuana and LSD had given way to harder drugs like cocaine and heroin. One also hears shades of Gaye's own drug use. "I've been open to grass since I was a kid," he told *Rolling Stone* in 1972. "I've also been open to alcohol, cigarettes, uppers and downers, heroin, cocaine, but I mean, you know ... what I dig and what's good for me are two different things." When asked what gave him control over what substances he used, Gaye responded simply, "Wanting to live."[8]

Coming out of the nightmare of "Flying High," the album segues into "Save the Children." All is suspended as brooding strings hover over the restless bass. The singer asks who cares to save a world in distress, before dividing himself into two voices, one putting his words out there tentatively, the second answering it passionately. At the song's emotional peak, the first voice calmly calls to save the children, as the second voice answers with the soaring "SAVE THE BABIES!" For a song so focused on the future, it was firmly rooted in the call-and-response music of the Black church. "Maybe today is the result of yesterdays spent in wooden churches," Gaye mused on the 1983 television special *Motown 25: Yesterday, Today, Forever*. "Singing the praises of our Maker in joyous harmony and love. And part of it has to be the songs we sang working under the blazing sun to help pass the hard times." He then lists a free-association naming past influences, listing "gospel choirs" followed by "slavery," as though they were the cure and the symptom, respectively. For Gaye, music's roots are never far away.

The music becomes joyous and upbeat, as the somber "Save the Children" gives way to "God Is Love." Clocking in at well under two minutes, "God Is Love" is essentially a transitional bridge between "Save the Children" and "Mercy, Mercy Me," but stands as a minor gem on its own (best heard in the beautiful standalone version that appeared as the B-side to "What's Going On"). It provides a rare happy moment on the first side and continues Gaye's call-and-response singing in a more exuberant setting. The singer declares that God is his friend and that He asks us to give each other love. "And all He asks of us, I know—" the song finishes, cut off mid-line as the music of "Mercy, Mercy Me (The Ecology)" flows out of it.

In an album revered for its prescience, perhaps no track is timelier than "Mercy, Mercy Me (The Ecology)." Continuing the groove of "God Is Love" but taking it down a notch, Gaye returns to his quieter ballad side with his own vocal overdubs filling the song in genuine care and concern. The singer laments our oil spills, mercury-filled fish, radiation, and animals dying in "this overcrowded land." But the magic of "Mercy, Mercy Me" is its laid-back groove with a lilting melody that you can sink into like an old couch. This disconnect between the lyric and the sound doesn't take away from the song—it actually adds to it. To have such a clear message over perfectly placed rhythm guitar, drums, strings, horns, and voices means that as a pop artifact, it will reach more people. And it did—"Mercy, Mercy Me" was Gaye's second of three consecutive #1 R&B hits from *What's Going On*.

The second side of *What's Going On* begins with the ringing church hall piano of "Right On," sprawling into a holy Latin-tinged, Santana-like jam. The track keeps its groove for some seven-and-a-half minutes, with the singer providing an overview of all different kinds of people—rich, poor, healers, soldiers, and slaves—for the bulk of the song. Towards the end, it shifts to a lofty, wistful feel as the strings take over and the singer sings of love—for your brother, for God, for love's own sake. Saxophones come in and briefly threaten to turn the song back into a groove, but the singer's not finished yet, echoing the "love can conquer hate" line from the album's title track and promising to take his lover "where love is king." The groove then comes back with a vengeance and clears the way to the following song. In his review of *What's Going On* in *Rolling Stone*, Vince Aletti largely praised the album, although he allowed that some "cuts don't hold together quite as well ('Right On,' the longest number, misses) but the album as a whole takes precedence, absorbing its own flaws."[9] Indeed, heard a half century later, *What's Going On* plays even more like a singular document, and removing a song would be like removing a gospel from the Bible.

"Right On" ends with the singer promising to take you where love is king. Given the hot rhythms of "Right On," one might expect that to be sex, but the calm, sweeping drift of "Wholy Holy" elevates us to the clouds of heaven. As Gaye was known to say, "Beyond sex is God."[10] The juxtaposition between "Right On" and "Wholy Holy" illustrate this and provide a spiritual center to the album. For the third time on the album, the singer calls to conquer hate, while also wanting to holler "love across the nation," as rooted in a love for God. This is soul music at its most soulful, as the listener is elevated to the highest level possible: witnessing the Lord Himself. Horns and strings swirl around each other twinkling and it is here, for a rare moment on the album, that all is calm and the music fades away into peaceful silence.

But the album isn't over, not just yet. There's still one more place for it to go—into the depths of time and history with a song so powerful, it erases all the hope and faith found in *What's Going On*'s first eight songs like they were scratches in the sand. "Inner City Blues (Make Me Wanna Holler)" finds Gaye turning away from the community of gospel to the isolation of the blues. The title of "Inner City Blues (Make Me Wanna Holler)" alludes to the work holler, an African American work song that was often performed solo. While hollers reach back to the times of slavery, LeRoi Jones noted in his *Blues People: Negro Music in White America*, "Many Negroes who were sharecroppers ... worked in their fields alone or with their families. The old shouts and hollers were still their accompaniment for the arduous work of clearing the land, planting, or harvesting crops. But there was a solitude to this work that was never present in the slave times."[11] The holler was a kind of music that thrived in a lack of community and reached back to an unknowable past in the African American soul.

In *The Souls of Black Folk*, W.E.B. Du Bois wrote about the Sorrow Songs, the "weird old songs in which the soul of the black slave spoke to men."[12] He called these "the true Negro folk-song," mysterious songs of a forgotten world still living in the hearts of people.[13] "They are the music of an unhappy people, of the children of disappointment; they tell of death and suffering and unvoiced longing toward a truer world, of misty wanderings and hidden ways."[14] Du Bois laces various Sorrow Songs through his work, ending the book with his children singing the spiritual "Let Us Cheer the Weary Traveler," who travels "along the heavenly way."[15] These words describe Marvin Gaye in this period, a weary traveler on a holy road, finding his own way forward in an echo of the past.

Grounding "Inner City Blues" in an ancient drum pattern and a spare, slinking bass line, Gaye tells a tale of the modern blues in a falsetto cry—the story of the man who leaves the old wilderness of the country for the strange, new wilderness of the city. Its singer finds himself at the end of a great journey—from South to North, from nineteenth century to twentieth, from acoustic to electric, from rural to urban—but instead of reaching freedom, he finds one set of problems exchanged for another. One can hear traces of former Mississippi sharecroppers like Muddy Waters and B.B. King, as well as countless voices from the Great Migration. Furthermore, many of the issues mentioned—trigger happy policing, panic, soldiers sent off to die—lay the groundwork for the title track of *What's Going On*. In this way, "Inner City Blues" takes the question of "What's Going On" and turns it into an answer—*this* is what's going on. A reprise of "What's Going On" appears toward the end of "Inner City Blues," like a quick breath of air before submerging back into the murky swamp of the lost soul. And as the ritualistic drumming and falsetto cries of "Inner City Blues" return to close out the album, the circle remains unbroken.

Just as Marvin Gaye predicted, *What's Going On* was a huge album, and its impact was almost as deep as its music. It became the best-selling Motown album up to that point and spawned three top ten hits on the *Billboard* Hot 100 and R&B charts. It remains an artistic and cultural landmark, earning the #1 spot in *Rolling Stone*'s "500 Greatest Albums of All Time" poll in 2020. And in May 1972, just a year after its release, Marvin Gaye came home to his native Washington, D.C., to commemorate the album's one-year anniversary with a concert at the Kennedy Center—his first live performance in almost four years. Gaye performed *What's Going On* in its near entirety (he left off "Mercy, Mercy Me" for unknown reasons), complete with many of the album's original musicians, hired horns, and an orchestra. There were confused circumstances surrounding the performance—Gaye, nervous and stoned, began the album with its second side, apparently by mistake—but it didn't mar the impact of the moment. When Gaye sat down at the piano to sing the album, he completed a journey that he began several months earlier: he finally became the preacher in the flesh, inspiring the almost exclusively African American crowd to fervently clap and sing along.

True to his obsessive drive, Gaye remained unsatisfied, wanting his sermon to God to be perfect. "I want to thank you for being here at my attempt to return to a live performance," he announced to the audience. "We hoped to perform the album exactly as you can hear it in your home ... but I'm a perfectionist and I wasn't completely happy with the way things sounded, so if there's anything we did that you'd like to hear again, we'll try to do it."[16] He concluded the show with a reprise of the bookends of his masterpiece, "What's Going On" and "Inner City Blues (Make Me Wanna Holler)," hanging one beside the other in the nation's capital, a hopeful modern pop song answered by an ancient work holler, as brought together by a weary traveler who wanted nothing more than to reconcile the two.

Notes

1   "Marvin Gaye on The Making..."
2   Ritz, 140.
3   Robinson, 3.
4   Warner, 42.
5   Fong-Torres.
6   Dyson, 11–12.
7   Ritz, 140.
8   Fong-Torres.
9   Aletti.
10 Ibid., 26.
11 Jones, 61.
12 Du Bois, 155.
13 Ibid., 156.
14 Ibid., 157.
15 Ibid., 163.
16 Ritz, 161–2.

7

I Am on a Lonely Road and I Am Traveling: *Blue*

In 1970, the Beatles' breakup shook the rock world to its core. More than any other group, the Beatles united rock and roll, creating a community that ushered the genre from a teenage music to an adult one. Now the community had no center. Increasingly, artists turned away from rock's greater community to look inward at themselves instead of outwards for inspiration. One of the earliest and most extreme examples of this was newly ex-Beatle John Lennon's first post-Beatles solo album, *John Lennon/Plastic Ono Band*, from late 1970. The album found him reeling from his recent scream therapy, and writing songs to, for, and about himself. The finale, "God," was a Cartesian exercise into what constitutes reality, in which he famously sings that he doesn't believe in Beatles—only in himself (and wife Yoko Ono). "The dream is over," he concludes, surveying the 1960s landscape that cast a shadow over the new decade. When pop/folksinger Joni Mitchell released the similarly introspective album *Blue* in 1971, some saw a connection, even though Mitchell was subdued and melancholy where Lennon was raw and unflinching. "In four albums, Joni Mitchell has gone from sparkling newcomer to larger-than-life superstar in the fast-moving whirl of pop music," Al Rudis wrote in his review of *Blue* for *The Cincinnati Enquirer*. "Thus, like John Lennon, she can now lay her soul bare and expect us to be interested."[1]

Lennon's main contribution to the singer-songwriter era was one of substance, not sound. Most classic singer-songwriter music was quiet with subtle, introspective lyrics set to pleasant, folk-derived melodies. James Taylor led the way in early 1970 with *Sweet Baby James*. A year later, Carole King released *Tapestry*, the best-selling album of the singer-songwriter era, but the era's finest album was Mitchell's *Blue*. It's telling that these latter two landmark albums were made by solo female performers. For a rare time in rock and roll, here was a style that audiences were prepared to give just as much (if not more) credibility to female performers as male ones. But where some heard gender, Mitchell heard only humanity. "*Blue* is just human," she once reflected. "Everybody, if they've got a soul, is going to go through those changes, and yet in the spotlight, nobody had ever written them in song ...."[2] As a master of songs about journeying both internal and external, Joni Mitchell was a true pioneer.

Blue evokes a sense of contemplative introspection that is unmatched in rock and roll. Her songs tempt us to read into them like pages in a diary, as though we are using her public act releasing *Blue* as a way to connect to her very private expression; indeed, Mitchell once commented about her intimate songwriting style, "The songs have simply been private letters that were published."[3] Making the album was a private affair. When asked about the sessions for *Blue*, she said they were the only sessions "where we locked the door."[4] "Was it a nervous breakdown?" she posited about the sessions in a much later interview. "People became transparent to me. People thought I had the evil eye. That's why we locked off the *Blue* sessions. Nobody could come in. If anybody came in, I'd burst into tears."[5] But Mitchell's pain proved fertile soil for her art. All of her journeys—physical and otherwise—added up into something beautiful and remarkable. Indicative of the restraint that characterized the album, she included an austere image of her face on the cover, printed in blue.

A dulcimer lays out a punchy rhythm, soon met by the thick chords of an acoustic guitar. The two instruments blend together as the singer begins "on a lonely road" and "traveling, traveling, traveling, traveling," as she looks "for something, what can it be?" Much of the opening "All I Really Want" plays like a stream-of-conscious response to this question, landing on one answer—a love that will "bring out the best in me and you"—before the melody grows somber and she broods deeper, charting a new path of thought. "'Blue' is less a collection of songs than a piece of music divided into sections," Ellen Willis wrote in *The New Yorker* in 1973. "Its central theme was travel, literal and spiritual—a familiar folk metaphor, except that instead of a man on the road the traveler was a woman pursuing her female identity through the byways of the pop world."[6] And by the end of "All I Really Want," the singer reveals her goal: "I want to make you feel free."

But if freedom is a major inspiration for and subject of *Blue*, what did the term mean to Joni Mitchell? In 1972, an interviewer noted how there can be a kind of deception in freedom. "Freedom is deceptive, though," Mitchell agreed. "It's like that line of Kristofferson's 'Freedom's just another way of nothing left to lose.' Freedom implies a lot of loneliness you know, a lot of unfulfillment. It implies always the search for fulfillment, which sometimes is more exciting than the fulfillment itself."[7] Two years later, Mitchell was asked to define freedom. She responded, "Freedom to me is the luxury of being able to follow the path of the heart."⁸ *Blue* puts both of these definitions of freedom into practice. On one hand, the album explores the duality of freedom, especially how loneliness can be the flipside of freedom. Meanwhile, the entire project was a document of an artist following the path of their own heart. And as a travelogue, *Blue* chases an elusive freedom that focuses on the thrill of the search over the empty promise of a destination.

The following "My Old Man" picks up on the romance of the first song, focusing in on the male recipient of the singer's love. Most of the song is descriptive, filling out the song's subject with the elegant piano and melody. Songs like "My Old Man" seem to invite, if not demand, the listener to try and decode the specifics that inspired it. In this case, the song is generally associated with singer-songwriter Graham Nash, Mitchell's lover who she broke up with just before she began *Blue*. Mitchell needed to break free from their domesticity and go into the world for an adventure. But first, she reflects upon one of the most significant events in her own life. "Little Green" tells of a baby put up for adoption. The song is likely the oldest one on *Blue*. Mitchell wrote it in 1967, not long after she gave her own infant child up for adoption, rather than raise it alone and penniless. This private event wasn't made public until three decades later when the two were reunited through internet posts. Mitchell has said that the emptiness left by her daughter led her to write songs in the first place, and indeed, she's only released a fraction of new songs compared to her output before reuniting with her daughter. "Little Green," She sings towards the end of the song, "Have a happy ending."

Cashing in on her claim on traveling in "All I Want to Do," while processing the breakup of "My Old Man" and the lingering pain of "Little Green," the singer flees California and heads to a cave-dwelling hippie commune in Matala, Crete, as Mitchell herself did before recording *Blue*. While there, Mitchell met Cary Raditz, a tough and rootless rambler. They became acquainted and she moved into his cave, beginning a relationship that lasted about two months. She wrote a song about him that she misspelled as "Carey," and included it on *Blue*.⁹ It is the album's closest thing to a pop-rock song, as the rhythm section grounds the soaring melody and sing-along refrain. But the relationship was short-lived. Mitchell originally went to Matala to be anonymous, but Cary noticed a change when she was approached by reporters and invited them to join her and Cary. In hindsight, Cary saw this as "when she really changed her whole life, from being somewhat at the effect of other people, to becoming the cause itself."¹⁰ Raditz's observations provide an interesting context for *Blue*. The idea that Mitchell had gone from an "effect" to a "cause" shows a woman taking her own initiative, and framing the world on her own terms. As an emotional document, this is what *Blue* is all about.

Closing out the album's first side is its title track, a song as guarded and stark as "Carey" was opening and inviting. "Blue" is one of the most uncompromised songs on the album, with lines that grow and shrink over a melody that rises and falls depending on the feeling of the lyric. After its killer opening line—"Songs are like tattoos"—it keeps hanging up words like clothes on a clothesline, until it cascades with a decade's worth of angst in a few choice lines: "Acid, booze, and ass," followed by "Needles, guns, and grass." But if the lyrics looked backward, the music looked ahead, creating a blueprint for countless female singer-songwriters in the 1990s. Still, as the singer puts it, "Blue" is just "a foggy lullaby," a eulogy for a recent era that already felt like a thousand years ago.

The second side of *Blue* opens with the singer sitting in a park in Paris, France. In the second verse, she is in the Grecian Isles; by the third, she is on a plane to Spain. In each place, her heart longs for her home that comprises the song's title, "California." Like so many things on the album, the singer takes an idea and personifies it, singing to the state as though it were a lost lover. She even flashes back again to Cary/"Carey," now describing him as a goat-dancing rogue who stole her camera to sell. (The real-life Raditz maintains that Mitchell gave him the camera as a gift and when he warned her that he would probably sell it, she said to go ahead.) The question she asks of California—"Will you take me as I am?"—hangs over the album, summing up the entire singer-songwriter movement in seven simple words. Her question marks a turning point, a conscious shedding of the carnival masks and psychedelic costumes in favor for something far more revealing. "That's how I felt," she later explained. "Like my guts were on the outside. I wrote *Blue* in that condition."[11]

In true narrative style, the album's following song, "This Flight Tonight," answers the homesick longing of "California" by placing the singer on an airplane descending over the sands of Las Vegas. The song works as a snapshot of a mind in several places at once—on one level describing the literal events of the flight, on another level thinking about her love she's flying home to see, and on yet another level, deeper questions of a higher order. But there is a sense of hesitation in "This Flight Tonight," a pang of regret to which the singer keeps on returning: "Turn this crazy bird around," she sings. The singer finds herself trapped in a paradox—returning home makes her want to take flight once again. It is this insatiable feeling of restlessness disguised as freedom that gives *Blue* much of its power, and the energy to keep moving forward in a crooked line.

Mitchell begins the following "River" with a sound that comes from another universe: choppy piano notes playing the refrain of "Jingle Bells." The familiarity of the melody takes you away to a distant, nostalgic place that sneaks up on you no matter how many times you've heard "River." But then Mitchell weaves it into a song of her own. She sings in glimpses, watching people go about their holiday chores before unleashing a soaring refrain where she wishes for a river to skate away on. Now that it's a modern holiday standard, Mitchell gets frustrated by those who deny it's a Christmas song. "It's absolutely a Christmas song," she told *The Los Angeles Times* as *Blue* reached its fifty-year mark. "It's a Christmas song for people who are lonely at Christmas! We need a song like that."[12] Mitchell knew a thing or two about being lonely at Christmas. At the age of ten, she was diagnosed with polio and shipped off to live in a children's polio colony. Though she wanted to go home for Christmas, she ended up spending it alone in the colony, where the wheezing sounds of the iron lungs could be heard through the night. Songs like "River"—with the way Mitchell spaces out her words, the placement of chord changes, and the song's existential loneliness—speak to the secret musical source of *Blue*, a source so subtle it hides in plain sight: the blues. While *Blue* is not a blues album per se, it uses a stripped-down sincerity that accompanies the confessional element of the music that echoes the blues. As her title implies, her blues are not the blues, but rather they *are* Blue, something so personal that it must be capitalized and kept in the singular.

In the next song on *Blue*, "A Case of You," Joni Mitchell proves herself as the greatest writer of dialogue in rock music. In the song, the singer recalls how a former lover called her as constant as a northern star. She flips this on its head and interprets it to mean she's constantly in the darkness. She then turns away from her companion and tells them that if they need her, she'll be in the bar— and presumably, in the darkness. All of this is conveyed in an economy of words that she's even able to make rhyme. "A Case of You" grows from this intimate dialogue of secular love into a song about the intimacies of faith. "You're in my blood like holy wine," she sings in the refrain. Her song transcends from a confession into a holy rite, yet one that is made entirely unto itself; there's no priest to administer the sacraments, only the singer and whatever form of God she may believe in. And yet, by placing this on an album, she is confessing to everyone. Therein lies the paradox of the singer-songwriter movement: It is a style marked by the singer's private thoughts and introspection, but simultaneously had to reach a wide audience to be successful. If there is anyone in the equation who serves as the role of the priest hearing the confessions, it's us, the audience.

Blue concludes with the haunting "The Last Time I Saw Richard." The singer begins by bluntly putting the title question to rest: the last time she saw Richard was in Detroit in 1968. Richard tells her that all romantics are doomed to be "Cynical and drunk and boring." When the singer laughs at him, Richard chides her for liking flowers and pretty men. He then puts some songs on the jukebox, leading the singer to point out that, despite his cynicism, he selected sweet love songs. In the final verse, the singer descries how Richard married a figure skater, got the status symbols of suburban life, and drinks at home in front of the television with all the houselights on. That's where the singer draws the line. "I'm gonna blow this damn candle out," she sings. The difference between Richard and the singer is that where Richard sees a dead end, the singer sees a new beginning. For her, the bar is merely "a dark cocoon" where she can "get my gorgeous wings and fly." With the determined hope of "The Last Time I Saw Richard" at the end, *Blue* is an extended meditation of loneliness and love, and the dark places they can lead. And the singer uses the same little-girl imagery that Richard mocks her for and welds it to her song to break free like a butterfly.

Taken all together, Joni Mitchell's *Blue* more than lives up to its name. As one listens (and re-listens) to the album, the color blue springs up everywhere, almost always in a different form: An emotion ("we both get so blue" in "All I Want"), a genre ("keeping away my blues" in "My Old Man"), a color ("her eyes are blue" in "Little Green"), a muse ("Blue, there is a song for you" in "Blue"), an expression (reading the news "gives you the blues" in "California"), even the glow of a television ("blue TV screen light" in "A Case of You"). The songs that don't mention the color outright imply it in their imagery: the distant city lights of "This Flight Tonight," the icy waters of "River," the lunar imagery of "The Last Time I Saw Richard." The only song to shun it completely is "Carey," in favor of "clean white linen," "silver [jewelry]", and "the bright red devil."

Blue became Mitchell's first Top 20 album in the US, peaking at #15 on the *Billboard* 200, while "Carey" became her second single to chart on the *Billboard* Hot 100, peaking at #93. But if *Blue* was only modestly popular upon its release, many critics took to it immediately. "In portraying herself so starkly, she has risked the ridiculous to achieve the sublime," wrote Timothy Crouse in *Rolling Stone*. "The results though are seldom ridiculous; on *Blue* she has matched her popular music skills with the purity and honesty of what was once called folk music and through the blend she has given us some of the most beautiful moments in recent popular music."[13] Over the years, *Blue*'s stature would only rise. In 2003, it reached a respectable #30 in Rolling Stone's "500 Greatest Albums of All Time" (the highest ranking for a solo female artist), before rocketing to #3 in the follow-up 2020 edition, beaten out only by Marvin Gaye's *What's Going On* and the Beach Boys' *Pet Sounds*. And between these *Rolling Stone* polls, National Public Radio (NPR) chose *Blue* as the greatest album by a female performer in 2017.

For all of *Blue*'s private confessions, it has now reached a critical mass that has outweighed even peers like James Taylor's *Sweet Baby James* and Carole King's *Tapestry*. "The *Blue* album, there's hardly a dishonest note in the vocals," Mitchell told *Rolling Stone* in a rare 1979 interview. "At that period of my life, I had no personal defenses. I felt like a cellophane wrapper on a pack of cigarettes. I felt like I had absolutely no secrets from the world, and I couldn't pretend in my life to be strong. Or to be happy. But the advantage of it in the music was that there were no defenses there either."[14] Her own spiritual journey was a private work that turned her into a public muse, improving with age like a case of fine wine.

Notes

1 Rudis.
2 Yaffe, 145.
3 Watts.
4 Crowe (2021).
5 Yaffe, 133.
6 Willis.
7 Valentine.
8 Marom.
9 Mossman.
10 Ibid.
11 Yaffe, 133.
12 Crowe (2021).
13 Crouse.
14 Crowe (1979).

8

We'll Have Superman for President: *Thick as a Brick*

One of the results of rock and roll using the album format is that it could hold long songs. While classical and jazz had long explored this, rock was still widely seen as a singles-driven market; most pre-1965 rock albums were two sides of a hit single with ten tracks of filler padding it out. However, by 1966, things began to change. Bob Dylan's *Blonde on Blonde* and Frank Zappa's *Freak Out!* were ambitious double-albums that closed with a side-long epic in mid-1966. Dylan's "Sad-Eyed Lady of the Lowlands" was a hauntingly beautiful surrealist ballad, while Zappa's "The Return of the Son of Monster Magnet (Unfinished Ballet in Two Tableaux)" was a challenging piece of *musique concrète*; both reached for art and got it. By November, the L.A.-based band Love issued *Da Capo*, which contained the eighteen-minute "Revelation" as its second side. A little under a year later, the title track of Arlo Guthrie's *Alice's Restaurant* took up the album's entire first side and proved to be one of the most enduring of the album-side songs of its era.

It was in this period that the Who experimented with an extended rock narrative in their first rock opera, the nine-minute "A Quick One While He's Away." Like *Tommy*, it improved as they played it live, with the definitive version captured at *The Rolling Stones' Rock and Roll Circus*. Originally taped in 1968, the television special went unreleased until 1996, supposedly because Mick Jagger thought the Who played a better set than the Stones (which they did). Performing right before the Who in the special was an early incarnation of Jethro Tull, who performed their second single, "A Song for Jeffrey." Although all the members except for leader and flautist Ian Anderson would soon change, the blueprint of the band was already in place. Anderson led the charge—one leg planted on the ground while the other flailed around like it was possessed—ranting and raving like a madman through a tempest of folk- and blues-based driving hard rock. "Don't see—see—see, where I'm goin'," Anderson sang like a man who embraces willful ignorance as a badge of honor.

The Rolling Stones' Rock and Roll Circus captures a moment of transition for rock and roll. While it may seem like a psychedelic happening—a sort of "Being for the Benefit of Mr. Kite!" brought to life—it was promoting the Stones' new album, *Beggars Banquet*, which marked their abandonment of psychedelic rock after their concept album misadventure, *Their Satanic Majesties Request*. The Stones now channeled a grittier, back-to-basics sound. Meanwhile, the concept album was carried on by bands like Jethro Tull, who pioneered what became progressive rock, alongside bands like King Crimson, Yes, and Genesis. For some, this more decidedly sophisticated music was transcendent; for others, it reeked of pretension.

And many would put Jethro Tull in that same category. In 1971, they released their breakthrough album *Aqualung*, which many believed was a concept album about God. Ian Anderson envisioned the group's next project to be a response to this assumption. "[T]he *Aqualung* album had generally been perceived as a concept album, whereas to me it was just a bunch of songs, as I've always said," he later explained.

> So, the first thing about *Thick as a Brick* was 'let's come up with something which is the mother of all concept albums and really is a mind-boggler' in terms of what was then relatively complex music and also lyrically was complex, confusing, and, above all, a bit of a spoof. It was quite deliberately, but in a nice way, tongue-in-cheek, and meant to send up ourselves, the music critics, and the audience, perhaps, but not necessarily in that order.[1]

Anderson gathered with his band mates—electric guitarist Martin Barre, keyboardist John Evan, bassist Jeffrey Hammond, and drummer Barriemore Barlow—and worked out their vision.

Released in March 1972, Jethro Tull's *Thick as a Brick* was the concept album to end all concept albums. It consisted of one nearly forty-five-minute song, split between the two sides of the record as "Thick as a Brick, Part 1" and "Thick as a Brick, Part 2." Ahead of the album's release, Anderson mischievously made up his own mythology around it. He claimed that the album's lyrics came from an epic poem penned by an eight-year-old savant named Gerald "Little Milton" Bostock. Jethro Tull used the album itself to flesh out the backstory with a fictional newspaper, *The St. Cleve Chronicle*. Anderson and his band mates wrote twelve pages of fake articles, which included a lead story on Bostock, and even a review of *Thick as a Brick* itself. The latter reads in part, rather accurately: "One doubts at times the validity of what appears to be an expanding theme throughout the two continuous sides of this record but the result is at worst entertaining and at least aesthetically palatable." Anderson reckoned it took longer to write and design the album cover than it took to create and record the music.

He later reflected: "I thought we steered a very good line between making it sound vaguely plausible as a concept, and being, so, y'know, quite silly." And many initial critics took Anderson at his word. "The album ... is based on an impressive poem by one Gerald Bostock," Chris Welch wrote in the *Melody Maker*. "It's one of those poems that fixes one with a penetrating gaze and snaps somewhat bitterly: 'I may make you feel but I can't make you think.'"[2] One can only imagine Anderson cackling at the irony here. For all the things that *Thick as a Brick* may or may not be—and it's many things at once, including brilliant, tuneful, complex, boring, esoteric, immature, sophisticated, and ambitious—it's aptly named. On one level, the title is a fancier way of saying "Stupid," which reflects the group's tongue-in-cheek grand concept album. But on another level, a brick reflects the opaqueness, the impenetrable nature of this work. Coming at you in a twenty-two-minute chunk followed by a twenty-one-minute chunk, it defies anyone who attempts to cut it down to size. Yet this presentation is essential to understanding the work. A depressing sign of our distracted digital era is that the fortieth anniversary edition of *Thick as a Brick* was broken down into eight tracks on iTunes.

The duality at the core of *Thick as a Brick*—the immaturity of it functioning as a prank and the maturity of artistic ambitions, no matter how satirical they may have been—is reflected in its central theme of boyhood and manhood. Rock and roll has always provided a caricature of the male ego, no more so than in the early 1970s, when *Thick as a Brick* was released within months of Led Zeppelin's untitled fourth album and the Rolling Stones' *Exile on Main St*. Jethro Tull simply took this machismo and double-downed on it, using folk-rock flair to create a cartoon magnum opus for a comic book music.

Even though *Thick as a Brick* formally consisted of one song, it was closer to a "rock opera"—if not the Who's *Tommy*, then definitely "A Quick One, While He's Away"—twisting and turning its way through various themes, styles, and shifts in mood. The album begins by addressing the listener. "The opening lines with that little acoustic guitar pattern ... that first minute or so was all I had, so I knew how it was going to begin with those words, 'Really don't mind if you sit this one out'—total rejection to the audience, saying if you don't like this then fuck off," Anderson later explained with laughter. While his peers like the Beatles joyfully announced to listeners that "We're Sgt. Pepper's Lonely Hearts Club Band," there is no "we" in Anderson's opening. It's not so much an invitation as a served notice of what's about to begin, take it or leave it.

The opening lyrics may be an insult to the listener, but the music surrounding it is a lovely folk melody, Anderson's acoustic guitar and flute flittering around the lyrics for the first verse and refrain. Already we find ourselves in a nondescript medieval or early Renaissance period—riding over fields, bartering farm animals, consulting wise men. By the second verse, the music grows as Jeffrey Hammond's bass and Barriemore Barlow's drums underpin the sound. And then, for one perfect refrain, the full band catches Anderson's folk refrain about new shoes and old peeling suntans, culminating with wise men who don't know how to feel thick . . . as a brick.

The singer leads us back down into the days of his youth, stopping to witness a son being born. "We'll make a man of him," the singer declares, before the music takes over into a swirling tempest, guitars churning upwards as organ spirals all around, all kept in check by an off-kilter time signature, parting ways briefly for acoustic guitars before coming back all in force in hammering blasts. Everything steps aside for the next movement, which pits the solider against the poet—the doer and the thinker—before the youngest of the family moves with authority as he builds sandcastles.

Most of the album is like this—winding musical passages that fluctuate between folk, jazz, and hard rock, all held in place by the album's secret weapon: Barlow's drumming. He has the rare ability to conjure whatever dynamic is needed at every point of the ever-fluctuating music. Barlow drives the music to grow from a mellow folksong to a storming rocker, as the oldest son bursts upon the scene from across the sea, challenging his youngest brother. The old man dies over tight, jagged riffs, until the music reforms into a regal march like knights on a crusade, led by John Evan's stately organ.

The music shifts into a distant, lilting organ melody that sounds a Renaissance fair; the rest of the band comes in to add muscle, turning it into a rigid, halting march. The singer reappears, only instead of a third-party narrator, he throws himself in the midst of the action. "I've come down from the upper class," he declares, "To mend your rotten ways." In a mere six lines, we get a sketch of the scoundrel: His father was a powerful man who people obeyed, until the singer killed him "twenty years too late." There's a bitterness in this voice that conveys both the wrath and regret of waiting two decades to do this to his father—and he will no longer waste any time.

The music melds into the opening riff that unleashed the whole thing, but this time it is turned into a child's sing-along, seeming to push things back into boyhood. It then returns to a section similar to the opening verses, calling upon childhood comic book heroes to save the day. The album reaches its conceptual apex as it imagines a society led by the British cartoon fighter pilot John "Biggles" Bigglesworth and Batman's loyal sidekick Robin. "We'll have Superman for president," the singer promises in what may be the most telling line of the entire work.

Comic book heroes like Superman are a caricature of manhood devised for young boys to emulate. The classic comic books of Anderson's day—who grew up in the 1950s—still had the traditional covers that promised an elusive thrill that the inside of the book almost never lived up to. And so, Biggles fights on the wing of a plane in midflight; Robin swings into action; Superman treats steel like cheap plastic. It is a fanciful, colorful world that takes the wonder of childhood and drives it into a literal cartoon version of manhood. For an album caught between the stages of male youth and adulthood, President Superman speaks both life stages better than the twenty minutes of music and lyrics that came before it. The side ends ominously, as the striking stabs of an instrumental piece reverberate into the sounds of nature.

The second side opens with nature sounds and an echo of the stabbing instrumental that closed of the first, before toughening up into a frenetic jazz fusion groove. Just as the first side announced the birth of a son, the second side announces the birth of a man. And in case any subtlety is lost, the music shifts into an over-the-top drum solo that puts the instrument front and center for the next few minutes even as the other instruments reappear alternately playing a winding folk melody and harder rock, before finally sputtering to a close.

The second side of *Thick as a Brick* is the more "progressive" one, which perhaps is a way of saying that where lyrics drove the first side, music drives the second. There's a dizzying array of moods, sounds, styles, genres, and time signatures—a revolving door of popular recorded sound. Once again, a folk riff similar to the one at the start of the first side plants the seed of the music and the second side (re-)starts in earnest. One can hear Jethro Tull flex their versatility by conjuring the sounds of other groups—at one moment, there's a ferociously strummed acoustic guitar like Pete Townshend's playing on *Tommy*, until the group joins in with heavy riffing straight out of an early Led Zeppelin album, before landing in a shimmering psychedelic section like the Grateful Dead's late-1960s albums.

The band shifts to a haunting, folk-based descending melody similar to the best parts of the first side, as we witness the ritualistic dawning of a new sun (son?). "Do you believe in the day?" the singer asks, drawing out his words. There is a remarkable instrumental passage that conjures the melancholy steps of some giant intergalactic being that grows into a light march, as if John Sousa wrote the score for *Forbidden Planet*. The music wanders away from the verses, but the singer still recaptures the music and bends it to his will, causing it to shift and change texture, as the organ bubbles all around the melody like a fugue. The flutes multiply to form a mad swirling sea, which the electric guitars try to tame with increasingly sharp howling cries. The music keeps marching ahead, going headlong into an instrumental break that grows in depth and menace, toying with the theme like a mouse being played with by a cat.

The singer warns of empty streets and gutters filled with blood, as "the fool toasts his god in the sky." The wrath of his words seizes the music, unleashing a hurricane of guitars and flutes, madly prancing around each other at reckless speed, falling into a call-and-response with the thundering drums in a new age symphony. The music oscillates between its laboratory of mutating themes, threatening to fall apart at any moment, only to land together at the top of the next verse like it was the only natural thing to do, as the sins of the father are fed with the blood of fools and the thoughts of wise men. Or something.

By this point, poring over the lyrics is futile—which of course is the whole point. Ian Anderson tosses words out like red herrings, referencing profound spirituality and juvenile bodily functions with equal abandon. But just when the lyrics nearly collapse into their absurdity, the music roars back to save them again and again, flexing its tricky timing and shrewd dynamics, if only to emphasize that this is serious music. And then, in the waning minutes of the album, there comes the only unnatural transition of the album, where the music bursts into a slower, churning rhythm that allows the band to return to their comic book heroes' refrain from the first side, before spiraling off into one last flight of musical fancy, the music climbing ever upwards, playing call-and-response with an orchestra, scaling higher and higher in a manner at once masterful and ridiculous, until the whole thing falls back into the solo acoustic guitar and vocal of the opening verse, in which ends the album as it began—staring you down, thick as a brick.

Jethro Tull released *Thick as a Brick* to mixed reviews. "Whether or not *Thick as a Brick* is an isolated experiment," wrote Ben Gerson in *Rolling Stone*, "it is nice to know that someone in rock has ambitions beyond the four or five minute conventional track, and has the intelligence to carry out his intentions, in all their intricacy, with considerable grace."[3] Dave Marsh was less charitable in *Creem*: "[T]o be perfectly frank, *Thick as a Brick* bores me to tears. It doesn't even have the calm chutzpah to offend. You can listen to it but it is beyond me why anyone'd want to."[4] Regardless, *Thick as a Brick* was Jethro Tull's first #1 *Billboard* album in America, staying for two weeks before being ousted by the default standard of rock and roll manhood, the Rolling Stones' *Exile on Main St.* This makes *Thick as a Brick* somewhat of an anomaly among the albums discussed so far, as the majority of them did not make it to the apex of the *Billboard* album chart. The fact that Jethro Tull could do so with such an uncompromised album speaks to *Thick as a Brick* hitting the perfect intersection of the band's hard work touring and an audience that was ready to meet the challenge of a one-song album.

Thick as a Brick was at once simple (comprising one song) and complex (comprising many different musical movements). For an album that regularly invokes fools and wise men, boys and men, high-minded themes and low-level jokes, perhaps it's only fitting that the album is itself a contradiction of terms. It's at once arguably the most ambitious concept album up to its time and a self-aware exercise in absurdity. And, forty years later, *Thick as a Brick* became one of the few concept albums to receive a sequel concept album when Ian Anderson released *Thick as a Brick 2* in 2012. The album provided an update on Gerald Bostock's life in five parallel universes. While it echoed the original, it did not surpass it, but still held its own whimsical charm—this time the cover of the album was from the fictional news website www.stcleve.com. Tellingly, Anderson released the album as a solo work, instead of with Jethro Tull. "I felt that it was better to have this [new album] be, at least in part, under my own name since it's not likely to meet with a great deal of commercial success anyway."[5] In other words, forty years later, he still really doesn't mind if you sit this one out.

Notes

1   Jethro Tull, Track 4.
2   Welch.
3   Gerson.
4   Marsh.
5   Eisen.

9

Like a Regular Superstar: *The Rise and Fall of Ziggy Stardust and the Spiders from Mars*

David Bowie made his first bid for rock and roll immortality with one of the great journeyman songs of the genre, "Space Oddity," in 1969. Rush-released to coincide with the moon landing, it told of an astronaut named Major Tom who goes into space, loses contact with ground control, and drifts into the abyss. It had many of the hallmarks that Bowie would build his legend on: a sense of alienation, an eye on outer space, and a man testing the limits of his world. After Bowie hit with "Space Oddity," he became something of a cult hero, releasing classic albums like *The Man Who Sold the World* in 1970 and *Hunky Dory* in 1971, impressing critics but never breaking through to a mass audience.

That all changed in 1972 with *The Rise and Fall of Ziggy Stardust and the Spiders from Mars*. It was a concept album about an androgynous space alien named Ziggy Stardust who comes to saves the world, becomes its biggest rock star, and commits a rock and roll suicide. What made the Ziggy Stardust project so revolutionary was that Bowie pushed the limits of the concept album by breaking out from the album's narrative and trying to live it out in real life, as an actor might walk out into the audience in the middle of a play but still expect to be treated in character.

The Ziggy Stardust phenomenon was officially born on July 6, 1972, when he and his band, the Spiders from Mars, appeared on BBC 1's *Top of the Pops*. Bowie knew it would be the first time many would see Ziggy Stardust, and he was well-prepared. "My performances have got to be theatrical experiences for me as well as for the audience," he commented about his distinct brand of rock and roll, "I think it should be tarted up, made into a prostitute, a parody of itself..."[1] On *Top of the Pops*, Bowie did just that. Dressed in bright red boots and hair, pale face makeup and dark eyeliner, a multicolored one-piece outfit, and bracelets dangling above his white-painted fingernails, Ziggy looked exactly how Bowie wanted him to: shocking, androgynous, and new.

The song he chose for Ziggy's debut, "Starman," was the perfect introduction to the Ziggy Stardust project. In a shrewd mix of concept and theatrics, it told of a rock and roll space man who comes to earth with an octave-leaping refrain lifted from "Somewhere over the Rainbow." This might have been enough, but Bowie—or, rather, Ziggy—outdid himself. He draped his arm around lead guitarist Mick Ronson during the song's refrain, which sounds completely tame today, but was seen as a wildly flamboyant act in the UK at the time. Coupled with a recent statement he had made to the press that "I'm gay and always have been," Bowie's carefully calculated actions laid the dynamite for an explosion.[2]

The Rise and Fall of Ziggy Stardust and the Spiders from Mars was the soundtrack to David Bowie's grand theater. Through its songs, the album sculpted the story for the project's unlikely superhero. Bowie knows that this is not just Ziggy's big chance but his own as well, and he constructs the album masterfully, filling it with concise, driving pop-rock songs brimming with hooks. Each song is cutting-edge mainstream rock and roll, the gritty sound of the Velvet Underground camped up with mad theatrical flair like Iggy Stooge (later Pop) and filled with the warmth of an acoustic guitar. In 1972, Bowie was asked to describe the album in an American radio interview. "I'll try very hard," he responded. "It's a little difficult, but it originally started as a concept album, but it kind of got broken up, because I found other songs I wanted to put in the album which wouldn't have fitted into the story of Ziggy, so at the moment it's a little fractured and a little fragmented."[3] Despite Bowie's words here, *Ziggy Stardust* forms a very cohesive narrative, one of the tightest of the rock era. Together, these pop songs tell the ultimate rock and roll myth, the rise and fall of a space-age rock and roll savior.

Ziggy Stardust begins with the ominous drumbeat of "Five Years," a song warning about an approaching apocalypse. It plays like a half-forgotten doo-wop song, stripped of its backing vocals and stretched out into a funeral march. We see newsmen weeping, stores looted for irons and televisions, and cops kneeling to kiss the feet of priests. Yet despite all this chaos, its final and most powerful verse is laser-focused, as the lyrics close in on a wistful image of innocence lost ("Thought I saw you in an ice cream parlor ..."), before totally losing it. The singer explodes into the desperate madness of the refrain: "FIVE YEARS—*AND THAT'S ALL WE'VE GOT!*"

The following "Soul Love" settles into its bouncy acoustic groove, providing a panorama of different versions of love—new love, sacred love, idiot love—setting the stage for the cosmos from which Ziggy will emerge. After the 1950s influences of "Five Years," "Soul Love" pays homage to the 1960s with its kaleidoscope of all-inclusive love. And when the fading beat of "Soul Love" continues into the thundering guitars of "Moonage Daydream," Ziggy Stardust emerges with an identity that bridges the 1950s ("I'm an alligator," alluding to Bill Haley's 1956 hit "See You Later, Alligator") and the 1960s ("I'm a mama/papa," alluding to the mid-1960s folk-pop group the Mamas and Papas), before introducing himself in contemporary terms as a "rock and roll bitch" for all of us. Meanwhile, the refrains evoke the essential weirdness of outer space. As Ziggy sings about keeping an electric eye on him and putting your ray gun to his head, the music opens up like a vista. Piano chords splash around low voices humming a strange countermelody, as though it's grounding the otherworldly sky with unknown spacecraft calmly hovering by. In later refrains, the voices are replaced with strings that heighten the drama, pulling away from Ziggy's vocal to create a beautiful, suspended tension, putting Ziggy on the edge of breaking into Earth's atmosphere.

It is here where Ziggy becomes the "Starman," and the first public signs of his arrival are told by a young boy discovering the music. This puts the focus back on the rock fan and the sudden way that an artist can arrive almost overnight. The way Ziggy's popularity spread by word-of-mouth feels organic, shifting the narrative from Ziggy's nearly unfathomable scale to an intimate small-town portrait. Fandom is very important to this work because fans are the living proof of one's superstardom. And as a statement of self-fulfilling prophecy, "Starman" marks a key moment in the Ziggy project. As the kids in the song tell that you can pick Ziggy up on television, it correlates with Bowie's real-life performance of "Starman" on *Top of the Pops*. For Bowie, life doesn't imitate art, it plays out the script that his art has written.

The last song on the first side is the only filler cut on the album, a cover of Ron Davies' "It Ain't Easy." Davies was an American country singer-songwriter who first recorded the song in 1970; later that year, Three Dog Night used it as the title track of their third album. While it's a solid song, it can be taken out of the album's narrative flow without disrupting it. Perhaps Bowie was attracted to it because it maintains a perspective from its holy-on-high mountaintop imagery— it begins with the singer looking down from a mountain and then jumping to the rooftops—but most likely, it was the song's ringing refrain that did it for him. "It ain't easy to go to heaven when you're going down," he sings again and again, in words that mirror Ziggy's descent down to earth from the heavens. Ziggy has arrived.

The second side begins with "Lady Stardust," a sweeping piano-driven ballad that tells of Ziggy's debut concert on Earth. The singer recounts how people stared at Ziggy's makeup, laughed at his long black hair, and his "animal grace." While the song was reportedly based on Marc Bolan, the leader of T. Rex who was seen as Bowie's biggest glam-rock rival, "Lady Stardust" raises questions about who Ziggy Stardust is modeled on. Despite the many names offered, as I hear the song's opening lyrics I can't help but think of that first great wild and androgynous (and seemingly overnight) rock star, Elvis Presley, who wore eye shadow in his early television appearances, had long slicked-back dyed black hair, and whose body was once compared to a snake in a *Newsweek* profile from 1956. But even more so, "Lady Stardust" is a love letter to the star-making phenomenon. The critics nod, the audience lose themselves, and the star charms; all are described together without sacrificing the magic of the situation. Buried in the second verse is perhaps the finest line on the album, sung by a member of the audience: "I smiled sadly for a love I could not obey." It captures that fleeting, bittersweet moment that connects the star and the fan, the legendary and the anonymous. "Lady Stardust" further teases reality by presenting a relatively unknown entity (Bowie) staking his claim to immortality (Ziggy)—and for a moment, catches it.

"Star" finds the singer turning "Lady Stardust" into pure stardom. For Ziggy, the role is just that, a role. Becoming a rock and roll star isn't just a natural progression of Bowie's career, but a *conscious decision*, a place where one can become a role merely by acting it out. It is here where Bowie and Ziggy's un-reality become one. Ziggy doesn't so much sing his words as he discovers them and realizes that the most enticing and exciting way to change the world is to "make a wild mutation as a rock and roll star." The stomping piano prods him, the distorted guitars surround him, and the campy backing vocals support him as he soars to become the star he sings about. "*Just watch me now—*" he mutters at the end with a wink—and indeed, the remainder of the album will play these words out.

The album's next song, "Hang on to Yourself," was used to open most Ziggy Stardust performances. Theoretically, it's the most complicated song on the album, as exemplified in its tagline, "If you think we're gonna make it, better hang on to yourself." It is as though Ziggy is singing to Bowie, which is really Bowie singing to Ziggy, which itself is again Ziggy singing to Bowie. The words go back and forth forever as any separating identity is crushed as the actor absorbs the role. The song's refrain becomes a cruel joke: in order to make it, the singer must hang on to himself—a self that, the more it is hung on to, the more it disappears. To live out the song's warning is to lose yourself between the endless layers of fantasy and reality.

The album's title track takes this riddle and captures it in the glory of performance. It's also the song by which the whole Ziggy Stardust project is best remembered. If "Ziggy Stardust" is the hardest-rocking song on the album, it's only because it cuts the deepest, using hard-rock riffs to accent what is essentially a mid-tempo ballad. The song tells of a rock and roll star who is simultaneously at his peak but "takes it too far," ultimately eclipsing his band and, in the end, this better judgment in the process. It was the story of Janis Joplin with Big Brother and the Holding Company, of Jim Morrison with the Doors. But most of all, this left-handed, space-age guitarist was the story of Jimi Hendrix and the Jimi Hendrix Experience. When Ziggy makes it big enough to be found "making love with his ego," the brilliant image hangs over the rest of the album in a vision of success and failure morphing into one.

So, the title track again begs the question, who is Ziggy Stardust? Like Jesus Christ in the Bible, there are relatively few direct physical descriptions of him. In "Lady Stardust," Ziggy first appears as a female with long black hair and makeup on her face; here, Ziggy is described as a well-hung left-handed male, singing with screwed up eyes and a screwed-down hairdo. Ziggy appears to be some sort of a cosmic shapeshifter, an intergalactic rock and roll reincarnation of Herman Melville's Confidence-Man. Furthermore, the name "Ziggy" remains elusive. Many saw it as a tribute to Iggy Stooge, a key influence on Bowie. It also echoes Twiggy, the androgynous model and actress who came to represent swinging 1960s London. Meanwhile, the surname was a nod to outsider musician Legendary Stardust Cowboy (real name Norman Carl Odam), who Bowie saw on television in the 1960s; four decades after *Ziggy Stardust*, Bowie covered Legendary Stardust Cowboy's "I Took a Trip on a Gemini Spaceship" on his 2002 album *Heathen*. But in the end, Ziggy Stardust was its own creation, stealing from everyone until it became wholly new.

The following "Suffragette City" provides the backstage for the center stage of "Ziggy Stardust," and does so more succinctly. Unlike all the enigmatic allusions of the previous song, "Suffragette City" is all sex and swagger. Now Ziggy truly does make love with his ego as sex takes over his entire life, forming a world of permanent ecstasy that many rock stars aspire to. But it is a false, hollow, and impossible existence, and it's after "Suffragette City" that the dark, tolling chords of "Rock and Roll Suicide" begin ominously.

"Rock and Roll Suicide" disguises itself as an abstract 1950s love song, complete with 12/8 time and doo-wop style backing vocals. But then, the singer leads the song astray, rips off its 1950s mask, and leaves it stranded with its haunting refrain, near spoken in isolation with only the cold heartbeat of a bass drum behind it: *"You're a rock and roll suicide."* The singer continues, building each verse upon the nervous restlessness of the first, increasing the pressure until his entire life becomes a late-night bad trip that fails to be redeemed by the new morning's rising sun. Finally, the verse-verse-verse structure cannot be stacked up any further and the singer's entire world closes in on him—

OH, NO LOVE—YOU'RE NOT ALONE!

In the song's final sweep, Ziggy turns to his audience to for proof of community against his loneliness. While some might interpret it as an actual suicide, it could also be a metaphoric one, a fever dream from which Ziggy awakes in a cold sweat. That said, the way Ziggy cries out for people's hands has a desperate anguish that feels unmistakably real.

By the time *The Rise and Fall of Ziggy Stardust and the Spiders from Mars* came out on June 16, 1972, David Bowie was already working to turn Ziggy Stardust into a real-life star. In July, influential members of the rock press were invited to witness a Ziggy Stardust show at the Royal Festival Hall. "Hello, I'm Ziggy Stardust and these are the Spiders from Mars," he stated at the beginning, letting everyone know that this was not a David Bowie concert but a Ziggy Stardust one, before tearing into "Hang on to Yourself." By the time he concluded the show with "Rock and Roll Suicide," there was evidence he was becoming the pop phenomenon that he aimed for. "When a shooting star is heading for the peak," wrote Ray Coleman in his review for the *Melody Maker*, "there is usually one concert at which it's possible to declare, 'That's it—he made it.' For David Bowie, opportunity knocked loud and clear last Saturday at London's Royal Festival Hall—and he left the stage a true 1972-style pop giant, clutching flowers from a girl who ran up and hugged and kissed him while a throng of fans milled around the stage."[4]

Following this breakthrough performance, Bowie constructed a complete world for Ziggy Stardust that became a twenty-four-hour-a-day proto-reality show. After conquering the UK, where the country's small size and concentrated music press can make an artist the next big thing, Ziggy set his sights on America. Although virtually unknown in America, he set up a tour headlining arenas and acting like rock and roll royalty. It was an entire tour built upon the idea that one can simply make themselves a first-class superstar, and the results were tragicomic. Ziggy's manager set up an American branch of his company to run the tour, many of whom were drawn from Warhol's inner circle, hired primarily on how outrageous they looked, as opposed to their knowledge or experience. Amazingly, the illusion held for the initial dates, where a good buzz in cities Cleveland and New York provided evidence of Ziggy's claims to stardom. But as the tour progressed into the heartland, the illusion fell apart, as hundreds showed up to arenas that were built for thousands. In time, Bowie was forced to learn that America was simply too big to wrap a fantasy world around.

And so, on July 3, 1973—nearly a year to the day that Ziggy Stardust debuted on *Top of the Pops* with "Starman"—Ziggy stood onstage at the Hammersmith Odeon in England, preparing for the last song of the show. Before he starts the song, he addresses the crowd. "Everybody," Ziggy begins, "This has been one of the greatest tours of our life, we really—" his thought is abandoned in the crowd's cheer. "Uh, of all the shows on the tour, this, this particular show will remain with us the longest because—" The crowd cheers again, but this time he raises his hand with a wry smile, signaling for them to wait, "Not only is it the last show of the tour, but it's the last show that we'll ever do." The crowd shouts in denial, but the star simply takes a bow with a sincere "Thank you." The final song he sings is "Rock and Roll Suicide." Usually it only refers to Ziggy Stardust, ending each night in grand tragedy while David Bowie continues on to the next gig, but this time is different. The song takes on new meaning in the shadow of Bowie's words; the rock and roll suicide now applies both to Ziggy on stage and Bowie in real life. While many were shocked that David Bowie appeared to be retiring from touring, it soon became clear that it was only Ziggy Stardust who was retiring— David Bowie would continue to play shows for the rest of his life.

And so, when Ziggy calls out at the end for the audience to give him their hands, they oblige, breaking the fourth wall between performer and audience. Yes, he was alright, and the song went on forever.

Notes

1   Miller, 299.
2   Edwards and Zanetta, 153.
3   *Far Out.*
4   Miller, 301.

10

And If the Band You're in Starts Playing Different Tunes: *The Dark Side of the Moon*

Pink Floyd released *The Dark Side of the Moon* on March 1, 1973. Sixteen days later, it entered the US *Billboard* Top 200 at #95. Forty-two days after that—April 28—it peaked at #1 for a single week. And *fifteen years* after that—July 16, 1988—it fell off the *Billboard* Top 200. *The Dark Side of the Moon*'s chart run saw four presidential administrations, three popes, two American-hosted Olympics, and once-in-a-lifetime milestones like Watergate, the end of the Vietnam War, the identification of the AIDS virus, and the Challenger explosion. To put it another way, *The Dark Side of the Moon* was on the chart for a longer period of time than the Beatles were an active band. In a genre of supposedly ephemeral music, *The Dark Side of the Moon* is an institution unto itself. It stands like a towering obelisk, so omnipresent yet so intimate, weaving itself into the lives of millions, each in entirely personal ways that belie its mass appeal.

Few could have predicted that Pink Floyd's popularity and influence would become so huge. The London-based band began as architecture's greatest gift to rock and roll. Three of its core members—bassist Roger Waters, pianist Rick Wright, and drummer Nick Mason—were architecture students when they formed Pink Floyd under the leadership of painting student Roger "Syd" Barrett. A psychedelic iconoclast, Barrett wrote the group's first singles—including the acid masterpiece "See Emily Play"—before embarking on Pink Floyd's debut album, 1967's *The Piper at the Gates of Dawn*. This was music that reached for the stars and got there, sending back strange signals from a distant galaxy. But Barrett grew increasingly withdrawn and unreliable, likely the result of his own mental instabilities and diet of hallucinogens. Before Barrett lost his way completely, Pink Floyd brought in a new singer and guitarist to augment him, David Gilmour. A five-member version of Pink Floyd lasted briefly, as Barrett soon left for good. It was now up to Waters, Wright, Mason, and Gilmour to pick up the pieces.

Waters increasingly stepped in as the role of leader, writing more of the songs and overseeing the group's creative direction. But when Pink Floyd began planning *The Dark Side of the Moon* in early 1972, the whole band pitched in. "Making *The Dark Side of the Moon*, we were all trying to do as much as we possibly could," Waters later explained. "It was a very communal thing." Although Waters was the chief lyricist in the band, *The Dark Side of the Moon* was a very much a full-band effort—and was made at the most collaborative phase in the band's history. The band shared ideas for the album around Nick Mason's kitchen table. Mason recalled that at first, there was "no coherent theme to help Roger develop his initial work. As we talked, the subject of stress emerged as a common thread."[1] He further explained how they "assembled a list of the difficulties and pressures of modern life that we particularly recognized. Deadlines, travel, the stress of flying, the lure of money, a fear of dying, and the problems of mental instability spilling over into madness ... Armed with this list Roger went off to continue working on the lyrics."[2] Other band members saw the concept through a slightly different lens. "It was madness, I suppose—to put it briefly," David Gilmour explained. "The pressures of modern living, and all the elements that one goes through that conspire to send some people insane."[3]

But *The Dark Side of the Moon* is not just about stress or insanity. It is an album that finds the profound in the ordinary, an extended meditation on the things we do without even realizing it. Most actions on the album are so routine, we don't even realize we're doing them. They are the mundane tasks that blur together to create the busywork of our lives. And so, people breathe, they wake up to alarms, they run, they dig holes, they transfer flights, they scribble lines on a page, they buy things with money, they come home, they get the daily newspaper, they go up, they come down. They hang on in quiet desperation.

The Dark Side of the Moon is also an album about space—the space through which time passes, the space within ourselves, the space between the people in our lives—all orchestrated with a sound that itself conjures space. No rock band has ever conveyed the sound and feel of the solar system than Pink Floyd. There is a vastness in the band's sound, an inherent distance that washes over the listener like an interstellar dream. It may aim for the darkness between the stars, but it winds up burrowing into the darkness of our inner-being.

The Dark Side of the Moon begins with a heartbeat, pounding through the darkness of inner-space in an echo of the galaxies beyond our own. Or, at least, it sounds like a heartbeat. It's actually Nick Mason's drum recorded to sound like a heartbeat when it became apparent that the album's pace is far slower than an actual human heartbeat. The album emerges on its own terms. Part of the album's power is that it sounds incredible. If engineer Alan Parsons did nothing else after this album, his place in the annals of rock production would be secure. *The Dark Side of the Moon* was recorded with a crisp fidelity that allows it to sound more contemporary than virtually everything else released in this period, and the album immediately puts its sound to striking use. The heartbeat gives way to an overture of sorts, a brief sonic preview of what's in store later on in the record—we hear the cashbox of "Money" and the mad laughter of "Brain Damage," before the sound of an airship comes closer and closer as a voice screams like a flock of birds—and then we are deposited into the laid-back, shimmering groove that is the album's signature. "Breathe" invites us to breathe in the air, before reminding us that everything we touch and see "Is all your life will ever be." "If there's any central message," Waters once explained, "it's this: This [i.e., life] is not a rehearsal. As far as we know, you only get one shot . . ."[4] For a song so mellow, it sets the album's dire tone about how now is all you've got. It's like a lullaby sung by Nietzsche.

"Breathe" spills into "On the Run," a mad dash of an instrumental fueled by a gurgling, churning synthesizer, and footsteps racing through the airport. The intensity only builds as the song enters a sonic texture of an airplane getting ready for takeoff, rising into the sky, hitting a comfortable cruising altitude, and then crashes down in flames like the Hindenburg. *"Live for today, gone tomorrow, that's me, Hahaaaa!"* says a creepy old voice right before the plane crashes. Voices like this one heard in "On the Run" haunt the record like ghosts, balancing the severity of the music with inane gallows humor. Pink Floyd assembled these voices from people around the studio, handing participants a set of cards and asking them to read the question and provide an answer. The questions were about people's biggest fears, opinions about life and death, and violent incidents in their lives. From this assortment of people and responses, the group chose the best ones and panned them across the album's vistas at carefully chosen times to enhance the songs.

After "On the Run," we hear silence, until, out of nowhere, we're dropped into a clock factory. It clangs, buzzes, and rings like everyone unwelcome wakeup call you've ever received all at once. This initiates "Time," which is the only full group composition on the record and one of its finest moments. The song works itself up into an easy R&B groove as the singer coolly kills off the hours of the day. And then, the whole thing shifts into a remarkable, lilting bridge, warning how a decade can go by without even realizing it. If time is an illusion, then the song "Time" flattens it until every year, every month, every day, every hour, every minute, every second is cut down into arbitrary units that become one in the same—a bunch of meaningless units when we are always just "one day closer to death." But then, it's gone. "The song is over," the singer ruefully observes, "thought I'd something more to say." "Time" then segues into a reprise of "Breathe" so effortlessly that you don't even realize they're two different songs. The singer makes his way home as church bells toll in the distance, and for a brief, fleeting moment on the album, everything is at peace.

Rick Wright's "The Great Gig in the Sky" is next, his soft, haunting piano chords invoking the sad grace of a funeral. And then out of the music comes the wordless vocal of singer Clare Torry, whom Alan Parsons invited to take part in the recording session. Her impassioned, soaring voice rises all around, like a spirit being conjured out of their casket at a funeral. Death is everywhere, and we can almost hear the soul twisting and turning its way forever upwards into the afterlife. The incidental interviews now discuss death—"*If you can hear this whispering you are dying*," whispers one—and the song becomes a tempest from earth to purgatory and beyond. Eventually, the vocal winds back down to the nothingness from which emerged. Wright plays the final chord of the song until the sound wavers slightly, and the first side of *The Dark Side of the Moon* is gone.

The second side of *The Dark Side of the Moon* begins with a cash register ringing and change being emptied into its drawer. The receipt paper's tear and jingling change complete a small loop that dances like a symphony of capitalism. Roger Waters' bass picks up on the unlikely groove source, soon joined by Nick Mason's drums, Dave Gilmour's guitar, and Rick Wright's keyboards into a funky rhythm. "Money" is the most recognizable song on the album and its only hit— as well as the first Pink Floyd song to make the *Billboard* Hot 100, peaking at #13. Its memorable sound effects and catchy hook fit perfectly with the simple, relatable lyrics, while the song's structure finds room for both a boogie section and an assist on the tenor saxophone by Dick Parry. When one thinks of the money that Pink Floyd would get from the sales of *The Dark Side of the Moon*, it adds an extra layer of irony to a song already overflowing with it.

Following "Money" is the album's second single, "Us and Them," which peaked one notch below the *Billboard* Hot 100 at #101. Rick Wright had been kicking the song's chord structure around for years, haunting enough to be a funeral dirge, yet stately enough to be a royal procession. "Us and Them" is filled with contrasting word pairings—me and you, black and blue, up and down, with and without—all of which imply starkly drawn lines but are actually just subtle shadings. Perhaps the most masterful part of "Us and Them' is how it captures the hypocrisies of war. "Forward he cried from the rear," the singer recounts, "and the front rank died." The economy of these words is immense. The commanding officer is ostensibly leading the men, but does so from the back, using his troops as a shield to protect himself. The singer coldly notes the general sitting watching the "lines on the map" move "from side to side." There is an eerie sense of inevitable gravitational movement, like a ball rolling around a tilting wooden labyrinth maze. And yet, for a song couched in death and violence, "Us and Them" is lovely, an evocative piece of music that can be soothing to the casual listener. In this way, this song about contradiction itself becomes a contradiction.

And then, after a storming bridge, the textures of "Us and Them" realign as "Any Colour You Like," an instrumental piece that reprises "Breathe" to create the musically freest thing on the album. "Any Colour You Like" is a testament to the fact that *The Dark Side of the Moon* is truly a group effort, with all members contributing to the final result. Wright's textured keyboards and synthesizers weave an intricate fabric only to be blasted by Gilmour's sharp electric guitar, as he brings things down to a sparer, funkier sound, with the rhythm section of Waters and Wright shadowing him every step of the way in a sliding, almost psychedelic groove. This is Gilmour's moment to shine, and the song peaks at his manic call-and-response guitar riffs, bouncing back and forth across the spectrum like a space-age "Dueling Banjos." Wright's keyboards swell to bolster Gilmour's guitar so that it can usher the song to its final lingering note, which lights the fuse for the album's grand finale of "Brain Damage" and "Eclipse."

Gilmour's guitar steps back to initiate "Brain Damage" with a shimmering pattern like the Byrds on Quaaludes. There is a palpable anticipation in the sound. Over the main guitar pattern, another guitar squeals back against the music in a perfect arc; Mason keeps time on a high-hat as everything hovers. For the first time on the album, Roger Waters sings lead. He begins by intoning, almost speaking the song's first six simple words: "The lunatic is on the grass." For a song about a stark raving madman, Waters sounds eerily calm. The music plays ominously, until it builds, Gilmour's guitar pushing ahead as Wright's organ blasts behind him like rocket fuel, and Mason's drums tumble triumphantly into four-wheel drive. "And if the dam breaks open—" the singer warns as the music gushes out like a tidal wave, illustrating the disaster as he sings it, he promises to see you on the dark side of the moon. After a second verse that embellishes the madness—the lunatic is now in his head, the singer declares, answered by the mad laughter from an interview clip—the sky changes. The music swells to a second refrain of clouds bursting and thunder sounding in your ear, an apocalypse of a thousand dams bursting as the walls of Babylon crumble to the ground. But then, things get strangely personal—

And if the band you're in starts playing different tunes—

For an album that wears its universality as its coat of many colors (an entire spectrum, in fact, of any color you like), this line seems oddly specific, tipping their hand. For such a seemingly simple sentiment, there's a lot to unpack. On one level, a band is a small community in which everybody does their part to contribute to the overall wellness of the collective whole. But "Brain Damage" tells of a broken band, a splintered community. We can imagine ourselves playing a song in a band, only to look around and realize that the other members are playing something else entirely. It is a disorienting image, a band member estranged within their own group.

It is impossible to hear this line and not think of Syd Barrett. "There *was* a residue of Syd in all of this," Waters explained. "It was pretty recent history. Syd had been the central creative force in the early days—maybe I provided some of the engine room—and so his having succumbed to schizophrenia was an enormous blow ... it really concentrates the mind on how ephemeral one's sensibilities and mental capacities can be." Waters further explained his fear "that one is not necessarily the master of one's own identity; that we're all marionettes, and the strings of our lives are pulled by our history, our backgrounds, our parents, our ancestors, and so on. I did feel at time close to madness myself."[5] Waters takes the external crisis of Barrett's madness and makes into a personal one: If Syd can go mad, then why not I? The answers provided by the album—the notion that the pressures of modern society make us all mad—turns the personal back into the universal.

The album's finale, "Eclipse," thrashes out of "Brain Damage" with a wild, rollicking tempo with Wright's organ playing like a gospel revival tent. In fact, it's barely a song at all, but a litany of verbs piled on top of each other—all that you touch, see, taste, feel, love, hate, etc.—that together approximate the structure of the human condition. In case it missed anything, "Eclipse" concludes by declaring that everything's in tune under the sun, and yet, "the sun is eclipsed by the moon." As the music fades, a barely audible voice steals the entire show: "*There is no dark side in the moon, really. Matter of fact, it's all dark.*" This is the voice of Gerry O'Driscoll, the Irish doorman at the studio where *The Dark Side of the Moon* was recorded. Among those interviewed, O'Driscoll gave the best responses among and his closing words pull the trick of eclipsing "Eclipse"—and the rest of the album. The only sound to follow on your way out it is Mason's heartbeat drum, bringing it all back to the beginning.

In many ways, *The Dark Side of the Moon* is the quintessential concept album. Its iconic cover of a black triangle splitting a line into a spectrum of light captures both the album's universal big picture as well as the subtly changing hues it contains. It's both a grand statement and all about the details, rewarding repeated close listening with the nuance of a Renaissance painting. And yet, *The Dark Side of the Moon* has enough concepts to fill several concept albums. Some hear it as one person's journey through life and subsequent madness; others hear it as a rumination on the arbitrary categories we've imposed upon our lives without ever questioning it. The band saw it as a study of the difficult parts of life, and you can hear that, too.

I personally hear it as Pink Floyd grappling to understand the trauma of their founder's mental disintegration, filtered through their own ideas of what brings you to the edge. In under forty-five minutes, they cover a lot: life ("Speak to Me"/"Breathe"), space ("On the Run"), time ("Time"), religion ("The Great Gig in the Sky"), wealth ("Money"), society ("Us and Them"), art ("Any Colour You Like"), and madness ("Brain Damage"/"Eclipse"), all bookended by the human heart. It's as though the entire record exists as a figment in Syd Barrett's fragile mind. While many consider Pink Floyd's 1979 double-album *The Wall* to be their greatest concept album, *The Dark Side of the Moon* is earlier, tighter, and more iconic. And not coincidentally, *The Wall*'s focus on a person's struggle with the stresses of life and madness continues many of the same themes as *The Dark Side of the Moon*. *The Wall* also found Waters taking increasing leadership of the band to varying degrees of success. Never again would Pink Floyd function as a unit like they did for *The Dark Side of the Moon*. The result was their masterpiece, in which they were able to come to terms with Barrett's psychological demise by creating the most popular concept album of all-time.

Notes

1 Mason, 165.
2 Ibid., 166.
3 Harris, 74–5.
4 Ibid., 75.
5 Ibid., 81–2.

Part Three

The Modern Era (1975–89)

11

Tear the Roof off the Sucker: *Mothership Connection*

By the mid-1970s, George Clinton made a name for himself with a pair of musical projects: Parliament and Funkadelic. Both were groups that mixed rhythm and blues, rock, soul, and a sprinkling of jazz to help foster a new kind of dance music: funk. Clinton built upon the music pioneered by James Brown and Sly and the Family Stone, with a different focus for each group. Parliament was the funky offspring of Clinton's first project, a doo-wop group called the Parliaments. This was the more commercial of the two outfits, focused on hooks that aimed for the radio and were put over by horns. Funkadelic's music was more rock-oriented with long guitar jams and messier ideas. Despite the two groups being on different record labels, they both used the same revolving door of musicians. In fact, the assemblage of musicians would often just go in the studio and cut tracks built on grooves, with Clinton later designating which tracks were by "Parliament" and which were by "Funkadelic."

In 1975, a notion struck Clinton as he was listening to the playbacks of the hours of riffs, jams, and layering tracks. "As I sorted through all the tracks, I knew that they needed a unifying idea, too, not just a theme but a kind of plot," he wrote in his autobiography.

> *Mothership Connection* was that idea. Now, with almost forty years of hindsight, people can look back and take it in stride: a concept album based around a crazy alien funk mythology. But at the time, it was harder to understand exactly where the idea came from. Drugs may have had something to do with it: they furnished confidence and momentum and sometimes turned sparks of ideas into bonfires. But it was also the natural—or, if you'd prefer, unnatural—step in our thinking. In [Parliament's previous album] *Chocolate City*, we imagined a black man in the White House. That would take thirty-four years to come true. For *Mothership Connection*, we went even further afield and imagined a black man in space.[1]

Some people at Clinton's record company interpreted this more narrowly as a spaceship coming down into the ghetto. "In their mind there was a black-liberation dimension, alien beings coming down to save all the poor people," Clinton explained. "I saw it differently. To me it was pimps in outer space, the spaceship as a kind of high-tech Cadillac."[2]

And while space travel has its risks of isolation and estrangement—such as we have seen with *The Dark Side of the Moon*—Parliament turns this notion on its head in *Mothership Connection* by using space as the ultimate unifier. Parliament's vision was shaped by LSD and the promise of the 1960s. While other groups abandoned psychedelic drugs in favor of heavy metal, punk, or soul, Parliament remained on its cosmic trip. Instead of chasing the music until it became an anachronism, Parliament forged their own patented brand of funk that evoked the depths of hallucinogenic drugs while keeping an eye on the dance floor.

Despite the precision of the music, the songs were often written communally. "Very few of our songs were planned," recalled bassist Cardell "Boogie" Mosson. "'Hey Boog, you got a tune?' 'Yeah—' 'Oh, yeah, that's slick. Put that on there.' And it just happens. I come in, hear something—'Hey, I got something for you, G.' 'Okay, I'll keep running the track.' George was the referee."[3] Boogie could have called Clinton a producer or mastermind, but instead opts for referee. This implies that the musicians are like teammates playing a game, making the studio into a more communal and enjoyable environment. It also indicates that Clinton takes a step back from the action. If he is the referee—as opposed to say, a coach, trainer, or manager—then he simply lets the teammates play and only gets involved when someone goes offsides. He can mold the proceedings to an extent, but the players have an autonomy that is unusual for a major rock band. They are free agents playing on the field of funk.

For Parliament, life was a never-ending party in which everyone was invited, and they were the house band. Theirs was an ethos of freedom, inclusion, and community that went beyond the graphic boundaries of this planet. The supposed inspiration for *Mothership Connection* was when Clinton and bassist Bootsy Collins encountered a UFO that beamed light on their car while driving home. "We thought the Mothership was mad at us for giving up the funk without permission," Clinton later recalled. "And then it hit the car again head on. We accepted that as proof and said, 'Let's go funkin'.' We had been endowed."[4] But with inspiration came trepidation. "We were very nervous about the project," Clinton later explained. "We had a concept that was the bomb but black audiences have never really bought a concept album. We decided to save most of the concept for the second album (*The Clones of Dr. Funkenstein*) and put the hits on the first release to grab attention."[5]

And yet, *Mothership Connection* has more than enough of its own central concept. The album reaches back into rock and roll's original means of connection: the radio signal. *Mothership Connection* documents an interstellar radio show that takes the lost funk from Earth and returns it through a spaceship. "Space was a place but it was also a concept," wrote Clinton in his memoir, "a metaphor for being way out there the way that Jimi Hendrix had been. Imagining a record in space was imagining artistry unbound, before it was recalled to Earth."[6] And the album more than lived up to this vision.

A deep voice begins over a fat, anticipatory groove:

> *Ah, good evening. Ah, do not attempt to adjust your radio, there is nothing wrong. We have taken control as to bring you this special show . . . Welcome to W-E-F-U-N-K, better known as WE-FUNK, or deeper still, the Mothership Connection. Home of the extraterrestrial brothers. Dealers of funky music. P. Funk, uncut funk, the* bomb.

A second voice cuts in, slightly sped up like a cartoon:

> *Coming to you directly from the Mothership, top of the Chocolate Milky Way, 500,000 kilowatts of P. Funk-power . . . I'm known as Lollipop Man, alias the Long-Haired Sucker. My motto is—*
>
> MAKE MY FUNK THE P. FUNK
> I WANTS TO GET FUNKED UP

The instruments, which had been fluttering about tentatively—a hi-hat cymbal keeping time here, some jazzy horn riffs there—fall into place as everything locks into one funky groove. The voices are a mob of tones and timbre, seeming to be the voices of an entire city melding together. Sly Stone pioneered this sound in the late-1960s in his classic string of singles with the Family Stone, before making darker, heavier music in the 1970s. Parliament flipped the script—they took this heavier feel and applied it to the uplifting party music that kept the spirit of the 1960s alive. It's a thick sound, dripping with acid, yet musically adventurous. And like Frank Zappa or Jethro Tull, it didn't take itself (or anything) too seriously. The lyrics were often silly inside jokes or chants carried on simple hooks that plowed into your brain. The music was dense, weird, experimental, and wild. But most of all, it was *fun*.

The instant that "P. Funk (Wants to Get Funked Up)" recedes into silence, the groove of the next song abruptly begins. "Well, alright!" the DJ pops in, keeping the patter strong:

'Star Child,' Citizens of the Universe, recording angels. We have returned to claim the Pyramids..."

What might first seem like a spaced-out DJ's patter is the key to this entire album. Building upon the work by 1950s avant-garde jazz musician Sun Ra (who claimed to be an alien from Saturn), Jimi Hendrix's otherworldly *Electric Ladyland*, and Ishmael Reed's 1972 novel *Mumbo Jumbo*, Parliament's masterpiece helped define what would become later would become known as Afrofuturism. The term was coined by journalist Mark Dery in his 1994 essay "Black to the Future":

> Speculative fiction that treats African-American themes and addresses African-American concerns in the context of twentieth-century technoculture—and, more generally, African-American signification that appropriates images of technology and a prosthetically enhanced future—might, for want of a better term, be called "Afrofuturism." The notion of Afrofuturism gives rise to a troubling antinomy: Can a community whose past has been deliberately rubbed out, and whose energies have subsequently been consumed by the search for legible traces of its history, imagine possible futures?[7]

In *Electric Ladyland*, Afrofuturism was one of many diverse elements that helped give the album its shape. On *Mothership Connection*, it's a central issue. George Clinton uses the album to propose that the community culture of the future—which is to say, the party on the Mothership itself—can be used to claim an ancient and forgotten past. The Pyramids are a testament to the ancient civilization of Egypt, one of the oldest civilizations known to man. By returning to claim the Pyramids, the album pulls the rug out from under Western Culture, using the African past to prove that they were miles ahead of everyone in the future. By finding the past in a vision of the future, *Mothership Connection* answers the question posed in "Black to Future" some twenty years before it was asked.

None of this is to take away from the fact that "Star Child" is also one great funky groove—in fact, it only enhances it. George Clinton spent too many years toiling as a Motown staff writer not to think in terms of musical hooks. Before the main words are sung, he's already feeding the riff to the listeners: "Alright, hear any noise, ain't nobody but me and the boys, gettin' down—hit it fellas!" These words are sung like a Greek chorus of funk, an endless group of voices that chant in unison, a crowd one can join but never stand opposed to.

"You have overcome," the DJ announces, "for I am here." The music suddenly shifts into a haunting, hypnotizing groove featuring a new vocal hook:

Swing down, sweet chariot
Stop, and let me ride

Anyone hearing these words in 1975 would have likely thought of the African American spiritual "Swing Low, Sweet Chariot," written around the end of the Civil War. The song evoked the gospel of Elijah, who was taken up to heaven in a chariot: "Swing low, sweet chariot, coming for to carry me home." The first known recording of the song was by the Fisk Jubilee Singers in 1909 and has remained a standard ever since, continuing strong into the rock era. Elvis Presley cut it in 1960, Sam Cooke made it the title track of his 1961 album *Swing Low*, and Joan Baez sung it at Woodstock in 1969. Meanwhile, the phrase became so potent that Chuck Berry paraphrased it in his 1964 single, "Promised Land," turning the chariot into an airplane.

However, people hearing the "sweet chariot" refrain of "Star Child" who were born after 1975 would likely think of Dr. Dre's "Let Me Ride," from his classic 1992 gangsta rap album, *The Chronic*. For many younger listeners, this song is where they first encountered Parliament's "sweet chariot" refrain, only this time, the freedom it evokes is through a tough guy stance on the streets of Compton. "Let Me Ride" is as much a shout-out to the West Coast G-funk gangsta community as "Star Child" is to the P-Funk empire—only instead of futuristic spaceships, Dre uses old-school lowriders. On a strictly musical level, *Mothership Connection* does predict the future, as its grooves would be sampled in countless hip-hop classics.

And yet, Parliament was as much an inheritor as it was an influencer. The following "Unfunky UFO" appears to borrow elements from Sly and the Family Stone's 1971 song "Luv N' Haight," such as a similar tempo, rotating vocalists, and a similar cadence. After having created "P-Funk (Wants to Get Funked Up)," "Star Child," and "Give Up the Funk (Tear the Roof off the Sucker)," the latter of which anchors the album's second side, the rest of the songs were tailored to fit the concept. "With those three songs nailed down, I went into the vault of unreleased tracks and began to retrofit the strongest ones to this new concept," explained Clinton. "'Unfunky UFO' was a funky track that I knew I could link to the same theme."[8] The song's hook about how you could feel so much better if you could show them how to funk ends the first side on a high.

The second side of *Mothership Connection* begins with "Supergroovalisticprosifunkstication," one of many multisyllabic, seemingly impenetrable titles that Clinton released over the years. The song featured one of the best hooks on the album about how if you give people what they want when they want it, then they'll want it all the time. For an album about community, "Supergroovalisticprosifunkstication" reads like a Declaration of Independence and Constitution rolled up into one. It picked up where Parliament's previous album from April 1975, *Chocolate City*, left off. "They still call it the White House, but that's a temporary condition too," Clinton famously said at the beginning of *Chocolate City*'s title track. The following song on *Mothership*, "Handcuffs," was an outtake left over from *Chocolate City*. Tellingly, it's the track that least fits into the album's theme. It's also the song that has aged the poorest, with its sadomasochistic lyrics dripping with male chauvinism. For an album so fixed on visions of the future, this feels like a tunnel into the past. Mercifully, it's the shortest track on the album and the song's groove keeps the party flowing.

A funky drumbeat signals the album's finest track, "Give Up the Funk (Tear the Roof Off the Sucker)," suspended in its first ten seconds, while "Sting" Ray Davis's impossibly low bass voice chants over the groove:

Tear the roof off
We're gonna tear the roof off the mother sucker
Tear the roof off the sucker

Anyone who doubts George Clinton's doo-wop roots should look no further than here. Davis's intro is a love letter to every bass man who ever boomed, but it wouldn't be worth anything if the song that followed couldn't live up to its opening. And it does. "Give Up the Funk" is perhaps Parliament's greatest recording—only 1978's "Flash Light" can touch it—and it was, not coincidentally, their biggest hit up to that point. Frustratingly, the edited version of the song that became the hit omitted Davis's classic intro part because of its use of the phrase "mother sucker," providing a rare moment when the real radio stations put a check on *Mothership Connection*'s fictional one.

Even without Davis's classic into, "Give Up the Funk" has a joyous, infectious vibe, pitched somewhere between the disco club and the church house. Employing only around forty different words (counting contractions like "We'll" as separate words), any deepness lacking in the words is more than made up for by the music. The mix of countless voices bounce on top of the music's groove, with Fred Wesley and Maceo Parker's horns providing a slithering countermelody, as Bootsy Collins's bass plays from another dimension, snaking all around the song, hitting notes that support the groove without ever sacrificing creativity. Everything is held together by the strutting, stuttering drums of Jerome Brailey, the secret hero of the song. He remembered: "George would usually be sitting behind the board, and we'd be in the room playing and jamming—me, Bootsy, [guitarist] Garry Shider—and George would say, 'Let's take that one,' and we'd take it, you know. And then he'd come up with the lyrics. Whoever he thought about giving writer's credit to—usually it was Bernie or Bootsy. For 'Give Up the Funk,' I was just excited to be in the group, I didn't go say, 'Don't forget to put my name down.' He just remembered to do it."[9] Despite the spontaneity that fostered the track, the whole thing works because it keeps returning to its immortal hook:

We want the funk
Give up the funk

Including one more iconic counter-hook—"We're gonna turn this mother out!"—"Give It Up" is music feel-good, healing music that not only moves the body but also soothes the soul.

The final song on *Mothership Connection*, "Night of the Thumpasorus Peoples," is a fitting close to the album. It's largely instrumental, as the only words are nonsensical chants. It sounds like the soundtrack to a sci-fi fantasy movie in which a spaceship from the future crashes into an ancient earth. The music remains hard, joyous, and funky as ever, while the singing sounds like the chanting of some undefined, primitive people. A buzzing sound emerges during the song, at times threatening to overtake it, sounding like a cross between a giant jug, a 200-pound bee, and a whoopee cushion. There is a sense of novelty that permeates the proceedings until an unlikely alliance is formed between the heavy funk of Sly and the Family Stone's *There's a Riot Goin' On!*, the atmospheric rhythms of Curtis Mayfield's *Superfly*, and the adolescent humor of Frank Zappa's *We're Only in It for the Money*. And yet, the horns on the track have never sounded so graceful, rising above the music in terms of both their performance and sophistication. But mostly, this is Bootsy's show—you can spend the entire song simply listening to the bass filling out the bottom with slippery notes that dance between the hard grooves of the down beats, refusing to ever be pinned down, as he eventually helps usher the album into the silence.

Considering all the conceptual planning that went into *Mothership Connection*, it's a bit surprising that George Clinton does not end the album with a radio sign-off of some sort. That said, the album still holds together remarkably well. One gets the feeling that the album doesn't so much end as it recedes into space, a radio signal fading away as it grows farther away from its listener.

Clinton's Parliament and Funkadelic may have created conceptually-tighter albums (like Parliament's *The Clones of Dr. Funkenstein* in 1976) and ones that reached the same—if not greater—artistic heights (like Funkadelic's *One Nation Under a Groove* in 1978), but Parliament's *Mothership Connection* was the album that put them over, giving them one of their highest-charting albums, as well as their highest-charting pop single ("Give Up the Funk"). And while some purists might argue that 1977's *Funkentelechy vs. the Placebo Syndrome* is an even stronger album, one can't deny that *Mothership Connection* had the strongest idea—which is to say, concept—in part for its simplicity: A radio show from the space-age future.

One listen and it is irresistible to put a glide in your stride and a dip in your hip—and come on up to the *Mothership*.

Notes

1 Clinton, 140–1.
2 Ibid., 141.
3 Mills, et al., 92–3.
4 Patoski.
5 Needs, 208–9.
6 Clinton, 141.
7 Dery, 180.
8 Clinton, 142.
9 Mills, et al., 93.

12

Fairy Tale High: *Once Upon a Time . . .*

As we have seen, the Broadway cast album was a key precursor to the concept album, as soundtracks to shows like *Oklahoma!, South Pacific,* and *West Side Story* were blockbuster albums of their day. One reason why these sold so well is because they targeted the older album-buying demographic who were not interested in rock and roll. However, with rock's growing sophistication, crowned by *Sgt. Pepper's Lonely Hearts Club Band*, rock was seen as a music serious enough for Broadway. The anti-war rock musical *Hair* revolutionized the American stage in 1968 and reverberated worldwide.

Among the countless up-and-coming performers to get their break in *Hair* was nineteen-year-old African American singer and actress Donna Summer (then known as LeDonna Gaines), who played one of the leads in the 1968 Munich production. "It was all part of my fairy-tale existence in a beautiful country that I had completely fallen in love with," Summer wrote of Germany in her autobiography *Ordinary Girl: The Journey*.[1] She later explained:

> Imagine falling asleep in a quaint little German bed-and-breakfast to awaken with the dawn to the smell of *lebkuchen* (gingerbread) and [my then-boyfriend] Ronnie calling me from outside in a horse-drawn carriage. I quickly ran to the balcony, threw open the doors, and stepped barefoot into two feet of white, virgin snow. It was a real-life Christmas snow globe, with Neuschwanstein castle towering above us. (Neuschwanstein was Walt Disney's inspiration for Cinderella's castle.) It was a mystical and surreal vision that I will never forget, one every girl should be allowed to experience at least once.[2]

This fairytale scene stayed with Summer. A few years later, she was a single mom in Munich struggling to make ends meet. Summer took singing jobs wherever available, which led her to Giorgio Moroder, an Italian-born record producer who worked with his partner, English-born Pete Bellotte, at his Musicland studio in Munich.

To Moroder, Summer was a true anomaly: A professional African American female singer in Germany. She sang on scores of demos, including a song they wrote together in 1975, "Love to Love You Baby." The record was little more than a hook, filled out by improvised sexy lyrics and sultry moans by Summer. Paul Bogart, the American head of Casablanca Records, liked what he heard and, to Summer's shock, released the song with her original vocal. It became an international hit, virtually creating an overnight sensation fairytale for Summer when she returned to America. However, the record's dripping sexuality—reinforced by Bogart's careful presentation of Summer as a seductive vixen—made her into a sex symbol that she was never quite comfortable with. "To this day I will approach a song as an actress approaches a script," Summer later wrote. "I do not sing; I act. When I sing, I sing with the voice of the character in the song. Because of that, I don't have to make every song something from my perspective; rather, it's something from the heart and soul of the character who is doing the singing."[3] Regardless of her methodology, "Love to Love You Baby" set the stage for her career.

Summer, Moroder, and Bellotte pioneered the burgeoning disco sound, ultimately resulting in 16 number one songs on the *Billboard* dance charts. And while many saw disco as degenerating rock from the album back to the single, Summer was allowed creativity that few others were granted. She used the album format to stretch out and showcase her talent, releasing a series of increasingly ambitious albums: *A Love Trilogy*, with a side-long song cycle of three disco love songs, *Four Seasons of Love*, containing one song for each season (plus a reprise of spring), and *I Remember Yesterday*, a tour of past musical stylings. The culmination of this period was Summer's first double-album, *Once Upon a Time . . .*, which was released in the fall of 1977. In his contemporary review for his weekly "Disco File" column in *Record World*, Vince Aletti wrote that the album "is a modern interpretation of the Cinderella story, a disco fairytale in four acts apparently designed to work as both a concept album and a musical score for [a] future film or play."[4] Over the course of the album, Summer allows herself to take on a role in musical theater while also seemingly drawing inspiration from a story that, if not autobiographical per se, tells of an overnight rags-to-riches fantasy that she could relate to.

Once Upon a Time . . . is one of the best-organized concept albums ever made. Unlike so many other concept albums, Donna Summer's masterpiece can be followed from its first listen. And yet, for all its reliance upon one of the oldest stories in human history, it maintains a clarity that never wallows in cliche. The album is divided into four acts—one for each side—three of which are programmed as an extended suite of music with no interruptions. (Indeed, upon its initial release, many discos played each side like it was one big song.) All the songs were written by Summer, Moroder, and Bellotte, which speaks to the team's versatility and focus.

Act One begins with the epic sweep of "Once Upon a Time," teasing us with the crescendos and strings of a Hollywood period piece theme for thirty seconds, before reinventing itself at a disco rhythm. Summer sings in a clear, cooing voice, spinning the tale of a girl living in the "land of dreams unreal." The song's haunting melody and stark lyrics of loneliness, futile cries, and bitterness belie the upbeat music underneath. The backing band cooks—drums setting the stuttering beat, bass grooving all around, wah-wah guitars bringing the funk, horns bringing the soul, and strings bringing the pop. Summer's voice is at the center of it all, singing with a childlike wonder that evokes the pure pop of a Supremes-era Diana Ross.

"Once Upon a Time" continues into "Faster and Faster to Nowhere" before you even realize that it's a different song. "Where am I going? What is this place?" Summer whispers in a claustrophobic urban dystopia that traps the singer. The song's brisk tempo bites at her feet like bloodhounds, the booming male backup singers pushing along the singer's trip to nowhere. Between the verses, Summer embraces the role, talking nervously to herself, to the listener, to anyone who might hear, eventually calling out for help. Hers is a journey into a heart of darkness that closes in on all sides.

She is rescued by the airy pop of "Fairy Tale High." The song is built around a lilting keyboard melody that nearly turns it into a nursery rhyme, as Summer sings like a radiant fairy godmother, taking the listener on a fairytale high and inviting us to "reach for a star." The song corresponds to the album's gatefold, which features Summer, clad in a white flowing dress sprinkling star-shaped fairy-dust over the skyline of New York City. She is a benevolent goddess who towers over the urban land that had previously trapped her album's protagonist. And the fact that it's a fairytale high speaks not only to her height in the photograph, but the effects of the substances (some of which can sprinkle like fairy-dust) deep in the city below.

Closing out Act One is "Say Something Nice," which deals with the insecurities of the protagonist. Despite the song's catchiness, the lyrics find the singer's self-worth seeming dependent on her lover's compliments. "From a contemporary standpoint, it's a message that doesn't flatter the singer; her neediness the negative image of modern female pop," Alex Jeffery writes in his book about the album.[5] But at the same time, Jeffery hears something else: "If you look at the song a different way, there's something about it that, in 1977, seems already to be commenting on the attention-starved economy of the social media-obsessed present."[6] Indeed, the song is the musical equivalent of a sexy Instagram post, begging for a "like." In terms of the album's greater structure, "Say Something Nice" brings the existential anxiety of the album's story from the societal to the personal. In fact, the song implies that one can trigger the other—after the singer feels the city closing in on her, she now finds her confidence closing in too.

Act Two is the most striking side of the album, a three-song suite strung together by the eternal pulse of electronic instruments. An undulating clicking sound fades in and sets the tempo for "Now I Need You," triggering a wash of whirring, hissing, and synthesizer sounds, a tundra of austere beauty. A bass drumbeat is the driving force while synthesized melodic fragments flicker and flash like the northern lights. Summer comes in like a ghost, singing a haunting melody about the unfulfilled promise of a departed lover. "Now I Need You" balances Summer's all-too-human vocal against the cold churning machines, all punctuated by the "NOW I NEED YOU, I NEED YOU" refrain sung by a chorus of lost souls in Purgatory. Yet there is a tenderness in the song that cuts through the sonic textures of the machines that frame it.

"Now I Need You" continues directly into "Working the Midnight Shift," with the only signal of the transition being a frigid arpeggio that drips down like icicles. Lyrically, "Working the Midnight Shift" is one of the most successful pieces in *Once Upon a Time...*, an elegant portrait of the working poor. The song uses short, simple statements that paint a vivid picture for anyone who's ever worked late hours to make ends meet: "When the city is waking up," the singer intones solemnly, "I'm going home." For many who grew up after the disco era, Summer's most famous song is "She Works Hard for the Money," her upbeat pop anthem from 1983. "Working the Midnight Shift" is a quieter, subtler prelude to the later hit, and a potent reminder of Summer's own working-class roots.

"Queen for a Day" begins with a churning sound not unlike "Now I Need You," before quickly assembling itself into a stately march. More than any other song on *Once Upon a Time...*, "Queen for a Day" taps into the element of the Cinderella story that gives it its American power: reinvention. The singer dreams of being queen for a day "So you'd never know ... it's me." If there is a fairy godmother who assists her in getting ready, the singer leaves her out, perhaps suggesting that she has pulled herself up. She imagines herself dressed in "ribbons and lace," and of course, "shoes made of glass"—and then it's off to the (disco) ball. The most compelling moment of *Once Upon a Time...* comes in about four minutes into "Queen for a Day," when a piano announces the song's shift from machines providing the music to a group of blood-and-guts musicians, who pick up the groove without missing a beat. The party is back on for Act Three.

In Act Three, we see Cinderella at the ball strutting her stuff to "If You Got It Flaunt It," which may be the great lost disco anthem. The band is back in full gear with the drums keeping the beat while the horns sway and the bass bubbles up like champagne. Employing fewer words than any other song on the album, "If You Got It Flaunt It" simmers on its own hypnotic groove. For an album filled to the brim with ambition, it is striking to hear a song that is simply *fun*. The following "A Man Like You" plays like a smooth ballad that takes its cues from one of Moroder's biggest influences, Motown Records. The song's focus on melody, sweeping strings, and warm backing vocals all speak to the 1960s soul hit factory's influence. As a vocalist, Summer was often criticized for her seemingly limited girly voice, but on "A Man Like You," she stretches her voice out like she did in *Hair*, cascading over the rolling melody. In her fleeting moments with the Prince, the protagonist recognizes its significance, a promise that she can finally be "home free." Those two words of the essence of Cinderella's dream—a home that allows her to escape from the dystopia of Act One and the machinery of Act Two. Now the trick is to not let it go.

The moody "Sweet Romance" follows, arriving with a dramatic instrumental opening that leaves a melancholy harpsichord in its wake. With the song being addressed to "Father dear," one imagines that the singer is praying to God, asking for assistance in the protagonist's hour of need. For all of Summer's reluctance to map her songs onto herself, "Sweet Romance" provides a rare chance on the album for Summer to invoke her strong religious background. The song masterfully rises and falls over its verses and refrains, creating dynamics that span from a lonely confessional to a gospel chorus. "My life's been so empty," she sings, knowing her Prince is what she needs to complete her.

An instrumental reprise of the title track is played for fifty-one seconds on the piano, temporarily taking us back to where we began, the land of dreams unreal. This helps to set up the finale of Act Three, "Dance into My Life," in which the protagonist imagines the Prince coming back to sweep her off her feet. There is an openness in the music of the verse, as the singer gets space to breathe, and the refrain builds things back into a party. The entire band is back in at a full-tilt groove, providing the soundtrack for the singer to dance on as she waits for the Prince's return. It's only appropriate that the album's triumphant third act leaves our hero on the dancefloor.

Act Four begins with "Rumour Has It," a funky dance groove that segues into a choppy, foot-stomping hook that builds the song's excitement. It's a spin on when the Prince searches for the girl with the glass slipper, but sidesteps those now-famous details of the story. Instead, the singer just learns of a rumor being spread around town that "someone" is trying to find "a girl like me." If the idea that a girl's happiness can only be found by the arrival of a man feels a bit passé, at least the song finds a wiser singer than the one who began this journey. She warns that one can change a lot of things "but not your destiny," and that you never know what you have won "until you lose." "Rumour Has It" did such an effective job of capturing the excitement of the protagonist's resolution, it was chosen as a single off the album, where it became a minor pop hit, reaching #53 on the *Billboard* Hot 100.

The following "I Love You" was the lead single pulled from the album, and the closest thing resembling a hit, inching into the *Billboard* Top 40 at #37. It's shocking that "I Love You" didn't do better because it's the finest track on the album. Featuring a majestic opening complete with strings and the twinkling of stardust raining down, the song shifts from the protagonist's perspective to that of a narrator, telling of the Prince searching for nights and days, until finally finding "the one he loved." When she sings the simple refrain—"He said, 'I love you'"—the music transcends itself, lifting the listener into the heavens on Summer's soaring vocal. And herein lies the power of the song—and in turn, the album. "I Love You" is able to take the tritest sentiment imaginable and render it into something impossibly new and exciting. Isn't that why we retell fairytales over and over? There is comfort in the blend of the novel with the familiar, something that is at once foreign and still rooted in our deepest societal values. Otherwise, there would be no value in endlessly rehashing the story of Cinderella—or any other fairytale for that matter.

Just in case we had prepared ourselves for any cynicism to rupture this tale, the final new song in *Once Upon a Time . . .* is called "Happily Ever After." It plays less like a song than the finale of a musical, the entire cast taking the stage in one big party, a loose and swinging sendoff. In a somewhat gratuitous epilogue, Summer offers a full-length retelling of the title track, this time intoning the lyrics with a heavy sense of drama. No words are changed; it simply completes the album's cycle. For someone who approaches singing like an actress, Summer ends on a theatrical soliloquy.

Despite its musical excellence and largely positive reviews, *Once Upon a Time . . .* was only a modest commercial success, overshadowed by her next three double-LPs issued over 1978 and 1979. All three hit #1 in *Billboard* and each had at least one #1 *Billboard* single: *Live and More* (featuring the #1 "MacArthur Park"), followed by the studio album *Bad Girls* (featuring the #1 "Hot Stuff" and title track), and the compilation *On the Radio: Greatest Hits Volumes I & II* (featuring the #1 duet with Barbara Streisand, "No More Tears (Enough Is Enough)"). This commercial arc has come to take prominence over *Once Upon a Time . . .* The album is marginalized or completely overlooked in many books about disco; even Summer herself curiously omits it from her autobiography.

Could this be because *Once Upon a Time . . .* was itself a first draft of her autobiography? Soon after the album's release, Summer told a reporter that it "is the first record I can really say is a part of me." If nothing else, it seems to be the musical embodiment of the "mystical and surreal vision" that she will never forget in the shadow of Cinderella's castle, so many years before. In this way, *Once Upon a Time . . .* is the most impossible fairytale of them all—the one that actually comes true.

Notes

1 Summer, 65.
2 Ibid., 66–8.
3 Ibid., 102.
4 Aletti, 24.
5 Jeffery, 57.
6 Ibid., 58.

13

There's No Returning on This Chartered Trip Away: *Zen Arcade*

In the early 1980s, hardcore punk emerged as a new kind of underground music. It took the punk rock ethics—loud, fast, and short songs—and upped all three elements to the extreme. Where the Ramones found a comfortable cruising altitude, these bands broke the sound barrier. Hardcore bands like Black Flag and Minor Threat had names as menacing as their sound, but this was not the case for Hüsker Dü. Formed in St. Paul in 1979 with guitarist/vocalist Bob Mould, bassist Greg Norton, and drummer/vocalist Grant Hart, Hüsker Dü's cryptic name comes from a Scandinavian children's board game that translates to "Do You Remember?" They chose it because it didn't sound like a typical hardcore band name. "[W]e don't want to be part of that hardcore thing," Mould explained in 1985. "Frankly, I don't think we ever were. Our music may have been inspirational for some people that like that kind of stuff, but we weren't doing it to placate them."[1]

Hüsker Dü's early albums crammed countless songs into a seemingly impossible amount of space. "*Land Speed Record* set the thrash-rock standard," *Rolling Stone* wrote of their 1982 debut album, which held twenty-five songs in under twenty-seven minutes.[2] These albums were recorded cheaply quickly on borrowed time as they toured America, sleeping on people's floors and popping amphetamines to keep their energy up and stave off hunger. "Hopefully we were going to just make enough money from the gig to get some food, maybe some beer, be able to buy smokes, and have enough gas to make it to the next gig," Norton remembered. "That's all that was important to us."[3] For many underground rock bands in the pre-Nirvana era, the road was a way of life, existing hand to mouth and relying on the kindness of strangers.

Hüsker Dü got a rare extended break in the summer of 1983, which they spent jamming and songwriting in an abandoned St. Paul church. They took this music and recorded a twenty-three-song double-album in forty-five hours—with nearly every song a first take—followed by a forty-hour mixing session.

When released on July 1, 1984, *Zen Arcade* challenged the notion of who could make a concept album and what it could mean. "'Zen Arcade'—it's a hard thing to explain," Mould once said. "We had that story together with all the characters. We knew it was going to be a double album, so it made sense to make the music a little more varied. It just hit us over the head one day that we were really growing, and that 'Zen Arcade' was going to be something special. It broke a lot of rules people thought we were following."[4] In maturing beyond their original sound, Hüsker Dü not only widened their musical palette, but also their stature in the world of 1980s indie rock and influence on rock music ever since.

Like many double-albums, Hüsker Dü's *Zen Arcade* is a sprawling rummage sale. With its twenty-three songs ranging from fifty-three seconds to fourteen minutes in length (and many of them a brash onslaught of noise and fury), it's not an easy album to get into. But those who do are rewarded with the rich themes, narratives, and nuances across its four sides. It was unusual to get so much new indie music in one place, especially by an underground punk band who built their reputation on brevity.

"Something I Learned Today" is the perfect introduction to the band and album—first we hear Grant Hart's tumbling drums, then Greg Norton's pulsing bass, followed by Bob Mould's distorted guitar, and finally Mould's screaming, anguished voice. The first thing the singer learns is that "Black and white is always gray." It's an apt lesson for the album that follows, alluding to how Hüsker Dü is cutting their dark punk sound with a lighter pop sensibility, as well as the album's protagonist, who spends much of the album confused, indecisive, and depressed, looking out into the world for delineation and seeing only gray. "Something I Learned Today" was such a succinct statement of Hüsker Dü's sound and purpose, they used it to open their live shows in this period.

"Broken Home, Broken Heart" fills in the protagonist's backstory, based on a punk riff like the Ramones' "Blitzkrieg Bop," only with a melodic bassline and fueled by amphetamines. The singer's parents fight while he cries himself to sleep at night, setting the scene for an album that does not shy away from the dark elements of life. "Many of the incidents in *Zen Arcade* were very personal," Bob Mould told the *Melody Maker* in 1985. "Those songs could well be all three of our autobiographies set to music. Some of us come from broken homes, some of us have had friends die, stuff like that."[5] In the first of many shocking transitions on *Zen Arcade*, the thrashing "Broken Home, Broken Heart" is followed by "Never Talking to You Again," a song with only acoustic guitar and vocals. For Hüsker

Dü's hardcore fans, "going acoustic" was akin to Bob Dylan "going electric" for his folk fans—a seeming act of betrayal. And yet, "Never Talking to You Again" is one of the best punk songs on the album. Clocking in at a mere 101 seconds, the song is a four-chord, fast and catchy kiss-off, written and sung by Grant Hart, whose melodic style nudged the band in a more mainstream direction.

Meanwhile, Bob Mould's style stayed closer to a harder punk aesthetic, crafting his songs as fast rockers in a haze of distortion. "Chartered Trips" is classic Mould, a barreling train of melody buried in noise that tells of our protagonist taking a chartered trip away. Some interpret this as the character briefly joining the military, or perhaps some sort of cult. The key lines are repeated at the end—"There's no returning on this chartered trip away"— implying a predestined fate in an unforgiving world. Not that you can really understand the words. Most of *Zen Arcade*'s lyrics are unintelligible, broken chards of sound cutting through the wall of noise. Yet these imperfections only unify the album under the DIY aesthetic of Hüsker Dü.

"Dreams Reoccurring" is *Zen Arcade*'s first instrumental, a brief song that freely mixes punk, psychedelic, and a touch of metal into a blistering sandstorm. Just when it sounds like it may all fall apart, it comes back even stronger, introducing a galloping riff riding through the fuzz of a thousand dead radio stations. "Indecision Time" returns to Hüsker Dü's classic punk style, speeding along as the protagonist unable to choose what's best for him, while holding on to his choice like it's a bid for freedom. Songs like "Indecision Time" are opaque, leaving us to decide what's happening in the narrative. Mould later explained that the band wanted "to leave things up to people's imaginations instead of making concrete definitions. We didn't want it to be a rock opera."[6] Although this statement conflicts with some other statements he has made over the years, it certainly describes a song like "Indecision Time."

"Hare Krsna" closes the album's first side with the singer encountering people chanting "Hare Krishna," a mantra associated with hippies since the 1960s counterculture. The singer initially thumbs his nose at the chanters, sounding uncannily like Frank Zappa's deadpan voice before chanting overtakes the song. They take the "Hare Krishna" chant and sing it to the tune of the Strangeloves' 1965 hit, "I Want Candy," which itself appropriated Bo Diddley's "Hey! Bo Diddley." Leave it to Hüsker Dü to take a fifteenth century spiritual mantra and turn it into primal garage rock.

Zen Arcade's second side begins with four of Bob Mould's punk rock compositions. First up is "Beyond the Threshold," which finds the singer in the big city with no place to stay. The oddly down-sloping verse melody is so buried in the mix, it nearly turns into one more layer of ambience. "Pride" continues this trend, as the song moves like lightning, as Hart's thundering drums, Norton's thumping bass, and Mould's relentless guitar suck the verse's lyrics down a garbage disposal as they're being said. They imply why the singer doesn't return home despite his misery: Stupid, selfish, pride. "I'll Never Forget You" ups the ante by adding wrath to the singer's pride. The protagonist has spilled his guts to a friend who turns their back on him. The singer addresses that person like they are trying to hold their own against a hurricane: "I WILL. NEVER. FORGET. YOU." The following "The Biggest Lie" features melodic punk underneath all of its noise and velocity, with Clash-like backing vocals. But the song is another dead end—in striking a heroic pose, the singer trades his "respect for no success."

"What's Going On" congeals around the best fist-pumping 1980s beer ad you never heard: "I WAS *TALKING*...WHEN I SHOULD HAVE BEEN *LISTENING!*" Hüsker Dü's "What's Going On" inverts Marvin Gaye's "What's Going On," applying the question inwardly to themselves as opposed to outwardly to the world. Mould's messy, scribbly guitar solos are the perfect compliment to Hart's rigid structure. "What's Going on" is followed by "Masochism World," in which the protagonist tries to feel something real from the outside world in an extreme way—through S&M. Sung by Hart, "Masochism World" is another song mixing punk aesthetics with pop elements, such as falsetto singing and harmonized backing vocals, but the experience only leaves the singer further confused, wanting an answer to a question he cannot even articulate.

"Standing by the Sea" closes the first disc of *Zen Arcade* with our protagonist on a trip to the beach. Norton's relentless three-note bass riff appears and reappears throughout the song, giving it a nervous edge, which is reinforced by the song's swaying, almost pirate-like shanty. At one point, he describes the sea as a place where your senses are bombarded by the roaring that you hear—which sounds like a description of Hüsker Dü's music. The first disc of *Zen Arcade* traces the protagonist from the most claustrophobic place (his home) to the most open one (the sea). And yet, he is still lost.

The third side of *Zen Arcade* begins with Bob Mould's electric guitar churning like a distress signal, initiating "Somewhere." Our protagonist is on a quest to find the truth but finds only lies. "Somewhere" was cowritten by Hart and Mould, but you can hear Hart's influence on the lead vocal and refrain, which has a pop edge and sounds like R.E.M. running on a treadmill. A psychedelic guitar solo that sounds like the musical break in the Beatles' "I'm Only Sleeping" further shows that even if the singer doesn't know where he's going, Hüsker Dü continues to chart their own path forward. The following forty-five-second instrumental "One Step at a Time" contains haunting piano chords counterbalanced by a lighter melody playing on top like a butterfly flittering around a lumbering elephant. Perhaps this is the sound of the singer finding love. If so, it is short-lived.

In "Pink Turns to Blue," the protagonist's girlfriend overdoses on heroin. The short, tough verses are followed by a falsetto refrain in which the singer doesn't know what to do "Now that pink has turned to blue." Unlike the person addressed with spite in "I Will Never Forget You," the girlfriend in "Pink Turns to Blue" was always by the singer's side. Now that she has gone, the singer's emotional center is gone too, and he's back adrift in the big city. "Newest Industry" is Mould's storming punk picture of a postapocalyptic dystopia, beginning with mass destruction and crumbling factories, as people now live in caves and sign up for the newest industry. Eventually, the singer decides to sign up as well. It seems better than sitting around and smoking cigarettes.

"Monday Will Never Be the Same" is a brief piano instrumental that is catchy yet sedate enough to be played over the closing credits of a 1980s prime-time drama. As with many of the instrumental tracks on this album, its meaning to the greater narrative is obscure, but perhaps it has something to do with the protagonist falling into his routine at the newest industry. "Whatever" plays like a recap for the album so far, with Mould's guitar up front and his vocals muffled underneath. The singer ran away from home to be by himself, "and now life becomes a test." Any feeling of independence is undercut by the flat chant of the refrain, acquiescing to whatever people want or say. Side three closes with "The Tooth Fairy and the Princess," a wispy psychedelic drone of voices chanting "Don't give up," "Don't let go," "In your bed," "Late at night," and "Don't get up," mirroring the overlay chanting of "Hare Krsna" at the end of side one. Only here, the track tells us that it was all just a dream and the entire album never happened. It's a lazy ending for an album that's otherwise tirelessly innovative.

The final side of *Zen Arcade* contains two songs: The anthemic "Turn on the News," and the fourteen-minute instrumental "Reoccurring Dreams." Written and sung by Hart, "Turn on the News" strikes an innovative balance between pop and punk. The "Turn on! (Turn on!)" call-and-response refrain that turns a social critique about media into a punk-rock sing-along that could have been written today. Although the "24-hour news cycle" was still in its infancy in the early 1980s, the media's omnipresence is already a given fact in this song. The singer lists examples of events that eerily correspond to a major issues decades after the album came out: Random shootings (Columbine and Sandy Hook), airplanes falling from the sky (September 11th), refugees filling the highway (the border crisis), and doctors learning about disease (coronavirus). Even more profoundly, the singer notes that despite "all the ways of communicating," we are unable to "get in touch with who we're hating." He's captured the division and polarity of American culture, twenty-two years before Twitter/X was launched. On *Zen Arcade*, Hüsker Dü predicted the future of indie rock, but on "Turn on the News," they predicted the future of American culture.

The instrumental finale, "Reoccurring Dreams" builds off the galloping riff of "Dreams Reoccurring" and extends it out to its real (or imagined) limits. Hart's drums perfectly match the peaks and valleys of the music, while Greg Norton's throbbing bass keeps the whole thing together. But this is Bob Mould's show, demonstrating his offhanded guitar work. Over the course of the album, his playing has evoked everyone from Chuck Berry to Jimi Hendrix to Johnny Ramone, and here, he mixes it all up in a performance that goes from psychedelic rock to experimental feedback to discordant attacks, all enshrouded in a sea of distortion. In his classic 2001 book about the 1980s underground rock scene, *Our Band Could Be Your Life*, Michael Azerrad suggested that "Reoccurring Dreams" "might be a summation of the rest of the protagonist's life—like all lives, it's a tumultuous improvisation, full of exhilarating highs and static lows."[7] The song ends with a single shrill, piercing note played—a flatlining, since the album is now dead.

Hüsker Dü's *Zen Arcade* is the most obscure and lowest-selling album profiled in this book. It is one of two albums not yet certified as Gold by the Recording Industry Association of America (RIAA) (*We're Only in It for the Money* is the other) and the only one never to grace the *Billboard* 200. The album was released by the California-based punk label SST Records, a legendary but disorganized and cash-strapped organization. They printed fewer than 5,000 copies to prevent eating the cost if it tanked. Instead, the opposite happened. Underground hype caused the album to blow up, leading to Hüsker Dü making appearances at stores that had long since sold out of the record. At least the critics got copies, and the album met with near-universal praise. In their review of *Zen Arcade*, *Rolling Stone* called it "probably the closest hardcore will ever get to an opera. A kind of thrash *Quadrophenia*, it traces a young buck's passage through a series of social and emotional wastelands ..."[8] While many may not call it a rock opera per se, it is almost always described as a concept album, although its actual story is somewhat obscure.

According to Bob Mould in 1989, "*Zen Arcade* is about a young computer hack from a broken home who dreams about killing himself after his girlfriend dies of a drug overdose. Instead, he lands in a mental hospital where he meets the head of a computer company who hires him to design video games. Then he wakes up and goes to school."[9] In Bob Mould's 2011 memoir, *See a Little Light: The Trail of Rage and Melody*, he further explained: "We didn't sit down and say, 'Let's write a semiautobiographical opera['] ... There wasn't a conscious effort to construct a composite character, but that seems to be the end result of the writing for *Zen Arcade* ... [it was] the beginning of video game culture, and we used that as the jumping-off point for the album's loose plot ... Once we saw what was happening with the narrative, the flow of the album became clear, and it becomes easier to put things in order."[10]

Despite Mould's focus on video game designing (the newest industry?), I hear nothing of the sort on this album. I hear the story of a young man running away from his small town and miserable homelife into the arms of the big city, only to find wrong turns everywhere—military racketeering, religious cults, S&M, betrayal, drugs, and death, before signing on to some sort of new industry and then waking up to realize it was all a dream. "Turn on the News" is the even harsher reality he wakes up into, while "Reoccurring Dreams" suggest that his vivid dreams may repeat to form a secondary "inside world," like the one referred to across the album. With *Zen Arcade*, a hundred different people could have a hundred different interpretations, but that doesn't make it unsuccessful—in fact, its versality proves its success as a concept album. It's the listeners digging for answers and insights nearly four decades later who prove that *Zen Arcade* holds up not in spite of its sprawl, ambiguities, and mysteries, but because of them.

Notes

1   Fricke, *MM*.
2   *Rolling Stone*.
3   Azerrad, 178.
4   Fricke, *MM*.
5   Ibid.
6   Lee.
7   Azerrad, 182.
8   Fricke, *RS*.
9   *Rolling Stone*.
10 Mould, 86.

14

As Soon as You're Born You're Dying: *Seventh Son of a Seventh Son*

Heavy metal music has always gotten a bad rap. It's long been the domain of adolescent white males, the tipping point at which rock goes from creative to, well, stupid. But it's such a fine line between stupid and clever, as immortalized in Rob Reiner's classic 1984 mockumentary *This Is Spinal Tap*, about the fictional titular British heavy metal band. At one point in the film, the band attempts to better their fortunes by reviving their conceptual stage show, as suggested by Christopher Guest's singer-guitarist Nigel Tufnel. "Stonehenge!" Nigel marvels to his bandmates. "Stonehenge. It's the best production value we've ever had on stage." Although this section of the film is best-remembered for the set designer who accidentally creates an 18-inch Stonehenge instead of an 18-foot model, I always appreciated the way Nigel's eyes light up when he initially suggests the idea, as though it is a profound work of art. Fewer than fifteen years after *Sgt. Pepper*, "Stonehenge" perfectly captured how conceptual rock already had been reduced to a caricature.

Fast-forward to May 8, 1987, when the famed British psychic Doris Stokes passed away. Among the many people who heard the news was bassist Steve Harris and singer Bruce Dickinson, who were on tour with their heavy metal band Iron Maiden. "I just had a thought: 'I wonder if she could foresee her own death?'" Harris recalled in a 2013 documentary. "Who knows? So, I started off with that sort of idea. I wrote 'The Clairvoyant' and then went to Bruce with it and basically, he said, 'Yeah, it's a great idea!' I started then having an idea for a song, 'Seventh Son of a Seventh Son,' because supposedly if you were born the seventh son of a seventh son you had the powers of a clairvoyant. So, I had those two ideas and Bruce went, 'You know what? We should do a concept album about this …'"[1] Dickinson remembers Harris coming up with the idea. "Steve and I reignited our songwriting partnership," singer Bruce Dickinson recalled, before getting nearly as overdramatic as Nigel. "He mentioned the words 'concept album' and my ears pricked up and my heart began to beat faster. Story, theatre: *Seventh Son of a Seventh Son* had it all."[2]

It's telling that the concept album had become such an established trope in the rock lexicon that what was once an artistic adventure had become a sort of tool, a device to be used from the rock and roll arsenal. It could make a grand statement or even predict the future. But for all of the potential pretension that could weigh a work like this down, Dickinson always kept his sense of humor. "In many ways, *Spinal Tap* has got it exactly right," he told a reporter just before *Seventh Son of a Seventh Son* was released. "The only sad thing is that people are laughing at heavy metal bands, without realizing that it's the whole business that's like that. Whether it's pop bands who go to the Montreux Festival, mime for 30 minutes and then collapse of nervous exhaustion, it's all bullshit."[3] And so Iron Maiden made *Seventh Son of a Seventh Son* in earnest, enjoying the fact that it was their seventh album.

Seventh Son of a Seventh Son begins with an acoustic guitar hitting chords as the singer eight lines, seven of which begin with the word "Seven"; the one line that doesn't arrives in the middle of the lines, with a reference to the journey that awaits: "And your trip begins ...". Guitar feedback radiates towards the listener, with a synthesizer riff dancing on top of it. The band comes in lockstep, as Dave Murray and Adrian Smith's guitars slash sustained power chords in unison, while Harris's bass underpins the sound and Nico McBrain's drum crashes turn the music into an oscillating force of nature. For an album about duality, it's only appropriate the opening music pits a catchy synthesizer line against a heavy metal band.

The band's tempo hunkers down and digs in like a full power frontal attack. "Moonchild" is the album's opener, as the singer introduces himself as the "fallen angel watching you." But this is not an album of halfway gestures. "Be the Devil's own—" the singer declares, "Lucifer's my name!" One is reminded of another British rock band's opening song on their seventh album—the Rolling Stones' "Sympathy for the Devil" on *Beggars Banquet*—which also began with the singer introducing himself as Satan. Only where the Stones invoked Satan as social commentary, Iron Maiden uses evil for evil's own sake.

"Moonchild, open the seventh seal!" Lucifer commands. The seventh seal originates from the *Book of Revelations*, the final book of the New Testament. After the war, famine, death, and chaos of the first six Seals, the Seventh Seal offers a respite: "Silence in heaven for about half an hour." Swedish filmmaker Ingmar Bergman used this quote to frame his 1957 masterpiece, *The Seventh*

Seal, about a medieval knight returning from the Crusades during the bubonic plague. Bergman was inspired by the silence of God in his film, and the human suffering that occurs in a world of sickness and mortal sin. Unlike other books of the New Testament that teach concrete lessons, the *Book of Revelations* is obscure, spinning fanciful imagery of surreal visions. Iron Maiden charges through the song like a well-oiled machine—Dickinson's careering wail rising and falling over the churning guitars and pounding drums, all at a breakneck clip. But what distinguishes Iron Maiden's sound is Steve Harris's bass rattling at the center of the sound's engine, an impossibly loose tone that still manages to hold the music together with cold precision. As the song finally barrels to a close, you can hear—to borrow a line from Don McLean about Mick Jagger—"Satan laughing with delight," in madness, fire, and fury.

"Infinite Dreams" starts off with a mellower feel, a study of nightmares that begins as a power ballad; it's like if Metallica played "Enter Sandman" in the style of their own "Nothing Else Matters." The verses stack up imagery and paranoia, until the tempo suddenly shifts, rollicking back and forth like someone tossing in bed for a thousand sleepless nights. Dickinson sings the haunting melody that oscillates between the churning guitars, but this is very much Steve Harris's song. "Steve's songs tend to be about dreams, nightmares, and obsessions, cos he has a lot of those, he's a terrible sleeper," Dickinson once explained. "He writes a lot of songs about out-of-body experiences, which he has more of than he likes to admit. I think he has a bit of a problem, with things like that, he's quite frightened of it."[4] Indeed, the song builds to one eternal question: "Where would you end—in heaven or in hell?" The only escape he sees is in death—and reincarnation.

The following song, "Can I Play with Madness," finds the singer attempting to resolve the issues of "Infinite Dreams." The premise is simple enough: The singer visits an old prophet to learn what his fate might be. Perhaps because it has a relatively straightforward narrative, "Can I Play with Madness" was the lead single for the album. Clocking in at three-and-a-half minutes and sounding close to a *Back in Black*-era AC/DC, the refrain's slick call-and-response is custom-made for classic rock radio, while the guitar wizardry and keyboards evokes Van Halen at their commercial peak. (An eye-catching video starring *Monty Python* legend Graham Chapman in one of his final performances didn't hurt either.) The song was their biggest hit up to that point in the UK, rocketing to #3 and kicking off a string of three Top 10 UK hits from this album.

After a deceptively smooth opening, "The Evil That Men Do" arrives with the nuance of a runaway train barreling down a mountain. There's an inherent speed to this song that overpowers everything else—the grind of the rhythm section, the distorted guitars endlessly reloading chords like bullets until they explode in synchronized rains of fire, the vocalist chanting in a defiant growl. Ostensibly, "The Evil That Men Do" appears to tell the conception of the Seventh Son of the Seventh Son (which implies that that the narrator is the latter Seventh Son), and there are plenty of images of baptism in fire, seventh lambs slain, and slaughter of innocence. When people dismiss heavy metal as mindless headbanger music for Satanists, this is the kind of music they mean. And yet, there is method to this madness, an underlying order that may sound like a riot but runs like a well-organized military siege. Otherwise, a song like this would be unable to build into its soaring crescendo of its refrain:

"THE EVIL THAT MEN DO LIVES ON AND ON"

For all of the apparent one-sidedness of its title and refrain, "The Evil That Men Do" succeeds because of it strikes a balance. The tension of the verses and pre-chorus reflects a moral balance in motivation and consequences. "I will pray for you," the singer declares, first to the mother and then to the son, still offering a gesture of hope, however futile it may be. As with "Can I Play with Madness," there's a pop element to this song that was novel for Iron Maiden—and most other metal bands of their generation. The song was chosen as the album's second single, and was nearly as big of a hit, reaching the UK Top 5. Closing with the one-two punch of "Can I Play with Madness" and "The Evil That Men Do," the album's first side shifts at its center from the elder seventh son to his clairvoyant offspring.

The second side of *Seventh Son of a Seventh Son* opens with its ten-minute epic title track. The singer witnesses the birth of "the seventh, the heavenly, the chosen one," which unleashes a war between good and evil forces over the newborn's powers. In less than three minutes, the verse of the song is over and the atmosphere shifts into an eerily hushed landscape of sustained guitar tones over a tensely meandering bass and the restless hiss of the drummer's cymbals. A voice emerges from the ether to deliver a seven-line poem about the birth of the seventh son of the seventh son, declaring him to have "the gift of the chosen sight." The music hovers while an odd, wordless vocal-like sound undulates like a storm cloud over a monastery. The jagged distorted guitars kick things back into gear, as they ascend the mountaintop where they unleash their solos. Although often overshadowed by Bruce Dickinson's singing and Steve Harris's songwriting, lead guitarists Adrian Smith and Dave Murray more than hold their own, trading wailing solos between the refrains in tight riffing unison. Murray's sound is precise but fluid, running up and down the fretboard through blues-based licks like Jimmy Page in his first solo and then getting a fast, fluttering sound in his second, reminiscent of Eddie Van Halen. Smith, on the other hand, brings a howl to his solos, a looseness that at first may seem like punk sloppiness, but is all perfectly calculated for maximum effect, giving way to colorful flights of fancy. Perhaps it is only appropriate that this saga of duality ends with blazing twin guitar coda.

"The Prophecy" is often cited as the weakest song on the album, a dizzying, if sometimes dazzling, cycle of time signatures that mostly work to push the album's plot along. It is sung by "the real seventh son" who warns that the village is doomed, but no one heeds his warning and blames him once disaster hits. The pre-chorus uses some gimmicky devil-on-one-shoulder-angel-on-the-other panning to represent the singer's confliction, but the lyrics are ultimately an overwrought cliché. The music saves the song, as its verses are bridged by a lilting 6/8 musical segues that could have come out of an electric Renaissance fair. But the finest moment is in the final minute, after the seventh son bemoans no one believing his prophecy and the electric music fades away to leave a minute of lovely acoustic guitars picking up the same riffs, like Iron Maiden had somehow transformed into Fairport Convention. It is a welcome sound that brings the record a surprising touch of variety. Such elements push a quintessential heavy metal band into something closer to progressive rock.

According to Steve Harris, the seventh song on the album, "The Clairvoyant," was the first song written for *Seventh Son of a Seventh Son*, and it plants the seed for the album's theme of duality—life and death, the real and the unreal, wisdom and ignorance. In terms of the album's plot, "The Clairvoyant" charts the fallout of the seventh son's "Prophecy," when his gift of foresight proves to be a curse. The singer notes a sense of irony that penetrates the song—despite his powers, the seventh son "couldn't foresee his own demise." All of this is told through some of the most effective music on the album. The verses have a haunting melody that is emboldened by Dickinson's all-or-nothing delivery. The refrain switches gears into a heavy, stuttering rhythm that almost feels like disco. "Isn't it strange?" the singer asks in one of the catchiest hooks on the album, that once "you're born, you're dying?" The group issued "The Clairvoyant" and issued it at the third single of the album and scored another Top 10 UK hit. Putting the three singles together—"Can I Play with Madness," "The Evil That Men Do," and "The Clairvoyant"—they play like a mini-version of the album, as they were released in the order they appear on the larger work. And while much of the album's themes are missed, the three songs form a clear path from madness to evil to death—except for the final line of "The Clairvoyant," which has a surprising shot at redemption: "And be reborn again."

Sure enough, an eighth and final song follows the seventh in a sort of epilogue to the album. "Only the Good Die Young" is a true group effort: Written by Harris and Dickinson, the song rides on the relentless drumming of McBrain, while Smith and Murray each get a guitar solo. Smith again sounds more spontaneous, at first playing his guitar like he is taking it apart, before finding his way up and down his guitar neck like it was a gyroscope. Murray is all precision and technique, fluttering and stinging at the perfect moments. Dickinson spews quasi-spiritual imagery wherever he goes—the red moon and the black sun, walking on water and measuring coffins by lust, and so on. "Until the next time," he winks, "Have a good sin." If there was any doubt as to how the Seventh Son of the Seventh Son ends his tale, "Only the Good Die Young" puts it to rest—born in a once-in-an-eon phenomenon, he is fought over by good and evil, given the power of prophecy, and is ultimately doomed by his own powers.

The album closes as it began, with Dickinson singing seven lines over an acoustic guitar, all beginning with the word "Seven." The only difference between the opening and the closing theme is that the latter omits the line "And your trip begins," as the trip is now over. For an album so bleak, using a variation on the intro as a conclusion is oddly hopeful. By evoking the beginning at the end, the album that reeks of death ends with a notion of rebirth. But even still, the album makes no guarantees. "It's a classic story of good versus evil, only with no guarantees whatsoever that it's the good guys who eventually come through," Dickinson once explained to an interviewer. "Nothing and nobody comes out of this story unscathed. Which is everyone's story, really, isn't it?"[5]

Seventh Son of a Seventh Son was Iron Maiden's first #1 album in the UK since their classic *The Number of the Beast* in 1982. It found an international audience, as the album hit #12 on the US *Billboard* charts, and they followed it with another triumphant international tour. The grand finale came in August, when Iron Maiden played the Monsters of Rock festival in Leicestershire, England, where they headlined for the first time over acts like Megadeth, Guns N' Roses, and Kiss, as some 107,000 of the faithful thrashed in the mud.

However, like so much of the music on *Seventh Son of a Seventh Son*, death lurked just around the corner. Two Scottish fans, eighteen-year-old Alan Dick and twenty-year-old Landon Siggers, died when the muddy land gave out underneath them and they were crushed by the crowd during the Guns N' Roses set. Iron Maiden were not made aware of this until after their set. "We took our responsibilities seriously, but we could never have foreseen the set of circumstances that led to those fatalities that day," remembered promoter Tim Parsons, who booked the festival. "It was just hideous. It was awful for Maiden, to hear what had happened just after their show, amid all that euphoria. But with very few exceptions, I wouldn't have wanted anyone else to be the headliner on that day. It was comforting because we didn't have to worry about them. They were utterly professional."[6]

Unwittingly, Parsons' words evoke one of the central themes of the album—*we could have never foreseen*, he explains. While this is no doubt true, it makes one wonder what would have happened if they could have foreseen the circumstances. If it could be foreseen, would anyone believe it? Would it be enough to perhaps cancel the festival and sacrifice any bottom-line profit margins? One would hope so, but if there was truly a prophet who actually foresaw this incident, my bet is that they would have been ignored. Perhaps the evil that often accompanies the gift of second sight isn't from an external source or even from the seer's own intentions, but rather with the doom of being confined to know the truth but never be believed. In this way, *Seventh Son of a Seventh Son* isn't merely a parable, folktale, or fantasy play, it's a meditation on prophecy that became a prophecy unto itself. "Only the good die young," sang Iron Maiden during their headlining set at Monsters of Rock, blissfully unaware of how true those words were.

Notes

1 Lawson.
2 Dickinson, 199.
3 Witter.
4 Ibid.
5 Ruskell.
6 Lawson.

15

This Is a Recording: *3 Feet High and Rising*

After the Beatles' *Sgt. Pepper's Lonely Hearts Club Band* introduced the concept album to a wide audience, countless artists tried to stake their claim with the new art form. One of the many less-remembered attempts was *The Turtles Present the Battle of the Bands* from 1968. In their review of the album, *CashBox* wrote that "the Turtles debut their first major 'concept' album, portraying eleven different rock bands"—marking the first time *CashBox* ever used the term "concept album" in their copy.[1] One of the album's biggest hits was "You Showed Me," a seductive, hypnotic song with haunting strings. It's a lovely yet mysterious record that could've been beamed from outer space.

Nearly two decades later, "You Told Me" was sampled in De La Soul's "Transmitting Live from Mars," the eighth track off their debut album, *3 Feet High and Rising*. De La Soul were a trio of two MCs, Posdnus (Kelvin Mercer) and Trugoy the Dove (David Jude Jolicoeur), and one DJ, P.A. Pasemaster Mase (Vincent Mason), who helped to introduce a quieter, more introspective approach to hip-hop. *3 Feet High and Rising* stood out in part because of the layers of samples it used—often running several at a time—that would break the mold for sampling. The result was a revolutionary sound.

But not everyone was impressed. In one of the first major lawsuits about the alleged unethical use of sampling, Turtles co-founders Flo & Eddie sued De La Soul over "You Showed Me." De La Soul's producer, Prince Paul, claimed that the group provided a complete list of samples to their label, but they "just cleared the ones they thought would be popular."[2] "This isn't just a financial objection," the lawyer for the Turtles argued. "Flo & Eddie are genuinely upset with the way De La Soul chopped up and mutilated their song." De La Soul's lawyer claimed that Flo & Eddie were "taking the position that if adopted would seriously hurt, if not kill [hip hop] outright." Flo & Eddie initially sued for $1.7 million; the matter was resolved out-of-court. But samples themselves are only one layer of the album.

3 Feet High and Rising is a two-tiered concept album. On one hand, there's the narrative within the album itself, which is a series of silly gameshow skits during which the songs function as commercials. "The game show concept was one of the last things we did, during the mixing phase," Posdnous remembered. "I think [Prince] Paul might have come up with that idea."[3] Others were less charitable to the concept. When asked by *New Musical Express* whether there was a concept in the album, Mase was defiant: "Hell, no. The game show? That was Trugoy and Prince Paul buggin' out in the studio ... Man, the whole game show shit was done in the last two days of the mixdown."[4] Regardless of how and when it was made, the gameshow concept structures the otherwise unwieldly album and gives it shape.

A secondary concept is the album's use of samples. Up to this point in hip-hop, no other album used such a varied, diverse, and numerous template of samples. They are the glue that holds *3 Feet High and Rising* together. "It's similar to the way folk musicians update the storyline of a popular murder ballad or put their unique pluck on a familiar set of chords," Christopher R. Weingarten writes in his history of *It Takes a Nation of Millions to Hold Us Back*, another hip-hop album from this era that pioneered sampling.

> Sampling, however, is a uniquely post-modern twist, turning folk heritage into a living being, something that transfers more than just DNA. Through sampling, hip-hop producers can literally borrow the song that influenced them, replay it, reuse it, rethink it, repeat it, recontextualize it ... All the associations that a listener may have with an existing piece of music are handed down to the new creation—whether it's as complicated as a nostalgic memory over a beloved hook or as elemental as a head-nod to a funky groove you don't specifically recognize.[5]

Samples are powerful things. They turn hip-hop artists into shapeshifters, able to speak in any voice from the dawn of recorded sound. But it was more than just a gimmick—it was a true democracy, limited only by the number of records on your shelf. In *3 Feet High and Rising*, the samples function as the music's second mind, a collective unconscious of a thousand radio stations playing at once.

The first sound you hear on *3 Feet High and Rising* is fanfare for a gameshow. After a cheesy organ intro, we hear host Al Watts (the album's engineer) get things started: "Hey all you kids out there, welcome to *3 Feet High ... and Rising*!" He introduces the four contestants—Trugoy as a flat-talking guy from Wichita, Mase as an Australian who swallows his words as he speaks them, Posdnus as a squirrely nerd who likes to say "your mama," and producer Prince Paul speaking in an overly-dramatic calm tone—and starts the game. Watts asks four ridiculous questions (such as, "How many feathers are on a Perdue chicken?") and tells the contestants to think them over during these messages. And then the songs begin.

"The Magic Number" starts with a scratchy groove until the song's samples fatten up the sound. The song is an extended riff on the Saturday morning kids' TV show *Schoolhouse Rock!* song "Three Is a Magic Number." De La Soul remake the song, rewriting the words and cutting in samples from the original version, as well as random samples such as a 1945 clip of New York Mayor Fiorella La Guardia: "I say, children, what does it all mean?" Like so many other voices on *3 Feet High and Rising*, La Guardia's voice is cut off, taken out of context, and put in conversation with a sea of other voices—James Brown ("One, two, three!"), Syl Johnson ("Do the shang-a-lang!"), Eddie Murphy ("Anybody in the audience ever get hit by a car?"), and Johnny Cash ("How high's the water, mama?"), the latter of which sets up the album's title.

"Change in Speak" was a reworked version of the B-side of De La Soul's first single, "Plug Tunin." Each verse cycles through the possibilities of a single rhyme that compliments the rappers' laidback groove, over the backbeat of the Monkees' "Mary, Mary," the wavering bass on Cymande's "Bra," and the horns on the Mad Lads' "No Strings Attached." And then there's the thirty-six-second sound collage "Cool Breeze on the Rocks," a dizzying array of blink-and-you'll-miss-it snippets of songs using the word "rock". Nearly two dozen samples pack the song, roughly one sample every one-and-a-half seconds. De La Soul could have chosen any word to build a collage around, but they chose *rock*. By constructing this statement of rock from old school rap records, De La Soul subverts the rock tradition while adding to it. "The record sounds complex," DJ Mase told a reporter. "But it isn't... We recorded the whole album in just over a month... It's like having a LEGO set and putting the stuff together out of all the little bits and pieces."[6]

More gameshow fanfare. "Contestant #1, do you have the answers?" asks Al Watts. Contestant 1 splutters, "Um, I wish my cousin Nat was here—he *knows* these things—no I'm sorry, I don't." De La Soul and Prince Paul may not have invented the "skit"—the short and often comic interludes between songs—but they were among the first to exploit its possibilities. There are nearly as many one-to-two-minute skits or goofy filler tunes as there are full-length songs, which gives the album its freewheeling spirit. "Can U Keep a Secret" is one of these, with each member spilling silly secrets about their band mates over a groove. While other MCs rapped about money and women, De La Soul accused each other of having dandruff.

"Jenifa Taught Me (Derwin's Revenge)" is one of the album's key songs. In his review for *Melody Maker*, Push (alias of Christopher Dawes), writes: "'Jenifa Taught Me (Derwin's Revenge)' is perhaps the best introduction to the world of De La Soul. It's a sexual adventure which begins with a savage scratch and a few James Brown whoops . . . But suddenly, in the middle of a verse, comes a shout of 'now wait a minute' and the song is lost for ten seconds or so. In the interim, somebody called Derwin hammers chopsticks out of a piano. It's impossible to hold back a smile."[7] Once again, the off-the-wall samples help bring the song to life. Here, "Chopsticks" is played by Liberace and some of the funky riffs come not from James Brown, but an obscure (and wonderfully bizarre) 1965 single called "Soupy" by Maggie Thrett. At the center of it all are De La Soul's clever wordplay ("Breakfast/Broke it fast"), which turn the boy-meets-girl cliché into something new.

The album switches gears for the socially-conscious "Ghetto Thang." "We all grew up in New York City itself and moved to Long Island later, so the situations in 'Ghetto Thang' we actually experienced ourselves," Trugoy once explained. "And we're now having to deal with them in our own neighborhood because those kinds of problems are starting to show up in suburban areas too."[8] The song throws us into a world of drunks, junkies, pimps, hookers, broken-down fathers, drug-using mothers, and neglected children. For an album so surreal, "Ghetto Thang" is a harsh dispatch from the inner-city.

The album then takes us from the deepest reaches of the inner-city to the farthest depths of outer space in "Transmitting Live from Mars." The track is one of the leanest on the album—there's no rapping, only a French instructional tape, the backbeat of Wilson Pickett's "Hey Jude," and the Turtles' "You Told Me" riff. Even if you don't understand the French (it translates to the lesson "At Mid-day": "What is there to eat?"; "There is sausage, probably."), the way the female voice repeats phrases like "*Quelle heure est-il?*" ("What time is it?") with the descending riff of "You Told Me" answering it, you will never forget it. It's that beautiful.

The following "Eye Know" used another of the album's most highly contested samples—"I know I love you better," from Steely Dan's "Peg." This time, the sample is used at the apex of each verse as Posdnuos and Trugoy calmly compete for the object of their affection. Some thirty seconds in, Otis Redding's iconic whistling from "(Sittin' on the) Dock of the Bay" pops up over the double backbeat of Lee Dorsey and Sly and the Family Stone. Redding's familiar tune adds a breeziness to the proceedings, helping to deliver the song's effortless charm. In the following skit "Take It Off," De La Soul shout to take off various clothing—Gazelle sunglasses, Kangol hats, Le Tigre shirts—that were all hallmarks of the 1980s-era rap stars De La Soul wanted to distance themselves from. "A Little Bit of Soap" follows with another short goof. Looping the opening riff of Ben E. King's "Don't Play That Song," the group tells the song's subject to "take your big ass to the bathroom and please use a—" then plays the title phrase of the Jarmels' 1961 hit, "A Little Bit of Soap," to fill in the blank.

Al Watts returns: "Okay Contestant #2, do you have the answers?" Contestant 2 nervously stammers, "No, no I don't." The following "Tread Water" is a surreal slice of fairytale-like proportions, as Trugoy and Pos spin tales about encountering a talking crocodile, squirrel, fish, and a monkey. Despite its silly trappings, Trugoy points out that "even something like 'Tread Water' has a deadly serious side to it. It's saying that when you're feeling down ... just keep going ... and even if it sounds like we're talking to little kids, we're really talking to everybody."[9] "Potholes in My Lawn" sounds like a cryptic message about inner-city life, but it was really De La Soul's inside-speak. Trugoy explained to *Rolling Stone* that the song's title "was like another way to say beat-biter or sucker MC, like songs from Run-D.M.C., songs from MC Lyte. The lawn was our rhymes and the potholes were the pieces missing."[10] As always, the samples added a new dimension to the song, especially the refrain's wire mouth-harp and yodel, which was lifted from Parliament's 1970 "Little Ole Country Boy." For a song about taking the words and music of others, this was one sample De La Soul didn't have to worry about. As George Clinton once rationalized: "If some poor nigger wants to get a start in music by using me, who am I to say no?"[11]

"Say No Go" is about the crack epidemic that Posdnuos formed around Hall & Oates' 1981 hit "I Can't Go for That (No Can Do)." Among the many samples that thicken the song is another cut from *The Turtles Present the Battle of the Bands*, in this case "I'm Chief Kamanawanalea (We're the Royal Macadamia Nuts)." This time, De La Soul only used the percussion and rhythm section's groove before the main song comes in—maybe that's why Flo & Eddie didn't notice. "Do As De La Does" is another short skit, constructed like an old-school hype track and executed like party. Posdnuos tells anyone with bad breath to "TAKE A LUUDEN," while Trugoy raps about Coca-Cola. "And now, for my next number, I'd like to return to the classics," says a voice. "Perhaps the most famous classic in all the world of music—" So goes Liberace's introduction of "Chopsticks" from his 1969 television show (while we already heard his "Chopsticks" performance itself in "Jenifa Taught Me (Derwin's Revenge)"), only now it's cut off to introduce a new version of De La Soul's first single, "Plug Tunin' (Last

Chance to Comprehend)." "A lot of people would listen to that song and say, 'What the hell are you guys talking about? I don't understand a word,' but if you listen to it, you can get it," Trugoy recalled. "What's really cool about that record is the style, the pattern and the cadence of the rhymes."[12]

Another skit follows, the tasteless "De La Orgee," featuring seventy-five seconds of simulated group sex. The skit provides a transition to "Buddy," a celebration of physical love. In an album filled with inside jokes, "Buddy" is the sleekest of the bunch—as many members of De La Soul's greater hip-hop crew can be heard on the record. The music video for "Buddy," featuring A Tribe Called Quest's Q-Tip, the Jungle Brothers, and Queen Latifah, is the document of a community. The ninety-second "Description," the three members of De La Soul introduce themselves in limerick form, followed by introductions from Q-Tip, De La's backup dancers, and Prince Paul. Next up is "Me, Myself and I," the most famous song from *3 Feet High and Rising*, becoming their only #1 song (on both the *Billboard* R&B and Rap charts) and only US Top 40 pop hit to date. And yet, the song was little more than an afterthought. It was recorded at the request of their label for something more mainstream. Built around a recognizable loop—Funkadelic's 1979 "(Not Just) Knee Deep"—and given an MTV-friendly video, the result was an instant-classic about personal autonomy. As Trugoy explained, "The vibe was like, 'I'm being me. Enjoy the music. If you like it, then don't worry about how I'm dressed.'"[13]

Enter Al Watts. "Contestant #4, do you have the answers?" The contestant answers in a rushed whisper: "*Uh, it's on the tip of tongue—I just can't—just can't think of it, I'm sorry.*" "This Is a Recording 4 Living in a Fulltime Era (L.I.F.E.)" was the final song recorded for *3 Feet High and Rising*. The track is centered around a sample of the phrase "This is a recording" from New Birth's 1972 "Got to Get a Knutt," a song laced with nursery rhymes, advertising jingles, and other assorted sundries. By lifting these four words, De La Soul turn the phrase "This is a recording" back on itself, in a gesture of modernism that destroys the notion of anything close to authenticity. It *is* a recording, of course, but at the same time, it's a recording of a recording, turning the idea of an "original" recording into an impossibility.

After "This Is a Recording . . .," the rest of the album feels arbitrary. The forty-one-second "I Can Do Anything (Delacratic)" that finds the group bragging about doing ridiculous things—"I could jump off this building"—over fast beatboxing. It sets the stage for the album's last official song, "D.A.I.S.Y. Age," which borrows from the Rascals' "My World" to declare the D.A.I.S.Y. Age has arrived. (De La Soul used D.A.I.S.Y. as an acronym for "DA Inner Sound, Y'all.") The verses have an unusual pattern, with Posdnuos and Trugoy throwing out two words and then spinning a verse out of them, and yet, the extended refrain feels like a homecoming.

And right on cue, we hear Al Watts: "Now that we're at the end of the show contestants, do you have any answers?" They mumble in the negative. Watts hands things over to announcer Don Newkirk, who provides very specific instructions for anyone at home who think they have the correct answers, promising a "specially selected grand prize" for any at-home winners. "Thanks and goodnight, for *3 Feet High and Rising*, this is Don Newkirk." The album then ends with the original 12-inch version of their first single, "Plug Tunin."

3 Feet High and Rising was released in the window of time between when CDs began outselling vinyl (1988) and CDs started outselling cassette tapes (1991). De La Soul's masterpiece clocks in at over an hour, which was a tight squeeze on vinyl (the last song, "Plug Tunin," was cut off), but fit comfortably on a CD, which could hold up to seventy-nine minutes. One trend seen in the remainder of the book is how the average length of the albums stretch out, some adding over an additional 33 percent of content than what would have been allowed on a single vinyl LP. But just because a group had this space didn't mean they had to use it all—for many albums made in this period, artists simply didn't have eighty minutes of things to say. Some of the finest albums of this era still clock in at under forty minutes, as Nas's *Illmatic*, Neutral Milk Hotel's *In the Aeroplane Over the Sea*, the Strokes' *Is This It*, and Amy Winehouse's *Back to Black* all demonstrate. De La Soul was a key exception to the rule.

3 Feet High and Rising became a surprise seller with its breakout hit, "Me, Myself and I," which helped the album secure the #1 spot on the *Billboard* R&B album chart. Furthermore, the album was likely the first rap LP to sell over 500,000 overseas, thanks in part to its rock-oriented samples and more laidback approach. This was especially true in the UK, where "Me, Myself and I," "Say No Go," "Eye Know," and "The Magic Number" all hit the Top 40, with the latter reaching the Top 10. De La Soul won a legion of European fans who remain loyal to this day.

In America, things were more complicated as the album was at once a masterpiece and a lawsuit waiting to happen. With Flo & Eddie leading the way, legal sharks circled the album, causing it to become a cautionary tale for sampling. Its artistic excellence and massive influence led it to become one of the first hip-hop albums inducted into the National Recording Registry, but hard to find for streaming or online purchasing. "We're in the Library of Congress, but we're not on iTunes," Posdnuos observed to *The New York Times* in 2016.[14]

After failed attempts to release *3 Feet High and Rising* on streaming platforms in 2019 and 2021, a deal was finally struck to release the material on March 3, 2023, the thirty-fourth anniversary of the album's debut. "Any song that had a sample in it and that sample was never addressed when the previous owners owned it," Posdnuos told *The Washington Post*, "we had to find out from the writers, the publishers—whoever owns the masters—and get them all on the same page and say 'Hey, can we now take care of this business and get this done with you?'"[15] Posdnous was pleased to find that nearly all of the artists were in favor of their music and they were able to clear all of the samples. Now, for the first time ever, *3 Feet High and Rising* is free to be streamed anywhere. This means "The Magic Number" can be heard alongside any song—even the Turtles' "You Showed Me"—as just another song on just another playlist. *This is a recording*, indeed.

Notes

1. *CashBox*.
2. Coleman, 154.
3. Ibid., 152.
4. O'Hagan.
5. Weingarten, 38.
6. O'Hagan.
7. Push, "3 Feet High."
8. Push, "Cadets."
9. Ibid.
10. Serpick.
11. Owen.
12. Serpick.
13. Push, "Cadets."
14. Cohen.
15. Bellware.

Part Four

The Postmodern Era (1990–9)

16

I Wanna Be Mesmerizing Too: *Exile in Guyville*

One day in 1991, a twenty-four-year-old Chicago-based singer/songwriter named Liz Phair stumbled across a cassette tape of the Rolling Stones' double album *Exile on Main St.* that someone had left behind in her apartment. "I listened to it over and over again," Phair remembered, "and it became like my source of strength—my involvement with *Exile* was like an imaginary friend; whatever [Rolling Stones' singer] Mick [Jagger] was saying, it was a conversation with him, or I was arguing with him and it was kind of an amalgam of the men in my life."[1] For Phair, the album was like an unfinished story, a script missing half of its dialog. She made it her mission to complete it.

Phair signed with Matador Records in 1992, which she secured after her homemade "Girly Sound" tapes became an underground sensation. As an unknown female artist betting her debut on a double-record response to the finest album by the biggest rock band in the world, Phair had her work cut out for her. "I took it like a thesis," Phair explained on MTV's *120 Minutes* in 1994. "What I did was I just took the *Exile on Main Street* album, like lyrically and just in terms of like arrangement, sequencing, and I answered it in my own way . . . I treated Mick's lyrics as sort of my love object. He was what the man was saying and this is what I was coming back with. And it was just kind of like this little dance between the two albums."[2] It was a special kind of concept album: an answer album.

Phair took the Stones' album and created a track-by-track response, even arranging the number of songs on each side to mirror the Stones' original. And while the Stones' album title referred to fleeing the UK on tax charges, Phair's exile was closer to home. Borrowing a word from fellow Chicagoans Urge Overkill's 1992 "Goodbye to Guyville," Phair named her project *Exile in Guyville*. As she explained in 2018, "'Guyville' was a specific scene in Chicago—predominately male, indie-rock—and they had their little establishment of, like, who was cool, who was in it, who played in what band.'"[3] Inspired to prove herself among the guys of Guyville, Phair crafted a record about gender in modern society, as modeled on an album by a group of men who *were* the establishment of male rockstar coolness. Phair's audacity outstripped everything except her talent, although being unknown worked in her favor. As Greil Marcus wrote in 2014 about Phair taking on the Stones: "It was a dare: someone no one's ever heard of can say as much, can say more, than someone everyone's heard of, whom everyone listens to, and in her own voice. Such a story is always new, and it's new now."[4]

Part of *Exile in Guyville*'s intrigue is that its concept hides in plain sight, so if one was not familiar with Phair's intentions and the Rolling Stones' back catalog, they would entirely miss it. As a testament to Phair's artistry, one can love the album without knowing the concept that drives it; for our purposes here, however, we will focus on how *Guyville* answers *Main St.* More than any other album we've looked at, *Guyville* is an interactive concept album, an unfinished puzzle, and one that requires active participation on the listener's part to put it together. At a time when the divide between indie and mainstream rock was shrinking, Phair further bridged the gap by creating a new indie album that spoke directly to a classic mainstream album. As a marketing strategy, it was clever; as a gesture to the male-dominated music industry, it was revolutionary.

Exile in Guyville begins with Liz Phair playing a chordal riff on her crunchy electric guitar, before co-producer Brad Wood's one-man rhythm section of bass and drums fill the sound. "6'1"" sounds like typical 1990s indie rock until Phair's vocals begin. "I be-ye-ye-ye-et you fall in bed too easily—" Phair sings in a weird, deadpan voice. Her sing-song melodies wind in unpredictable ways, riding guitar chords that twist and turn like a detour route. Appropriately for the album opener, "6'1"" has one of the strongest connections to its correlating *Exile on Main St.* track, "Rocks Off." Phair heard "Rocks Off" as when the singer (Mick) is "tripping home from being at someone's house sleeping with them and you run into your other girlfriend while you're doing your walk of shame—which is what I thought about 'Rocks Off.' So, I wrote a song like I was the girl he ran into, which was '6'1"."[5] And the fact that Phair is only 5'2" adds to the irony. Phair relays that this makes people come up to her and say: "'Oh '6'1"', I guess you're not that.' To me, it's the encapsulation of what the rest of the record is going to be delivering."[6]

"Help Me Mary" employs a rocking beat and Stones-like riffs as the singer bemoans guys who take over the house, rule the stereo, and get drunk. The parallel song on *Main St.*, "Rip This Joint," is a breakneck 1950s-inspired rocker that Phair saw as "all about sort of the attitude of these rock guys that would just kind of roll into town, create trouble, sleep with other people's girlfriends and leave a big mess behind. I was writing about my own experiences hosting these spontaneous gatherings of rock dudes and how just hidden my real self was in that male scene."[7] In doing so, Phair turns the Stones' song inside-out by taking it from the perspective of the bigshot male rockers to the anonymous female scenester who must put up with—and clean up after—their mess.

The following ninety-second "Glory" features Phair's hushed confessional about a real-life rocker from the Guyville scene who gets through to the singer. "You are shining some glory on me," she sings, as though her soul is being saved in a small club. Correlating with the Stones' "Shake Your Hips," a Slim Harpo cover that hypnotizes with its syncopated groove, Phair noted that "Glory" was an example in which "I would be in agreement instead of arguing with Mick, where I'd be like, yes, I too have seen a rock and roll hero who's sort of a bum and I think he's really tragic and beautiful—'Glory.'"[8] Next up is "Dance of the Seven Veils," which alludes the biblical story of Salome, who dances to receive the head of John the Baptist on a platter. The song is best known for its refrain, where the singer calls herself "a real cunt in the spring." And it's been noted that the Stones' correlating song on *Exile on Main St.*—"Casino Boogie"—also used the word "cunt" nearly twenty years earlier, but no one batted an eye.[9] To have a female artist sing the word so nakedly feels like a power move worthy of Salome.

The first side of *Exile in Guyville* ends with "Never Said," which Phair chose as the album's lead single—and for good reason. "Never Said" is *Guyville*'s earworm, with Brad Wood's steady rhythm section and engineer Casey Rice's guitar playing one note like a distress signal, while Phair's slashes at her guitar as her harmonies rise above it all. Lyrically, "Never Said" is a straightforward song with the singer declaring her innocence of any insinuation or rumor. Not coincidentally, it appears in the same spot as the Stones' lead single for *Exile on Main St.*, "Tumbling Dice." Phair's song functions like a conversation between Mick and Liz, with the first line of "Tumbling Dice" answered by the first line of "Never Said": "Women think I'm tasty," brags Mick; "I never said nothing," responds Liz.

The second side of *Exile in Guyville* opens with "Soap Star Joe," a mocking look at a guy who swings into town to become a star. The best part is at the end, where the singer describes Joe's thinning hair and aftershave: "Check out America," she sings, "You're looking at it, babe." The parallel Stones song, "Sweet Virginia," is an outsider's view of America—a campfire sing-along sung in an exaggerated drawl for a girl who shares her name with the state of both Jamestown and the capital of confederacy. "Soap Star Joe" and "Sweet Virginia" capture two different Americas—one slick and modern with thinning hair, and one old and unsettled with dirty shoes. "Explain It to Me" follows, setting a mellow vibe with obscure lyrics. Even Phair struggles to explain it: "It's about a ruined rock hero and seeing one of your greatest figures at their weakest, I guess."[10] The correlating track on *Main St.* is "Torn and Frayed"—which begins with a similar guitar riff— is another beautiful song with great atmosphere about a down-on-their-luck rock musician.

The haunting "Canary" comes next, a piano ballad full of verse lyrics like "I sing like a good canary" and "I come when called," contrasting the bravado demonstrated elsewhere on the record. In her book about *Exile in Guyville*, Gina Arnold writes about *Guyville*'s relatability, as it featured songs about "what it was like to feel voiceless and powerless in a nightclub, on a road trip, or during sexual intercourse."[11] "Canary" is a song that demonstrates the latter. Phair's song corresponds to "Sweet Black Angel" on *Main St.*, a well-intentioned (if poorly aged) protest song supporting African American activist Angela Davis. As Davis once said, "I am no longer accepting the things I cannot change. I am changing the things I cannot accept." This could be the motto of *Exile in Guyville*.

The hypnotic "Mesmerizing" finds Phair bending her voice like Bob Dylan over her churning guitar with a minimalist backing. The song opens up when she gets to the song's hook: "Wild and unwise, I wanna be mesmerizing too." This is her desire to escape Guyville. Using a word featured in "Rocks Off" ("It's so *mesmeriiiiiiiizing*—"), "Mesmerizing" corresponds to the Stones' "Loving Cup," about a hardscrabble farmer looking for a drink from his lady friend's loving cup. Hearing this as part of the Mick and Liz conversation, she challenges the metaphor. She's more than a cup to drink from, but rather somebody who can be mesmerizing in her own right—even when comparing herself to Mick Jagger.

The third side of *Exile in Guyville* opens with "Fuck and Run," about falling back with a guy—again—despite knowing you deserve better. "I want a boyfriend," the singer says at the first refrain, longing for "that stupid old shit" such as "letters and sodas." "Fuck and Run" corresponds to the Rolling Stones' "Happy," a straightforward enough song: The singer needs a love to keep him happy. "Fuck and Run" raises the stakes. When the singer of "Fuck and Run" confesses she wants an old-fashioned boyfriend, she exposes a vulnerability that much of the album masks under toughness. In the refrain, the singer shows her hand, confessing she feels like she's "gonna spend another year alone," before going into the "fuck and run" chorus. The singer is an outlaw on the road living through a series of one-night stands in search for something real. Up next is "Girls! Girls! Girls!" in which Phair's singer calls all the shots and gets away with murder. We hear only Phair's vocals and electric guitar, sexy and wavering on the edge like a sociopath. When asked about how it corresponds to the Rolling Stones' parallel track "Turd on the Run," Phair explained: "'Turd on the Run' is 'Girls! Girls! Girls!' and that to me was like, if you're a turd on the run and you can get away with it, well look what I can get away with . . . I get away with murder . . . that was my response."[12]

The following "Divorce Song" is easily the album's finest song. Ostensibly about a girl and a guy on a road trip, it begins *in media res* when the girl asks for a separate room after driving all day. Phair's eye for detail shines in a verse where the singer confesses that she stole the guy's lighter and lost the map, but when the guy says she's not worth talking to, she says, "I had to take your word on that." Relationships often seem like grand sweeps, but they often break down into tiny moments. Phair explained: "The stuff that's in movies never happens . . . it's just these micro-interactions with people. 'Divorce Song' is very much about that."[13] Corresponding to the Stones' "Ventilator Blues," a hard, gutbucket blues, the song's angular guitar riff keeping the singer down but not out. "Ventilator Blues" hits you over the head while "Divorce Song" is a study in subtlety, as the latter draws upon the same frustration as the former but finds wisdom instead of wrath.

Despite its title, "Shatter" is a quiet place in the album, beginning with Liz Phair's lead guitar work, followed by the singer describing a man who leaves a mark that she takes to heart, and she will carry with her "for a long, long time." "Shatter" is a love song that plays like a dirge—a beautiful, gray purgatory. The corresponding Stones' song, "I Just Want to See His Face," also sounds like a gray purgatory, only theirs is more mysterious; you can almost hear the skeletons rising in syncopation from the blurred corners of the sound, as Mick croaks about just wanting to see Jesus's face. "Shatter" makes no mention of Jesus but instead sings of love like it's a cross to bear. The album's third side ends with "Flower," a two-minute song that contains so many explicit phrases—"I want to fuck you like a dog" and "I want to be your blowjob queen," among others—that many critics found it unsettling. Phair sings a high vocal loop before her deeper monotone appears with obscenity-filled come-ons like a buried id. "Flower" correlates with the Stones' "Let It Loose," which Phair took as a rallying cry: "He's saying let it loose, stop being an uptight girl from the suburbs and I'm like, really, OK, here you go, here's what's in there!"[14]

The opening song of the album's fourth side, "Johnny Sunshine," plays like two songs grafted together: The first, a deadpan rocker with its singer providing a list of everything her guy took when he left her; the second, a chorus of angels lamenting the scene. The corresponding Stones' song "All Down the Line," shares the notion of hitting the road like a one-way train track, only Phair's singer can't follow—the guy took her car. One of the most fascinating *Guyville-Main St.* pairings is Phair's "Gunshy" and the Rolling Stones' "Stop Breaking Down." "Gunshy" is a confessional wrapped in a woozy, dreamlike wash of guitars and vocals. "There's no pretense or bravado," Phair once noted. "It's really saying, 'I don't know if I am cut out to do what it seems to be that society wants women to do.'"[15] The Stones' song, on the other hand, is all bravado. Originally written and recorded by Robert Johnson as "Stop Breaking Down Blues" in 1937, the song describes the singer's loving as a gun that blows women away. The Stones smash any nuance from Johnson's song and turn up the volume, making it into a hedonistic ritual. Though the Rolling Stones are covering Robert Johnson, Liz Phair comes closer to capturing his daring spirit.

"Stratford-on-Guy" was inspired by a flight coming into Chicago, turning it into a mystic quasi-spiritual experience. The parallel song on *Main St.* is "Shine a Light," a powerful gospel-influenced song about redemption. Phair's "Stratford-on-Guy" hints at a similar feeling, describing the earth as lit from within "Like a poorly assembled electrical ball." Phair later framed it as, if not quite a religious experience, then at least an epiphany: "There is this sense that you're literally at 30,000 feet above the scene that you are so involved in and this relationship you're so involved in and it's just a literal perspective shift above it. A lot of the bullshit just falls away."[16] And while the Stones sing of a light shined down, Phair's vantage point is from above, looking down at the lights. The final track on *Exile in Guyville*, "Strange Loop," begins by the singer announcing that the fire the guy likes in her "is the mark of someone adamantly free." Yet the confusion still lingers, as the singer is unclear about what she wants. In the final track of *Main St.*, "Soul Survivor," the singer says that being the soul survivor is going to be the death of him. Both songs try to reconcile ideas that end each album on an ambiguous note. The final words of *Guyville* are the words of a woman who has finally put everything into perspective: "I always wanted you, I only wanted more than I knew." In the singer's ability to learn and grow from Guyville, she proves herself as a soul survivor, too.

When *Exile in Guyville* was released on June 22, 1993, critics lost their minds. If there was ever an album built for a stereotyped 1990s-era record critic (white, male, straight, and socially awkward), this was it—a beautiful woman who sings like Lou Reed, writes songs laced with obscenities, and created a work based upon a cornerstone of the rock canon. Oh, and she's topless on the cover. As Sue Cummings wrote in *LA Weekly*, "Phair's conceptualizing gives her work a handle, but what seizes you on the album's first play is the simple production and her lyrics' frankness. In the end, it will be hard for critics not to like her, because she has made a meta-album: a feminist critique of a standard in the boomer rock canon, a record that reviews another."[17] Many agreed, as *Exile in Guyville* topped the year-end best album lists of *The New York Times*, *SPIN*, and the *Village Voice*, and appeared in dozens more.

Commercially, it didn't fare nearly as well, with no charting singles and peaking on the *Billboard* 200 album chart at #196. But in the musical world, where hype outweighs sales, Phair received lots of attention, which caught her off-guard. She had only played about a half-dozen gigs before being expected to tour for her album. Her first shows were awkward and stiff, which the real-life Guyville scene used as fodder to claim she got a free ride without paying her dues. While the rest of the rock press embraced Phair, the Chicago indie scene all but ostracized her. In this way, *Exile in Guyville* caused its title to come into being—during her initial wave of success, Liz Phair was literally exiled *from* Guyville.

As an unknown female artist to take on the self-proclaimed greatest rock band in the world and succeed, Liz Phair pulled off one of the greatest David-and-Goliath stories in rock and roll. "I met Mick Jagger and the way I understood that he understood it," Phair later told an interviewer, "I don't think he'd ever listened to it, but he essentially shook my hand and gave me a wide smile as if to say, 'You're welcome for using our name to get your fame.' And it was sort of like, 'We're gonna let you off this one time, you cheeky person.'"[18] But if all there was to *Guyville* was the way in which it was assembled, then we wouldn't still be talking about it today. It was one of the most influential albums of all-time and flipped the script on four decades of rock and roll male hedonism. That it did so while being one of the greatest and most complex concept albums is just one more notch on Phair's belt against the guys of Guyville.

Notes

1   Hopper.
2   "Liz Phair Interview plus Video . . ."

3 Trucks.
4 Marcus.
5 Hopper.
6 Spanos.
7 Ibid.
8 Ganz.
9 Arnold, 87.
10 Spanos.
11 Arnold, 18.
12 Ganz.
13 Spanos.
14 Ganz.
15 Spanos.
16 Ibid.
17 Cummings.
18 Ozzi.

17

I Am the Silencing Machine:
The Downward Spiral

"I know what I'm doing when I use the word *fuck*," Liz Phair once explained about *Exile in Guyville*, "but I think it's termed explicit only because I'm a girl. The thrill of it is like ... you look around at all the good girls and wonder what's going on in their heads."[1] Indeed, Phair's lyrics "I want to fuck you like a dog" raised many eyebrows. As if to prove her point, the following year Nine Inch Nails—an industrial project operated by mastermind Trent Reznor—released *The Downward Spiral*. One song on the album, "Closer," contained a refrain about wanting to "fuck you like an animal," and no one batted an eye; in fact, it became one of the album's most popular tracks. And what did the good girls think? "You haven't really lived, I think," wrote Jonathan Gold in his 1994 *Rolling Stone* cover story on Nine Inch Nails, "until you've heard a gang of Wayne State sorority sisters moan, 'I want to fuck you like an animal,' the chorus to 'Closer,' which has sort of the same resonance that 'I Want to Hold Your Hand' might have had thirty years ago." That would be a compliment if Trent Reznor didn't hate the Beatles.

For all intents and purposes, Trent Reznor *is* Nine Inch Nails. He may have had others on his albums or a touring band for concerts, but everything Nine Inch Nails creates adheres to his vision as the driving force. The project first came to prominence with its 1989 debut album, *Pretty Hate Machine*, which contained the song "Head Like a Hole." Although the album only reached #75 on the *Billboard* 200 album chart, it became one of the first independent albums to sell over a million copies and influenced the decade to come. In 1992, Nine Inch Nails released a follow-up EP, *Broken*, which left the more accessible synth-based music for a sound that was more industrial-based, using walls of machine-generated noise to create all-encompassing bleak soundscapes.

For Reznor, Nine Inch Nails' third release, *The Downward Spiral*, continued a progression begun by the first two. "[O]n *Pretty Hate Machine* I'm depressed by everything around me, but I still like myself ..." he told *SPIN* in 1996. "On *Broken*,

I've lost myself; nothing's better, and I want to die. *Downward Spiral* was searching for the core, by stripping away all the different layers."[2] He added in the same interview: "I had been working on the idea of *Downward Spiral* in my head for a while without writing any songs, just a concept. Originally, my pretentious aspirations were to make the dreaded concept record with a film that went with it ...you could maybe hark back to [Pink Floyd's 1979 concept album] *The Wall* as my inspiration."[3] *The Wall* tells the story of a rock star's descent into madness, something that Reznor could relate to. He made an album that was as disjointed as *The Wall* was polished, a mess of machines and noise that put you inside of the head of the protagonist. And with themes like control, machines, sex, BDSM, religion, madness, drugs, death, and you've got an album that's as powerful as it is polarizing.

The Downward Spiral begins with a sample from George Lucas's 1971 film debut, *THX 1138*, of a prisoner getting beaten by a guard. The slamming blows get faster and faster until they crash into the beginning of "Mr. Self Destruct." The song has an impenetrable loudness like a jackhammer stuck in a garbage disposal. "I am the voice inside your head," the singer intones through the clattering noise, as a voice whispers in response, "and I control you." As you listen, there is depth in the sound; *Spiral* is a tapestry of machine-made sounds. Synths emerge for the refrain, as "Mr. Self Destruct" demonstrates his power: "I drag you down, I use you up." And then, midway through, near-silence appears, as we can just hear the singer's echoed whisper: *"You let me do this to you."* The second half of the song explodes at full blast. "I am the silencing machine," he sings, foreshadowing the album's journey as a machine-corrupted descent into depression and suicide, as told by tools of technology. At the end, white noise increases before the song cuts off into a beautifully suspended loop of guitars and machines in a dance. And then this too is cut off by dead silence.

"Piggy" provides space after the claustrophobic opener with a funky drumbeat and seductive vocal—until you realize it's about an ex-lover the singer refers to as a pig. The pig imagery cuts deep. *Spiral* was recorded in the house where actress Sharon Tate and four others were murdered by Charles Manson's Family in 1969; the killers wrote "Political Piggy" in blood on the wall and "Pig" in blood on the front door. The latter was still visible when Reznor moved in, so he named the studio "Le Pig." Despite Reznor's interest in the macabre, he maintains he didn't seek the building out: "The Tate house was just a house. They didn't advertise that fact it was the Tate house when we were looking at it."[4] And once disclosed, it wasn't a deal-breaker. "Honestly," he remembered, "with the exception of the name of the studio [Le Pig], which I know was in very bad taste, most of the lyrics had been determined before I even leased the house."⁵ "Piggy" ends with a the refrain "Nothing can stop me now" because the singer no longer cares; he uses his pain and anger as a blank check to do whatever he wants. The only thing that can stop him is the song itself, which ends by cutting him off cold: "Nothing can stop—"

"Heresy" begins with a wavy keyboard line that is joined by a mechanical, pumping beat. Reznor sings in a falsetto voice, sounding like one of his heroes, Prince. Suddenly, the noise is back for the refrain, which hits like an ice storm: "GOD IS DEAD," the singer screams, "AND NO ONE CARES." As the third song on *Spiral* (a cruel invocation of the Trinity?), the singer addresses God by rejecting Him. Also, by following the "God is dead" line with one about going to hell, it implies hell as a real place, even without the structure of God and heaven around it. It's often said people go to hell because they choose to, but in "Heresy," there are no other options.

The following "March of the Pigs" is *fast*—featuring programmed drumming too quick for any human to play, a tidal wave of sounds and feedback unleash a descending riff like everyone in the band is getting kicked down the stairs. The singer screams commands, calling the pigs to march, to push, to crawl on their knees. The chorus scales things down to a running motor on a kickdrum as military jets soar overhead. "Take the skin and peel it back," the singer instructs, as the sound pushes out of the dark ground like a seed, blossoming like a rose growing out of concrete, as the industrial machine sounds are suddenly replaced by a piano and the singer singing a lovely hook—"Now doesn't that make you feel better?"—before settling back into an onslaught of noise. In an album so dark and challenging, this was a moment of peace. The goal of *Broken* "was to make a dense record," Reznor explained. "We approached [*Spiral*] from the opposite point of view—a record with holes everywhere."⁶ Reznor uses silence to let space into the music, giving the album—and its listener—room to breathe.

The next track, "Closer," samples the beginning of Iggy Pop's 1977 song "Nightclubbing," which Reznor made sound like pistons pumping and releasing steam in a void. The singer comes in as a wah-wah fuzz bass line appears over a faster clicking sound. "Closer" is a portrait in self-loathing through imagery of depraved sex. The infamous "I wanna fuck you like an animal" refrain was one of the great hooks of the era, but more interesting is the song's tagline: "You get me closer to God." One wonders what the singer means, since he declared that God is dead only two songs earlier. Regardless, the song's extended musical coda is a thing of savage beauty, overlaying rattling mechanical sounds with interlocking catchy riffs and a high synth line. Coming out of the dense yet multilayered sound is a haunting 11-note riff that is picked out by warped piano keys suspended in cold animation, creating notes that hang like icicles in a vacuum.

The final note of "Closer" rings on top of the first beat of "Ruiner"—a funky drum pattern over mechanical squeals and a pony's whinny. Grinding layers of noise obscures the rest of the verses, as the singer fleshes the ruiner out: He's "got a lot to prove" and "nothing to lose," he's "your only friend," he "ruins everything he sees." A dramatic, dystopian theme of synthesizers, hammered beats, and voices appear, like the final villain in an old video game. The song ends with the singer claiming that he is not hurt and that nothing can stop him, which, like in "Piggy," cuts him off at the end.

"The Becoming" follows "Ruiner," introducing an oscillating loop of people screaming and running—taken from the 1990 science fiction film *Robot Jox*—as the beat fires like gunshots. *Robot Jox* was about men operating giant robot machines, while "The Becoming" reverses the premise by placing the machine inside of the man. In a lopsided vocal that plays around the beat, the singer explains how he used to have feelings but he's "now made up of wires." The singer addresses "Annie," asking her to hold him tighter, a reaching for human touch over an acoustic sound. The singer says the machine inside of him wants him dead. Meanwhile, the acoustic guitar works its way out of the ether, only to be overpowered by mechanical white noise and rhythm at the end.

"I Do Not Want This" begins the second half of the album with the singer in anguish, although much of the first verse features just a few piano notes played under a thick, rigid beat. Everything is tension, waiting to break. The dam bursts when the singer screams in catharsis that he does not want this and no one knows how he feels. "To a large extent, the new record is me coming to terms with who I am and addressing that in a potentially ugly manner," Reznor explained in 1994.[7] "When you peel back the skin sometimes you find that what you see is not always the person you thought you were." "I Do Not Want This" is the sound of fighting a losing battle. A machine-filled instrumental section follows the main part; the singer comes out screaming about how he wants to know everything, be everywhere, have sex with everyone, and "do something THAT MATTERS."

"Big Man with a Gun" kicks like cartoon heavy metal with adolescent lyrics to match. Filled with tasteless gun-as-phallic imagery, it ends with the singer screaming "ME AND MY FUCKING GUN" over and over. Initially, Republicans took it as an attack on conservative gun advocates. Reznor saw otherwise, explaining in 1996 that "the original point of 'Big Man with a Gun' was madness ... But it was also making fun of the whole misogynistic, gangsta-rap bullshit."[8] More controversy came in 1999, when Dylan Klebold, one of the two assassins in the Columbine High School massacre, was revealed to have loved *Spiral*, referencing it in his journals. One imagines he did not hear "Big Man with a Gun" as satire. Instead, he may have been provoked by its final line: "Nothing can stop me now."

The nearly-instrumental "A Warm Place" comes next, with the only lyrics being an almost-inaudible voice speaking like a secret: *"The best thing about life is knowing you put it together."* The rest of the song creates a soundscape vivid enough to step into. "David Bowie's *Low* was probably the single greatest influence on *The Downward Spiral* for me," Reznor said a month after *Spiral* was released. Indeed, Bowie's landmark 1977 masterpiece was groundbreaking for its use of electronic music, especially its second side of four instrumentals, each conjuring its own fantasy world. For a work that uses silence like an instrument, "A Warm Place" embodies a calmness at odds with the rest of the album.

"As the record goes on, the structure of the songs gets worse and less predictable," Reznor told *Melody Maker* in 1994. "At one point I realized every song I'd ever written was a pop song and I wanted to destroy that, destroy everything, destroy my career and destroy myself in the process, maybe."[9] With this in mind, the last four songs of *Spiral* are darker and more abstract, beginning with "Eraser." There's a quiet mechanical swishing noise until drums kick in; high notes spin angular riffs as the sound slowly grows denser. The singer intones two-word phrases mirrored by keyboard and bass—"Need you" and "Dream you"—as the beat continues. When he gets to lines directed to himself—"SMASH ME!" and "ERASE ME!"—he's suddenly screaming over an huge sound with shredding electric guitars and layers of noise. For the finale, he keeps screaming "KILL ME!" until the song ends neatly on cue, leaving only silence.

"Reptile" has a grinding beat with a high wheezing noise, like someone trying (and failing) to start a lawnmower. The singer sounds like he's inside a machine, padded by guitar-like echo and a pulsating synth bass. The lyrics are among the most disturbing on the record, describing a woman with reptile blood who spreads herself to let insects into her body. The refrain builds as a distorted guitar joins in and the singer declares, "I am so impure." After the second verse, in which the singer learns his depths are limitless, comes the coda where the singer fights against the song: "Goddamn it, let me go!"

The title track of *The Downward Spiral* starts with warbling rhythm like an empty airport luggage conveyer belt. Over this, an acoustic guitar plays the haunting eleven-note theme first heard in "Closer." The acoustic guitar grows into a hard rock riff with bass following underneath. Machine noises build in strength, until the singer lets out a long scream, as drums smash in with electric guitars and keyboard playing the eleven-note theme in time with the music. The sound is sealed off, like it's bleeding through a neighbor's wall. Meanwhile, the singer intones: "He couldn't believe how easy it was," he reports, "He just put the gun into his face. Bang!" The stench of death all over the album finally makes it to the fore.

The final song on the album is "Hurt." Most of it features Reznor with an acoustic guitar as ambient machine sounds whisp by in a state of eternal, unbearable stillness. "Hurt" is a chilling tale of loneliness, a world where nothing is forgotten and everyone "goes away in the end." By the end, the full band plays a slow burn, as the singer warns that he "will let you down" and "make you hurt." The presence of "Hurt" after "The Downward Spiral" leaves the album's ending ambiguous. It implies that the suicide in "Spiral" was symbolic or not really the singer himself. Maybe "Hurt" turns the album into a junky's fever dream. Or perhaps it's the ghost of the singer reflecting on what he's done. But no matter how you interpret it, the singer remains alone.

For a song that evokes the afterlife, "Hurt" has had quite an afterlife of its own. In 2004, Johnny Cash recorded a stripped-down cover of "Hurt" for his album *American IV: The Man Comes Around*. "It was a good version, and I certainly wasn't cringing or anything, but it felt like I was watching my girlfriend fuck somebody else," Reznor told a reporter about hearing it for the first time. Then someone played him the video. "Wow. I just lost my girlfriend, because that song isn't mine anymore . . . I wrote some words and music in my bedroom as a way of staying sane, about a bleak and desperate place I was in, totally isolated and alone. Some-fucking-how that winds up reinterpreted by a music legend from a radically different era/genre and still retains sincerity and meaning—different, but every bit as pure."[10] In "Hurt," Johnny Cash seized on the pop songwriting driving much of *Spiral*, and turned the song into an unlikely American standard.

The Downward Spiral was released on March 8, 1994 to rave reviews. In describing "Mr. Self Destruct," *Rolling Stone* noted that while other bands used the soft/loud dynamic, "Trent Reznor takes it to sadistic extremes, especially since the song—without the power riffing and the howl, the distortion and the infinite layering—would essentially be as melodic as a late Beatles tune."[11] *The Chicago Tribune* hailed Reznor as "an amazing artist, maker of some of the most sophisticated machine music ever made. Like Dr. Frankenstein, Reznor has animated the beast, turned synthesizers into a symphonic swirl, given his drum machines a personality."[12] And *The Los Angeles Times* predicted that "'Spiral' is a major work that is likely to stand alongside Nirvana's 'Nevermind' as one of the twin towers of 1990s American rock."[13] All three reviews proved prescient.

But perhaps the most unexpected success for *Spiral* was that it debuted at #2 on the *Billboard* Top 200 album chart. The album hit the perfect tipping point of Nine Inch Nails' word-of-mouth growing popularity and endless touring intersecting their most accomplished work up to that point. "I think popular music sucks today," Reznor told a reporter in 1996. "For the most part, I cannot fucking stand the shit that's at the top of the charts. Now, I'm not saying my sole mission is to turn people on to other music. But maybe I can change things a bit."[14] *Spiral* earned Reznor a seat at the table—the next two Nine Inch Nails albums debuted at #1.

The Downward Spiral is one man's descent into madness, with each spiral ring a lower circle of hell. But even with the finality and despair of "Hurt," this is music that demands to be played again. Part of it is its depth of sound—it's a rare album where you can pick up something new with each subsequent listen. Furthermore, its lyrics entice you to go on the journey again to figure out what exactly is happening to the singer, or perhaps, whether you see any parts of yourself in the spiral. In this way, the spiral isn't a spiral at all—if you turn it to 90 degrees towards you and look at it from the top, it's a circle. Like the black vinyl or metal CD playing it, the journey retells itself like a snake eating its own tail. And as three different songs on the album tell us, nothing can stop it.

Notes

1 O'Dair, 537.
2 Weisbard.
3 Ibid.
4 Chirazi.
5 Steinke.
6 Garbarini.
7 Wiederhorn.
8 Weisbard.

9   Wilde.
10 Rickly.
11 Gold.
12 Kott.
13 Hilburn.
14 Weisbard.

18

I Feel Like Death Is Fuckin' Callin' Me:
Ready to Die

Before he reinvented himself as The Notorious B.I.G., Christopher Wallace was a kid who sat on a Brooklyn stoop because his mother wouldn't let him go into the street. He was adrift in life, but what he observed from his vantage point—seeing the same neighborhood people, watching drug deals, witnessing wads of cash going back and forth—made him a student of the streets before he even set foot to hustle on them. "It was hard," Wallace later reflected. "My mom was a single parent. And she just basically left me to do what I wanted to. Every time she left, she'd tell me to just use my discretion. The way I saw it, that just meant I could do whatever I wanted to. I just roamed the streets. From the age of twelve, I was hangin', doin' basic street shit—robbing, stealing, selling drugs. If I was hungry, broke, and wanted something, I just took it."[1] Wallace dropped out of high school at seventeen and became a full-time hustler. He robbed and stole to survive, but the real money was in drug dealing. In 1991, he was arrested for dealing crack in North Carolina and served a nine-month sentence before he could make bail. After this experience, he increasingly focused on a career in rap music.

Wallace first became known as Biggie Smalls, but after learning that name was already in use, he changed it to The Notorious B.I.G.—the "B.I.G." stood for "Business Instead of Game"—although he was also still known as Biggie Smalls. He made a demo tape that was featured in *The Source*'s "Unsigned Hype" column; eventually, it was heard by Sean "Puffy" Combs, an enterprising young mogul-in-the-making. Combs had started his own label, Bad Boy Records, and signed Biggie as one of his first artists. Biggie had an unusual work style. He would show up to the studio, ask the producer to play a sample, and then sat in the corner for an hour, smoking blunts and mumbling to himself. At some point—after an hour, or two, or three—he would announce "I'm ready," and go into the studio booth and cut the song, often in one take. And while Biggie handled lyrics, Combs shaped his hard sound into something more commercial. Biggie once explained that Combs "wanna make hits. That's what he thrives on. So, whatever he tell me to do, you know what I'm saying? If it ain't too outlandish, I'll roll ... I'm down."[2] As one of the greatest artist and producer teams in hip-hop, Biggie and Combs challenged each other to bring out the best in themselves.

For Biggie's first album, the label named it after the first song recorded for it, "Ready to Die." Despite its morbid title, the album gives us a grand sweep of one person's life, from birth through death, with lots of greed, wrath, and lust in between. But now we're getting into tricky territory. It's tempting to hear autobiographically-inspired songs as confessions by the artist, whereas it's often somewhere between fiction and reality. "Biggie is an entertainer," Biggie once told an interviewer, referring to himself in the third person. "He makes music and he makes videos. That's Biggie Smalls, but Christopher Wallace is the person. That's the one that has to take care of the family. The daughter, the wife—all of that. That's Christopher. That's the real person. I leave all that Biggie stuff alone. We don't blend too much."[3] This distinction between Christopher Wallace and Biggie Smalls is instructive; it helps us keep the album in perspective. Biggie Smalls is a fictionalized version of Christopher Wallace, a persona he can take on while telling his story. Biggie was a writer in the truest sense of the word, using facts to set scenes and adding fictions where needed to see them through. On *Ready to Die*, The Notorious B.I.G. switches styles, subject matter, and even voices to become hip-hop's finest storyteller.

Ready to Die begins with the ominous strings of "Intro," before turning to a heartbeat. We hear a three-minute overview of Biggie's life, with each era given its own soundtrack. In 1972, he's born to the sounds of Curtis Mayfield's "Superfly"; in 1979, his parents argue about him during the Sugar Hill Gang's "Rapper's Delight"; in 1987, we hear an adult Biggie executing a robbery over Top Billin's "Audio Two"; and finally, in 1993, we hear Biggie released from prison to the tune of Snoop Dogg's "Tha Shiznit." The use of vignettes sets the scene for what will be a very cinematic album. Taking us from Biggie's birth to his prison release the year before *Ready to Die*'s release, it provides a sketch of where he's been. As for where he's going, Biggie says at the end of "Intro": "I got big plans, nigga, big plans ..."

The first song on the album, "Things Done Changed," begins with a drum fill that leads into a lush tapestry of sound—a sample from Dr. Dre's 1992 "Lil' Ghetto Boy," as horns, harp strings, and record scratches thicken the sound. We hear a lyrical sweep of "back in the day" old-school fads, children's games, and neighborhood get-togethers, before contrasting this with the current streets as a wasteland of dead bodies and drug dealers. The third verse contains a line about how if you want to get by in the streets, you're either "slinging crack rock" or else "you got a wicked jump shot." These words frame the entire album, only with Biggie, he got out through his prowess on the mic instead of athleticism on the court. All put together, it's a visceral snapshot of the streets that's so strong, it's one of the few hip-hop songs included in Henry Louis Gates Jr.'s *The Norton Anthology of African American Literature*.

The following "Gimme the Loot" depicts two guys executing a robbery. The main voice is deep and assured, while the other is higher and tentative; both are played by Biggie. One imagines Biggie's own transition from a young teenage hustler to an adult professional allowed him to understand both sides of the picture. The album then shifts to a hardcore rap sound with "Machine Gun Funk." "This ain't Christopher Williams," Biggie raps early in the first verse. The song celebrates Biggie giving up his previous life of crime for music. And yet, he uses the language of a drug dealer to describe his music—"I got bags of funk and it's sellin' by the tons" in one line; "smokin' mics like crack pipes" in another—until the hustler on the street becomes the hustler on the mic.

"Warning" takes a straightforward idea—Biggie is tipped off that some acquaintances are going to rob him—and tells it in a compelling way. Biggie's beeper goes off at 5:46 a.m. It's his friend Pop, who warns him of Biggie's acquaintances who are planning to turn on them. Throughout the conversation, we hear Biggie in person and Pop through the phone, with Biggie again playing both roles. The most effective turn of phrase is when Pop tells him that they're aware of his mother's new home in Florida at the Fifth Corridor; Biggie cuts in: "Call the coroner!" The rest of the song finds Biggie stockpiling his guns until he hears somebody coming. We then switch to the two would-be criminals whispering in the night, killed by two blasts to the head.

The title track of *Ready to Die* comes next, beginning with Biggie putting a gun to someone's head and blowing them away. As usual, Biggie has full conviction in his voice that backs up his otherwise extreme claims. Given this buildup of threatening the listener, one might expect the hook to be something like "*You* should be ready to die," but it not—it's "*I'm* ready to die." Biggie's claim that he's ready to die turns his death threats into a death wish, as if he's going out all armed and dangerous because he doesn't care if he gets killed. "Yo, I'm not ready to die," Biggie—or perhaps, Christopher Wallace—once said. "That's just like an extension of how I feel. It's serious for me right now."[4]

"One More Chance" shifts gears to Biggie's prowess with women. Again, we get a cinematic opening—a series of messages from girls Biggie has apparently jilted—before hitting a laid-back groove, filled with slick (if vulgar) lyrics that stack rhymes on each other as Biggie describes his notoriously big anatomy. The refrain lifts its melody from the Jackson 5's "I Want You Back," while the verses introduce his line, "I love it when they call me Big Poppa," which grew into its own song. To keep the sexual vibe flowing, the ninety-second "#!*@ Me (Interlude)" features Biggie having simulated sex with a woman. It's a throwaway that, along with a similar interlude later in the album of Biggie receiving oral sex (at the end of "Respect"), feels more gratuitous than necessary. Indeed, in her mostly-glowing review of *Ready to Die* in *The Source*, Shortie mentions that "the two sex skits are annoying. A graphic depiction of Biggie gettin' a blow job? He can keep that gem to himself."[5]

"The What" is the only track with a featured artist, Method Man, from the Wu-Tang Clan. Where Biggie's voice is smooth and unflappable, Method Man sounds hoarse from yelling, hyped-up and ready to explode like a powder keg. The two work off each other brilliantly. And although most of the song is bragging about their skills on the mic, the refrain holds a message of self-determination: "Everything you get you gotta work hard for it." They mean it. "At the time I was making the album," Biggie told *Rolling Stone* a few months after its release, "I was just waking up every morning, hustling … just risking my life every day on the street selling drugs, you know what I'm saying? You could get killed easy, but I was doing that every day because I knew that's what I needed [to do] to eat."[6]

Up next is "Juicy," which was lifted as the first single from *Ready to Die* and was Biggie's breakthrough hit, reaching #27 on the *Billboard* Hot 100 and #14 on the *Billboard* R&B charts. "Juicy" is an ideal introduction to Biggie (and *Ready to Die*), telling Biggie's rags-to-riches story in miniature. Opening with "It was all a dream," this is a hip-hop fairytale, a retelling of *Once Upon a Time* … from the perspective of a hip-hop prince. Everything is so surreal and unexpected that even the singer is trying to piece it all together. Once again, it's the details that make it vivid—*Word Up!* Magazine, Bambú rolling paper, sardines for dinner—and put us into Biggie's world. This plus the internal rhymes he uses (one verse rhymes "landlord dissed us" with "Christmas missed us") and Combs' sleek production make for an all-encompassing experience. The following "The What" has a touch of prophecy when Biggie uses the line "blow up like the World Trade." Hearing these words, recorded 1993, one can't help but think of the attack on the World Trade Center in 2001. Of course, Biggie was dead for four years by that point, but in an album about the past and present, one can hear a hint of the future, too.

"Everyday Struggle" throws us back into the album's "ready to die" motif: "I don't wanna live no more," it begins, as the singer hears "death knockin' at my front door," enhanced by a knocking drumbeat sample. "Everyday Struggle" provides a picture of Biggie's days as a drug dealer, specifically detailing one of his trips down south. The relentless attack of words and rhymes backed by the snapping drums emulate the lyrics' stress and struggle. In an early *New York Times* profile, journalist Touré speculates Biggie "has put drug dealing behind him but retains the dealer's constant fear that his life is in danger."[7] "Everyday Struggle" is a song about being trapped by the streets even once you're no longer on them.

"Me & My Bitch" tells a fictionalized version of Biggie and his wife. Despite some misogynist lyrics, the singer makes it clear he respects his wife if only because she can keep up with him, if not get an upper hand. She uses his toothbrush to wash the toilet and throws his clothes out the window, yet the singer still proclaims, "I hope we fuckin' die together." But they don't. He learns his wife has been killed by a gunshot to the heart, which he knows was meant for him. He swears revenge, perpetuating the pattern of using murder as revenge for murder (as his own killing in 1997 allegedly did). A skit follows that features Biggie giving a brief interview to a female reporter. He defers on influence: "Ain't nobody really influenced me, you know what I'm saying? I was just tired of being on the streets, you know what I'm saying? I had get up off that, you know?" She then asks where's he from. The response comes swiftly: "Brooklyn."

The laidback groove of "Big Poppa" comes in, using the high-pitched synthesizer on top of the mix like an outtake from Dr. Dre's *The Chronic*. Some call this sound as the "Funky Worm," from a 1972 Ohio Players' song that used this sound and got sampled in countless hip-hop songs. It's a hallmark of 1990s West Coast hip-hop, but Biggie is always the first to remind you that he's representing Brooklyn. With its irresistible "I love it when they call me Big Poppa" refrain, the song was the follow-up single to "Juicy" and did even better, reaching #6 on the *Billboard* Hot 100 and #4 on the *Billboard* R&B chart in 1995. The song finds Biggie at his most seductive, at one point laying out his game plan to his potential lover, down to what food he will order—"T-bone steak, cheese eggs and Welch's grape"—with an effortless swagger that predicts later hits like "Hypnotize."

"Respect" features singer Diana King shouting the refrain in a Jamaican dialect, over one of the funkiest beats on the album—a sample of KC and the Sunshine Band (featuring George McCrae)'s 1975 "I Get Lifted"—slowed down and mixed heavy so you can sink your teeth into it. "Respect" reflects on Biggie's life as a whole, from his birth to his years as a teenage drug dealer, time in prison, and finally his redemption with music. And yet, death looms, from his birth with the umbilical cord around his neck. For Biggie, life and death are two sides of the same coin, and the fragility of life is always threatened by the finality of death.

"Friend of Mine" focuses on relationships, specifically chastising girls who sleep with a guy and then his friends. When played against "One More Chance," "Friend of Mine" is an exercise in hypocrisy. In the former, Biggie shrugs off the women who are mad at him for sleeping with their friends, while the latter finds the guys incredulous at such an act. What saves it is the refrain's hook—"You know that ain't right—with a friend of mine"—lifted from Black Mamba's 1984 song "Vicious." "Friend of Mine" sounds good, but once you try to break it down and square it with the other songs, it's an ethical mess. Next up is "Unbelievable," which finds Biggie in full hip-hop star mode, repping his home, toting guns, destroying MCs, and getting money. Biggie samples himself from "The What" to declare that "Biggie-Biggie-Biggie Smalls is the illest." Unlike many other tracks on the album, it is less a narrative than Biggie bragging about his cred. But Biggie's main theme pops its head up towards the end—"Get ready to die, tell God I said hi"—once again keeping death close by.

Tellingly, the final song on *Ready to Die* is "Suicidal Thoughts." Set up as a phone call from Biggie to Combs in the middle of the night, "Suicidal Thoughts" is one long verse, punctuated by Puffy's questions over the phone about what is going on. "When I die, fuck it, I wanna go to hell," Biggie begins, and things only grow more dire from there. He flashes back over his life and lets his sins and stress pile up with the lines of the verse. Biggie's final words on the album— "Matter of fact, I'm sick of talkin'"—are followed by a gunshot blast and more desperate cries from Combs before the phoneline is disconnected. The heartbeats that opened the album return, only this time, they get slower and slower until they simply stop.

It's impossible to listen to *Ready to Die* today without the foreknowledge of Biggie's own death hanging over the album. Three years after *Ready to Die* was released, Biggie was about to release his double-album follow-up, *Life After Death*, when he was killed in a drive-by shooting in Los Angeles on March 9, 1997. Many saw it as retaliation for Tupac's fatal shooting six months earlier on

September 13, 1996. In real life, Biggie and Tupac were initially fast friends, but a rift grew between them. The point of no return appeared to be when Tupac accused Biggie of orchestrating the 1994 shooting that nearly killed Tupac. "I had nothing to do with any of that Tupac shit," Biggie explained, two months before his own death. "That's a complete and total misconception. I definitely wouldn't wish death on anyone."[8]

Except, perhaps, on himself.

On *Ready to Die*, Biggie makes the case that he's ready to die, but for modern listeners, he's already dead. Part of *Ready to Die*'s power lies in this prophecy. It predicts a death that came before Biggie could release a follow-up album called *Life After Death*. *Ready to Die* plays like an autobiography but sounds like a last will and testament. Navigating this album is like weaving around tombstones in a moonlit graveyard—death is everywhere. Throughout the album, Biggie sees dead bodies piling up in the streets, identifies dead bodies, threatens death to his enemies, causes the deaths of others, listens to the prayer "If I should die before I wake," hears death knocking on his front door, finds his lover dead at the hand of his enemies, and finally causes his own death with a gun. This is the work of a man haunted by, if not paranoid about, death. "I'm not paranoid to the point where—" Biggie once told a reporter with a pause, before changing course. "Yes, I am. I'm scared to death. Scared of getting my brains blown out."[9] The way he allows death to define his life is eerie—especially when you know how it will end for him. Because Biggie seems to know, too.

Notes

1 Nelson, *Billboard*, 30.
2 Tinsley, 168.
3 Ibid., 6.
4 Ibid., 162.
5 Shortie.
6 Fernando.
7 Touré.
8 Michael.
9 Touré, 42.

19

A Handshake of Carbon Monoxide: *OK Computer*

Although it's surreal to remember today, there was a time in the mid-1990s when Radiohead seemed little more than a one-hit wonder following their 1992 international fluke hit "Creep." At least in America. In their native UK, their second album, which flopped in the US, was a big hit with an influential string of singles. But it was on their third album, 1997's *OK Computer*, that the group—singer/guitarist Thom Yorke, guitarist/keyboardist Jonny Greenwood, guitarist Ed O'Brien, bassist Colin Greenwood, and drummer Phil Selway—made their bid for rock immortality. Although the album's title came from a line in Douglas Adams' humorous satire *A Hitchhiker's Guide to the Galaxy*, *OK Computer* was a beautifully stark and brooding album. In a 1998 interview with *NME*, Yorke described the songs as "'Polaroids in my head,' a succession of snapshots that form a larger whole."[1] Nigel Godrich, who co-produced the album with Radiohead, noted, "You have to sit through the whole album because it's a whole piece."[2] Immediately upon release, *OK Computer* was branded a concept album, which feels right considering the record's reoccurring themes and otherworldly vibe. But what exactly was it a concept album about?

Mark Kemp wrote in *Rolling Stone* that "Radiohead have released a concept album whose theme—based on rock's age-old fear of the imminence of a world run by computers—unfolds gradually during the course of the album's twelve songs,"[3] while James Oldham posited in *NME*: "Radiohead have created an album motivated and unified by one overriding theme: three years away from the millennium, Yorke wants to leave the planet and escape from the routine and clutter of life. Not that Radiohead have chosen to [make] a concept album; at least, not consciously. It's just that virtually every track on 'OK Computer' is driven by a feeling of impotence with the world around it."[4] And *SPIN* described it as a "soaring song-cycle about the fate of the soul in the digital age (or something)."[5] The "(or something)" is the most 1990s way of describing one of the decade's most iconic albums.

For Thom Yorke, the album came out of the exhaustion after the endless traveling and touring for *The Bends*: "We were living in orbit, on a bus, so when you stepped back into the real world it didn't compute. I felt very little connection with my fellow human beings."[6] Beginning with a jackknifed tractor-trailer in a car crash, *OK Computer* chronicles all kinds of journeys: in cars, tramlines, flying saucers, escaping on foot, going forwards and back, climbing up walls, crashing down in a plane. The album may be slow in tempo, but it's going everywhere at once. "Though Thom Yorke insists that 'OK Computer' was inspired by the dislocation of non-stop travel, it's now understood as a record about how overreliance on technology can lead to alienation," wrote Amanda Petrusich in *The New Yorker* on the album's twentieth anniversary. "Critics (and some fans) approached its reappearance with trepidation . . . Even Thom Yorke . . . has been nearly sheepish when discussing its legacy. 'The whole album is really fucking geeky,' he recently told *Rolling Stone*."[7]

In truth, *OK Computer* is all these things and more, depending on how you listen to it. I hear it as an album of journeys—away from society, into machines—many of which end in crashes or confusion. After all, its opening song is called "Airbag."

The first sound you hear in *OK Computer* is the jagged, whirring notes of Jonny Greenwood's electric guitar. As the music grows, Phil Selway's drums come in with a strange, sputtering fill, which settle into an off-kilter pattern that dictates the lurching pace of the song. To compensate, Colin Greenwood's bass tethers itself around periodic beats, producing as much silence as notes. Jonny's guitar distortion fades and Thom Yorke comes in with his high, careening vocals, singing about a jackknifed juggernaut in the next world war. "I am born again," the singer announces at the center of each verse, starting the album with a vision of reincarnation. The airbag that saves the singer's life gives him the feeling of an immortal superhero: "In an interstellar burst," the singer croons, "I'm back to save the universe." After two decades of hindsight, Yorke puts an optimistic spin on the song: "I was really frightened of cars back then, but 'Airbag' was almost the opposite of that. If you get into a crash or a potentially disastrous situation and walk away, you feel a thousand times more alive regardless of what that is. It's more about that."[8] The cascading soundscapes of "Airbag" dissolve into a final crash, as three succinct mechanical chirps set the pace for the next song.

"Paranoid Android" is a six-and-a-half-minute, multi-section rock opera that Radiohead released as the lead single for *OK Computer*. Starting with a ringing acoustic guitar pattern over a gentle backbeat as a spacey electric guitar hovers around, Yorke sings his short verses about resting and revenge slowly, carefully, as a computerized voice can be heard under his shimmering "What's that?" refrain: "*I may be paranoid, but not an android.*" The guitars shift into a hard rock riff, causing the sound to layer and grow. "Ambition makes you look pretty ugly," sneers the singer, before Jonny Greenwood plays an angular guitar solo that begins in chaos and ends with a wail that crashes everything down. The song is resurrected by the album's most gorgeous moment, when monk-like singing rescues the music from its hard rock ashes into a thing of beauty. "Rain down on me," the singer calls to the sky, "From a great height." The solemn progression of music over the steady, slow drumbeat feels like a both a funeral and a baptism by rain. The sophistication of the song suggests progressive rock, which Radiohead generally disdains. Whether or not it's progressive rock per se, "Paranoid Android" was a gambit that paid off—despite label skepticism, the song was a huge hit, peaking at #3 in the UK, where it remains their highest-charting single to date.

"Subterranean Homesick Alien" hijacks its name from Bob Dylan's 1965 classic "Subterranean Homesick Blues," but the song is a mellow, lilting waltz with sparkling guitars and warm electric piano running underneath. The singer lives in a boring town in which he feels aliens hovering. Only the frantic "They're all uptight! Uptight!" refrain with its descending guitar pattern and thundering drums break the sleepy mood. In the second verse, the singer wishes the aliens would take him on their ship, even though he knows his friends would never believe him. The idea of isolation from one's community for following aliens is a trope that runs deep; "That was like *Close Encounters of the Third Kind*," remembered Yorke in 2017.

OK Computer is a very cinematic album, its music fluctuating between subtle background music and storming crescendos. "Exit Music (For a Film)" was created for Baz Luhrmann's 1996 *Romeo + Juliet*. Yorke only saw a few scenes from Luhrmann's film, so he based it on Franco Zeffirelli's more traditional film version from 1968. The result is a beautiful, haunting folk song about two young lovers escaping. The first part of the song features only Yorke singing with an acoustic guitar, all unnerving anticipation. When the drums finally tumble in for the last section, joined by high synthesizers and a fuzz bass, the song fattens up from an eerily still evening on the beach to a tsunami, until the singer is yelling just to be heard. By the time he's crawled out of the tempest, he sounds like a man who's barely survived a shipwreck. He appears to address those who challenged the lovers. "We hope, that you choke," he rasps, "That you choke."

"Let Down" lands the album on a more familiar pop sound—at least in the music. Built around the picked notes of shimmering electric guitars, the song has all the sonic richness of an early Byrds song. The drums take a backseat while the musical interplay between the guitars and bass fill out the sound into a densely layered tapestry. Guitarist Ed O'Brien described the production as "a nod to Phil Spector," but beyond the all-encompassing prettiness of its sound, the lyrics are devastating.[9] One of the album's most pointed travelogues, starting with "Transport, motorways and tramlines," watching them start and stop, as people are filled with empty disappointment: "Crushed like a bug in the ground." The singer wishes to grow wings from a chemical reaction, only to realize this is "hysterical and useless"—he is confined to his world. It is a portrait of detachment, in which every journey blurs into stagnation.

"Let Down" was an obvious choice for a single, but Radiohead nixed it when they didn't like their music video for it, so the following "Karma Police" was chosen instead. Lifting the chord progression of the Beatles' "Sexy Sadie," Yorke tapped into "fridge buzz," which is what he referred to as "the combination of incessant information and background noise that always threatened to overwhelm him."[10] ("I recorded the actual buzz from a fridge for that on the demo," remembered Yorke.[11]) Meanwhile, karma is a noticeably human-centered concept in an album about the omnipresence of machines. In one verse, the singer calls the karma police to arrest a man who "talks in maths" (perhaps in the binary code of "Ones and Zeroes"—an early title for *OK Computer*) and "buzzes like a fridge." The chorus is a haunting piano-led melody, with a twisted delivery: "This is what you'll get—if you mess with us." Halfway through the song, the sound becomes a dense avalanche of fuzzing and whirring as the vocals become distant and echoed. This shift in texture mirrors the man-vs.-machine schizophrenia of the album, where the human element (karma) and the computer capabilities (police) combine to create one absurd unit. "It's not entirely serious," Yorke said of "Karma Police." "I hope people realize that."[12] But as O'Brien's mechanically cloying guitar fuzz takes over at the end, it sounds like a win for the machines.

If the following "Fitter, Happier" is a victory lap for the machines, then it's a discomforting one. Although it's the shortest track on the album, it's a buzzkill, consisting of a Stephen Hawking-like voice (which isn't Hawking, despite the rumors) dictating how to live more productively. Man and machine become one, as the words are spoken by an android voice with diminishing returns of logic. It closes starkly: "*Fitter, healthier and more productive. A pig. In a cage. On antibiotics.*" For many people, one listen was enough and it's likely the most-skipped track on a major album since the Beatles' "Revolution 9." And yet, this track is central to Radiohead's vision. It's placed as the seventh song, beginning the second half of the twelve-song album. Haters should be grateful though—Radiohead had originally pinned it to begin the record. Instead, it comes at the heart of the record, which is to say it's as warm as the one given to the archetypal android, the Tin Woodsman.

Radiohead follows the *musique concrète* "Fitter Happier" with *OK Computer*'s hardest-rocking song, "Electioneering." The song is built around a catchy, driving guitar riff, before drums jackhammer in and a cowbell keeps the pace frantic. "Electioneering" proved popular among the new songs played on their tour for *The Bends* and was earmarked as a lead single; however, everyone agreed the studio performance did not come close to the live experience. It was also one of Radiohead's first overtly political songs, blasting those who say whatever they need to get votes. The only progress that the politician cares about his is own, which makes your own wellbeing an arbitrary factor. For an album so obsessed with the bleakness of the binary world, the politician of "Electioneering" represents where a human can be as cold and calculating as a machine.

While "Electioneering" and a few other songs were recorded at Radiohead's rustic Oxfordshire recording space, Canned Applause, the studio's isolation and tensions between the band soon proved difficult. Looking for a restart, co-producer Nigel Godrich booked St. Catherine's Court, a fifteenth century mansion near Bath. "Climbing Up the Walls" was the first song to take shape in the mansion. Recorded during a hailstorm, it paints a slow, haunted world covered in ice and filled with ghosts. Radiohead was convinced the mansion was haunted and Yorke remembered ghosts spoke to him while he was sleeping. But despite any supernatural events at the time of recording, "Climbing Up the Walls" was primarily inspired by Yorke's stint working at a facility for the mentally ill. "Depression for example at the time was something that everybody just went, 'Oh, well, you're just depressed,'" he once explained. "But now it can lead into other things like if someone gets ill, they can be a danger to themselves and to other people. That's what I think about when I play ["Climbing Up the Walls"] now."[13] All too often, depression left unchecked can lead to suicide, which sets things up for the album's next song.

"No Surprises" begins with a chiming opening guitar directly inspired by the Beach Boys' *Pet Sounds* (specifically, the opening notes of "Wouldn't It Be Nice").

It is a slow song, but a comforting one, allowing the rhythm section to lay low while a glockenspiel doubles the guitar riff like a child's music box. At first, "No Surprises" seems like a lilting lullaby, but the lyrics prove otherwise. The singer calmly describes being at the end of one's rope—heart like a landfill, a job slowly killing you, bruises that won't fade. In a world filled with noise, he wants to hit the ultimate mute button, longing for "a quiet life." The singer can get this with "a handshake of carbon monoxide," which is to say that machine-generated carbon monoxide can meet him halfway and greet him in a gesture of friendship and death. The second and third verses are two lines each, the first marking his final fit and bellyache, and the second with mysterious lines admiring a pretty house and garden. Is this a flashback? Or a fleeting glimpse into a new, better world? Or something else entirely? The ghostly backing vocals answering the refrain with "Get me out of here" seem to imply that the singer remains trapped.

The album's penultimate track, "Lucky," begins with about twenty seconds of machines whirring before the singer announces that he feels like his luck could change. Then he asks "Sarah" to kill him, albeit with love. Is this a callback to the Shakespearian-era slang of "dying" for "orgasming"? Or does he truly want this Sarah person to kill him? The refrain raises more questions than it answers, as the singer asks to be pulled out of the air-crash and the lake. The singer then declares "I am your superhero" and that "We are standing on the edge . . ." The notion of death by transportation machine leading to rebirth as a superhero is key, mirroring the near-death machine crash of "Airbag." In the second verse, the singer declares "It's gonna be A GLORIOUS DAY," the instruments getting louder, but the singer standing up to them like he was staring down a wind tunnel. After some of Radiohead's most thoughtful guitar solos, the singer leaves everything unresolved: "We are standing on the edge—"

Based on the sound of the album's closer, "The Tourist," the singer in "Lucky" might be standing on the edge of some sort of afterlife. "The Tourist" is a distant, ghostlike waltz that seems to play through a layer of cotton. The opening lines may in fact be sung by a ghost, although the singer himself may not be aware of it himself. He sees sparks, gets overcharged, and, most tellingly, travels at "a thousand feet per second." The refrain encapsulates the song's central message: "Hey man, slow down." After an album of the pressures and paranoia brought about by modern society, politics, and machines, "The Tourist" floats through the world, cautioning everyone to not rush through everything so quickly. The song ends with its layered guitars merging into a single ring of a triangle, a childlike instrument named after a geometric shape. Perhaps an angel has gotten their wings.

When *OK Computer* was released, it was meant with near-universal acclaim. "Truly, this is one of the greatest albums in living memory," wrote James Oldham in the *NME*, as he gave the album a perfect 10/10.[14] And somehow, *OK Computer*'s reputation has only gone up from there. Some heard *OK Computer* as the end of an era—the last of the great guitar-era "classic" rock albums—while others claimed it was the first album of the new millennium, three years ahead of schedule. But what makes it so impressive and cohesive?

I hear *OK Computer* aligning into four interrelated suites. "Airbag," "Paranoid Android," and "Subterranean Homesick Alien" start the album with an interstellar burst, an android in self-denial, and a man who dreams to be taken by aliens. All could be made into a happy space adventure, but each song drips with dread, paranoia, and isolation. This sets up the escape found in "Exit Music (For a Film)" and "Let Down," from the perspective of two doomed runaway lovers and a singer sprouting wings to defy the emptiness of public transportation, respectively. With the first song ending "We hope that you will choke" and the second singing of getting "Crushed like a bug in the ground," the freedom of escape proves elusive. The next four songs—"Karma Police," "Fitter Happier," "Electioneering," and "Climbing Up the Walls"—take things from the personal to the societal. We hear fridge buzz corrupting minds, life wisdom from a talking machine, and pushback from greedy politicians, before falling into a depraved mental state because of it. The final three songs, "No Surprises," "Lucky," and "The Tourist," make the album. "No Surprises" explores death as a way to silence the noise, "Lucky" tells of rebirth as a superhero standing on the edge, and the dreamlike purgatory of "The Tourist," which tells us to slow down.

With big sales in the UK and slow but steady sales in the US, *OK Computer* has become a cornerstone of modern popular music. Its dispatches about the psychological trials of humans in the mechanical/digital age makes it the rare album that gets more relevant with every passing year. It built a dystopian world, the essence of which remains—and continues to remain—just out of reach, even as its details of artificial intelligence, talking machines, human anxiety, and displacement are becoming more real every day. *OK Computer* is a prophecy of the future that somehow always feels like the present.

Notes

1 Oldham.
2 Footman, 53.
3 Kemp.
4 Oldham.
5 *SPIN*, 86.
6 Aizlewood, 88.
7 Petrusich.
8 Greene.
9 Randall.
10 Footman, 36.
11 Greene.
12 Aizlewood, 84.
13 Greene.
14 Oldham.

20
I Chose to Use My Heart:
The Miseducation of Lauryn Hill

When Lauryn Hill was six, she found her parents' old soul 45s, introducing her to artists like Marvin Gaye, Curtis Mayfield, and Aretha Franklin. "There was something sacred about those old records," she later explained. "They meant so much to me, and they ... had a lot to do with the soundtrack of my life."[1] Seventeen years later, in 1998, she released her debut solo album, *The Miseducation of Lauryn Hill*, which freely mixed soul and gospel, as well as reggae, pop, and hip-hop, in a way that felt both organic and new.

By this time, Hill was already an international star as a member of the Fugees, which she co-founded with Wyclef "Clef" Jean and Prakazrel "Pras" Michel. All three members were planning solo albums, and it was assumed that Clef would produce Hill's. However, once she began putting it together, there was radio silence from Clef, so Hill decided to go it alone. A few months later, when Hill played some of her new tracks for the heads of her label, Columbia Records, they were unimpressed, which devastated her. So, Hill tried another approach. She picked the album's hardest song, "Lost Ones," and took it to Ruffhouse Records, a joint venture label with Columbia. Ruffhouse agreed to print a limited number of singles to send to DJs and clubs, and the song took off. Columbia caved and released *The Miseducation of Lauryn Hill* on August 25, 1998.

The album's title, *The Miseducation of Lauryn Hill*, alludes to both the 1974 film *The Education of Sonny Carson* and Carter Godwin Woodson's 1933 book *The Mis-Education of the Negro*. Carson spent his early years fighting in gangs and doing time in prison, before making his name in advocacy for African Americans. Woodson was an influential professor who is now known as the "Father of Black History." Already we have two strong forces at play—the street education of Carson and the scholarly education of Woodson—the perfect combination for Hill, who grew up in sight of the Newark ghetto, but excelled at school and attended Columbia University.

"If we had a few thinkers we could expect great achievements on tomorrow . . ." wrote Woodson in *The Mis-Education of the Negro*, "Some Negro with [a]esthetic appreciation would construct from collected fragments of Negro music a grand opera that would move humanity to repentance."[2] Lauryn Hill's parents always kept a copy of Woodson's book in their home, like it was waiting for their daughter to answer its call. Indeed, the album's first song, "Lost Ones," calls for every man to "get down on his knees and repent."

But first, we find ourselves in a classroom.

The bell rings. A teacher reads his class roster and asks for the students to respond when he calls their name. After going through a dozen names, he gets to Lauryn Hill and receives no response.

So goes the "Intro" of The Miseducation of Lauryn Hill *and Lauryn Hill is nowhere to be found.*

The though beat of "Lost Ones" comes in, and Hill hits the ground running, stacking up rhymes with a vengeance against an ex-lover. It's presumably about Wyclef Jean, with whom Hill had a secret relationship while she was in the Fugees, even though Clef was dating (and eventually married) another woman. The song takes aim at his artistic ambitions—"Everything you did has already been done"—and establishes herself as an artist in her own right. "She booked a recording studio in New York City and gathered up every instrument she could think of—a harpsichord, a timpani, a trombone, a Hammond B-3 organ," reported *TIME*'s historic cover story on Hill from February 1999. "She wanted to create hip-hop with live instruments."[3] But staying close to home was a detriment, as Hill grew discouraged with all the people trying to influence her. Following one of her muses, Bob Marley, Hill left for Tuff Gong, a studio Marley co-founded in Kingston, Jamaica. "Lost Ones" features a key line, "I was hopeless, now I'm on Hope Road," referencing the 56 Hope Road address of the Bob Marley Museum. Much of the album was recorded here, which gives it a reggae second mind.

Woven throughout the album are classroom skits with a male teacher asking a class full of boys and girls about love and what it means. In the first, the teacher spells out the word love and asks the students if they know any songs about love. One boy answers "Love." The teacher thinks there's no song called "Love," but the kid says it's by Kirk Franklin. [Indeed, the song can be found on the gospel singer's 1997 album God's Property.*]*

The following "Ex-Factor" takes the broken heart scenario from "Lost Ones" and turns it from an attack into a torch song; this song was also likely about her relationship with Clef. Hill lets her voice unfurl with its smoothness countering the raw emotion it carries. At various points in the song, Hill sounds frustrated, confused, defiant, and despondent. The catchy refrain says it all—"This ain't working, this ain't working"—as though the singer already knows the situation, but cannot convince her heart what her mind already knows. For the singer of "Ex-Factor," love is a feeling that can only be created, but never be destroyed.

The notion of eternal love is further explored in "To Zion," one of Hill's most personal songs. While recording the album, Hill became close with Rohan Marley, a professional athlete and Bob Marley's son, and became pregnant with his child. "To Zion" chronicles her decision to keep the baby, despite pressure from the music industry and her friends not to see it through. The singer explains she was told to use her head, "But instead I chose to use my heart." Adding to the song's warmth is Carlos Santana's subtle guitar work, weaving its way through the production. The title "To Zion" has a double meaning—Zion is the name of Hill's first child as well as a Rastafari term for the promised land; the song is at once a dedication and a destination. Hill's voice rings triumphantly throughout, basking in the joy of her beautiful baby. "I've never been in love like this before," she sings, celebrating maternal love.

> *The teacher asks if you should know why you love someone. A girl responds that it's "because he stands out, it's like he's got a glow or something."*

The album's most famous song, "Doo Wop (That Thing)" comes next. It was the album's first single, which made Lauryn Hill the first solo hip-hop artist to debut at #1 on the *Billboard* Hot 100. With its rap beat, soulful horns, bluesy piano chords, and doo-wop breakdowns, "Doo Wop (That Thing)" was an amalgamation of a half-century of popular music. The song is structured around two verses— one verse warning girls about guys who just want sex, and a second verse warning guys about girls who just want money—and tied together by an irresistible refrain, where both male lust and female greed are "that thing." Then, midway through, everything steps aside for an unforgettable acapella doo-wop breakdown. One can hear traces of Marvin Gaye layering his own voice in *What's Going On*, the effortless singing of Donna Summer's *Once Upon a Time...*, and the street cool of Notorious B.I.G., among countless other works. Hill's album stands on the shoulders of giants.

The following song is "Superstar," which many hear as another diss track to Clef, if not the entire rap industry. Beginning with the Doors-paraphrasing refrain ("C'mon baby light my fire"), the song examines the role of an artist in music. "Music is supposed to inspire," the singer reminds us, but many artists are getting rich releasing mediocre stuff and coasting on their reputation. For Hill, music is something sacred, so she sees this as not just an artistic crisis, but a spiritual crisis as well. In the killer rap that comprises the song's third verse, the singer invokes the ultimate Superstar, Jesus Christ, then warns that, like him, "They'll hail you then nail you, no matter who you are." Given the controversy that Hill experienced in the years following her album's release, the song foreshadows her own struggles with stardom.

"Final Hour" is one of the few full-fledged hip-hop songs on *The Miseducation of Lauryn Hill*, but it remains unique for the fact that the instrumentation was created by live musicians and featured many unusual instruments, such as the harp, flugelhorn, and flute. The song's refrain promises that you can get money and power before its ominous warning: "But keep your eyes on the Final Hour." The rest of the song is chockfull of religious allusions—Muslim ("I make salat like a Sunni"), Jewish ("breaking bread sipping Manischewitz wine"), Rastafari ("Still be in the church of Lalibela"), and Christian ("I remain calm reading the 73rd Psalm"). Like the array of musical styles on the album, Hill freely shifts from religion to religion, as though they are all different genres playing the same song.

"When It Hurts So Bad" is one of Hill's finest breakup songs. It plays like a confessional but is really a meditation on the simple paradoxes about love. "But how could this be love," the singer asks at one point, "And make me feel so bad?" Recorded in Jamaica, the song features swirling harp strings leading into reggae-style drum rolls that punctuate the sound, while Bob Marley's backing singers, the I Threes, lend strength and empathy to the singer. Hill's vulnerability expressed through open gospel-like verses and pop refrains show how love can be a double-edged sword at best, and a traitor to your heart at worst.

> *The teacher asks if TV and music make people confused about love. A girl answers that there's a lot of TV and music that "sounds nice" but isn't necessarily right for you.*

"I Used to Love Him" takes the agony of "When It Hurts So Bad" and shuts it down with the help of a female friend—Mary J. Blige. The song begins with a stunning close harmony reading of the refrain that again harks back to the doo-wop influence blending soul and gospel influences. The voices complement each other perfectly—Blige's higher, smoother croon balances Hill's deeper, grittier sound, with its most exciting moments occurring when they switch off lines at the ends of their shared verses. With insights on love ("Addicted to love like the drug of a fiend") and spiritual guidance ("Father, you saved me and you showed me"), Hill uses religion in a similar way she uses music—taking pieces of what's all around her and assembling it into her own version.

"Forgive Them Father" continues the spiritual journey of "I Used to Love Him." Joining Hill is Shelly Thunder, a reggae pioneer who later became a devout born-again Christian. She recites the part of the Lord's Prayer at the beginning of the song and can be heard throughout, especially in the final verse. But what seems like a straightforward song about religious morals—"Beware the false motives of others," the first verse begins—has more going on. "Forgive Them Father" is a remake of Bob Marley's 1972 song "Concrete Jungle." While both songs are very different, one can best hear the homage in the pre-chorus, where the tension builds until it's relieved by the refrain. Only where Marley's refrain strikes a rare balance between a love song and a protest song, Hill's refrain is a smooth letdown, appealing to God that these sinners "know not what they do." The result is a song that basks in sacred love.

> *The teacher clarifies that what the girls feels is important. A boy responds that this is because he wants her to still love him.*

"Every Ghetto, Every City" is Lauryn Hill's reflection on growing up in South Orange. It is steeped in a 1970s/1980s haze with funky clavinet playing all around the sparse beat. The song evokes Stevie Wonder's "I Wish" from his 1976 opus, *Songs in the Key of Life*, approximating the older song's pop melody and dancefloor funk. Hill's eye for detail in citing people ("Biz Mark used to amp up the party"), places ("Moving Records was on Central Ave."), and things ("A beef patty and some coco bread"), draw you in, even if you don't get all the references. Everyone's own childhood is a secreted coded language, filled with local names, games, and expressions that get lost in translation. But "Every Ghetto, Every City" works because of Hill's clear passion for this world—and the way that she only refers to New Jersey as "New Jerusalem" adds a characteristically spiritual layer.

> *The teacher asks a boy what he thinks about love. The boy, dreamlike, says "Well, love is just a feelin'—"*

The slow jam "Nothing Even Matters" comes next, with Hill duetting with D'Angelo. It's an inspired pairing as both were incredibly talented relative newcomers who pioneered the 1990s new soul movement. After so many songs about heartbreak, it's inspiring to hear a paean to a passionate, secure relationship. One of D'Angelo's verses gives away the game with the singer admitting that he sometimes has "a tendency to look at you religiously." The sacred and secular love that has been invoked throughout the album now meld into one.

The album's penultimate track, "Everything Is Everything," continues to blend the sacred with the secular, with the singer finding value in everything in the world. The song invokes speaking in tongues, Baptists on the street, two female leaders of Ancient Egypt (Cleopatra and Nefertiti) and invites the listener to "roll with cherubims." It is, truly, as Hill raps towards the end, "where hip hop means scripture." But the key line in terms of the singer's development over the album is a much simpler notion: "Let's love ourselves and we can't fail." In other words, *The Miseducation of Lauryn Hill* has considered love in many of its facets and came down to self-love as the most important of all, for it is the seed from which all true love can grow. It is an equivalent to Descartes' "I think, therefore I am" thesis, only with "think" replaced by "love."

The title track appears last and plays like the conclusion of an epic. Instead of beats and percussion, we get swirling cocktail lounge piano and strings; only the continual pop and fuzz of an old record brings us back to a modern sound. Surveying the past and present, the singer realizes that trying to live up to someone else's expectations is a recipe for failure. She concludes that by looking "deep in my heart," she's learned that "the answer, it was in me," causing her to make up her "mind to define my own destiny." Building off the self-love of "Everything Is Everything," "The Miseducation of Lauryn Hill" shows how one can channel that self-love into one's autonomy over their own life. In this way, guided by love, Hill is able to break free.

The final two tracks on the album, "Can't Take My Eyes Off of You" and "Tell Him," stand apart. Technically, they aren't part of the official album because they were released as bonus tracks after a DJ started playing a dub of "Can't Take My Eyes Off of You" and it became a major hit. Heard after *The Miseducation of Lauryn Hill*, they use the wisdom gained from the album and applies it to the singer's world. "Can't Take My Eyes Off of You" is a cover of the 1967 Frankie Valli hit, capturing the moment of infatuation in a new relationship, and Hill renders it beautifully. "Tell Him" can be heard as an answer to this, as though the singer has gone from observing her beloved to taking charge of the situation and telling him how she feels. In other words, the singer makes up her mind to define her destiny. The secret tracks play not only as a coda for this album, but as a potential preview for a sequel.

Only a sequel never arrived—at least not yet. After Hill released *The Miseducation of Lauryn Hill* to great acclaim, she withdrew from public life. It appears that one cause of this was a lawsuit filed in late 1998 by several collaborators with Hill on the album who questioned her role as the sole producer and claimed co-production credit. All agreements were essentially done by handshake, with no paper trail. Hill contested the suit, but ultimately settled out-of-court in February 2001. Hill still maintains that she was the sole producer, but for many, the lawsuit put an asterisk on this claim.

In mid-2001, Hill recorded a concert for MTV that was released as *MTV Unplugged No. 2.0* the following year, in which she calls herself "crazy and deranged" and "emotionally unstable." Accompanied only by her acoustic guitar (which she was still learning how to play) and a ragged but soulful singing voice (she had blown out her voice the day before, but refused to reschedule), it's either a glimpse of an artist standing emotionally naked to their audience, or a document of an artist losing control. In truth, it was both. In the years that followed, she has sporadically played shows where she was hours late, or showed up but just went through the motions. She was found guilty of tax evasion, for which she was imprisoned for three months. She insisted on only being referred to as "Ms. Hill." In a 2009 cover story for *Essence*, Joan Morgan captured the post-*Miseducation* Lauryn Hill: "When Ms. Hill finally emerges for the interview, she is beautiful, petite, with an air that is palpably vulnerable, fragile even. Over the course of our hour-long conversation, one thing becomes exceedingly clear: Not only has [Lauryn] left the building, but the Lauryn Hill icon we helped create may well also have been an illusion. Her decision to become Ms. Hill liberates both herself and us from who we needed her to be."[4]

But even if our Lauryn Hill is gone, *The Miseducation of Lauryn Hill* remains. It grows in stature and influence with each passing year. Part of its power comes from it being an autobiographical confessional-type album, yet one focused on the simplest yet complex theme imaginable: love. And it still manages to build to a logical and emotional conclusion, completing the journey in a way that satisfies and deepens with each new listen. Hill's *Miseducation* is our missed education—wisdom about the heart that can only be learned through experience. These "collected fragments of Negro music" that form "a grand opera that would move humanity to repentance" are not just her story, but now our story as well.

Notes

1. Furman and Furman, 13–14.
2. Woodson, 91.
3. Farley.
4. Morgan, 111–12.

Part Five

The New Millennium (2000–16)

21

I've Been Taken for Lost and Gone and Unknown for a Long, Long Time: *SMiLE*

When Paul McCartney visited Brian Wilson in mid-1967 and told him to hurry up with his project, it was too late. After eighty-five recording sessions across ten months, *SMiLE* was officially scrapped a few weeks later. By that point, the last (and only) new material the Beach Boys had released since *Pet Sounds* in the spring of 1966 was the single "Good Vibrations" that fall. Unlike the songs on *Pet Sounds*, where each song captured a different emotional place, "Good Vibrations" comprised several emotional places—fragments of diverse musical ideas that created a whole greater than the sum of its parts. If *Pet Sounds* is a tapestry, "Good Vibrations" is a patchwork quilt. For the Beach Boys' next LP, Wilson planned to take the fragmented technique of "Good Vibrations" and apply it to an entire album. He ultimately named this work *SMiLE* (the stylized lowercase "i" was because he didn't want any ego in the project) and intended it to be "a teenage symphony to God."[1] Wilson teamed up with poet Van Dyke Parks, who crafted surreal lyrics for his melodies. Before long, Wilson mapped out an entire country by breaking it down into little bits and pieces—small artifacts of myth and legend—that he could pull together for anyone lucky enough to hear the original music.

But then Wilson got lost in his country's wilderness. His new music became too strange and avant-garde for the other Beach Boys to understand, while his label, Capitol Records, just wanted him to put something out already. But it wasn't that easy, especially as he became increasingly isolated in the creative process. "It was like putting together a jigsaw puzzle on a wall instead of a tabletop," Wilson later wrote. "It kept falling."[2] Further exasperating things was Wilson's own fragile psyche. His mental state deteriorated as he turned to psychedelic drugs to cope with what was later diagnosed as schizoaffective disorder, which causes auditory hallucinations, depression, and paranoia. This fueled Wilson's erratic behavior during the original *SMiLE* sessions, which is almost as famous as the ill-fated album itself: he built a large sandbox for his piano, installed a full-sized Arabian tent in his living room, and became paranoid that John Frankenheimer's film *Seconds* was secretly made by his idol, producer Phil Spector, to scare him. A turning point came on November 28, 1966, when Wilson recorded "Fire," a strikingly effective aural representation of the element, and believed it caused several fires in the area. Seeing his music as evil magic, he supposedly burned the tapes.

Only the tapes weren't destroyed. In 2002, after teaming up with a band called the Wondermints to play *Pet Sounds* live for the first time to widespread acclaim, Wilson agreed to work on completing *SMiLE* as a follow-up project. Wondermints pianist Damian Sahanaja went to Capitol Records and made an extensive digital library of the original *SMiLE* material. Sahanaja then worked with Wilson and Van Dyke Parks to assess and complete the work. On February 20, 2004, *Brian Wilson Presents SMiLE* debuted at London's Royal Festival Hall, followed by a series of triumphant concerts. Now they just needed to record it in a studio. Legally, they couldn't use any of the original *SMiLE* tapes from the 1960s, so they had to make completely new recordings, but all parties were up for the task. The result was *the* version of Brian Wilson's "teenage symphony to God," nearly four decades after it was first promised.

In early 2004, an interviewer asked Brian Wilson when *SMiLE* became "a fully-fledged concept album." "It just popped into my brain," Wilson replied. "It was very spontaneous. Just a case of getting it done. We recorded it in sections, little pieces, and then later we pieced it together. The theme is Americana. We never discussed it, we just did it. My friend Van Dyke wanted to capture the feeling of Americana, I loved what he was into."[3] Indeed, *SMiLE* is divided into three movements, the first of which is about American history.

SMiLE opens with "Our Prayer," an eighty-second acapella invocation to the heavens—voices rising, falling, billowing up into clouds, tightening down into hymns—before venturing into the album. "Our Prayer" is immediately answered by the refrain from the 1953 doo-wop classic by the Crows, "Gee," sounding like it was coming through an old-fashioned car radio. The music opens up into a prelude for the album's first song, "Heroes and Villains," as voices sing out chants and melodies while a piano rings out underneath. A trombone smear leads us into the song like a funhouse slide.

"Heroes and Villains," plays like a mini-version of *SMiLE* itself—shifting in mood and subject matter, but always returning to intricate vocal harmonies. The singer breathlessly explains how he's been in town so long that the city has "taken for lost and gone and unknown for a long, long time." To hear these words coming from a sixty-two-year-old Brian Wilson, his voice crinkled with age but still resonant, makes it poignant. Wilson's *SMiLE* had been taken as lost, gone, and unknown for the last thirty-seven years—and now it is found, present, and very well-known. Everything parts like the Red Sea for the "heroes and villains" refrain, sung slowly over terse staccato vocal percussion as haunting strings reel underneath. Later, a spaceship signal turns the music into a cantina ballad about a dancer named Margarita. A cop appears: "You're under arrest!" The singer reflects on his children growing up "healthy, wealthy, and wise." The backing vocals become a barbershop quartet behind the singer, who reckons he can still hold his own by the heroes and villains. A short variation of "Our Prayer" arcs across the sky, landing in an elegant coda that goes from swelling stringed instruments to light jazzy ones, making room for the clip-clop of an old horse, before finally winding to a close like the sunset in a Disney film.

The low, hollow drums of "Roll Plymouth Rock" bob like a buoy in the harbor, as people wave from ocean liners while beaded Indians cheer. We hear the hypnotic "Rock...rock...roll...roll...Plymouth Rock, roll over..." mapping the 1620 Pilgrims landing of the Mayflower onto Chuck Berry's 1956 hit, "Roll Over, Beethoven." A reprise of the "Heroes and Villains" refrain melody appears in a haunting, chiming piano rhythm, before voices come in—loud, beastlike chants coming from underneath, scorning the ribbon of concrete for ruining the church of the American Indian; a subsequent verse laments a similar scenario regarding native Hawaiians. The final verse sung in Hawaiian may be an attempt to atone the sins that the white man has unleashed since Plymouth Rock.

The happy-go-lucky "Barnyard" finds the Pilgrims becoming settlers as a simple one-string guitar riff leads into a variety of human-made animal noises. Wilson had intended to use childlike humor to make feel-good music for *SMiLE*, and "Barnyard" is perhaps the clearest example of this. "Old Master Painter" is a brief instrumental snippet of a cello playing the melody of the 1949 pop standard about God as a painter creating the world. But this is just an intro to a brief cover of "You Are My Sunshine," a country standard by Jimmie Davis. Wilson sings his version with a tinge of melancholy over suspended strings and a clicking beat, before a saxophone sweeps in and the strings return with a suspended fade that bends the music like a psychedelic record.

"Cabin Essence" heads west with an idyllic home on the range. Suddenly, the serenity is broken by a train barreling ahead, running on a track of low, ghostly voices. "Who ran the iron horse?" the song asks over and over, the unrelenting force of technology flying past the quiet cabins and homes on the range. Beautiful voices sweep in asking if you've seen the Grand Coulee Dam, which opened nineteen days before Brian Wilson was born. But then, the song returns to its cabin quaintness as "the crow cries uncover the cornfield," a swaying, lilting melody with perfectly obscure lyrics. With a last glance of pastoral paradise in a land increasingly dominated by iron horses and huge dams, the American History movement of SMiLE comes to a close.

The second movement of SMiLE is about childhood and aging, beginning with the stirring "Wonderful." There is a holy presence in this song about a girl who loved her liberty, parents, and was "Never known as a non-believer." She leaves her family and loses everything to a non-believer, before returning home to a trinity with her mother and father. When Wilson said he was making "a teenage symphony to God," one imagines he was thinking of songs like "Wonderful." The coda of "Wonderful" begins "Song for Children." Most of the song is a fluttering chant about the child being the father of the son, as the band plays a marching song with rolling drums and twinkling melodies. The fifes and woodwinds play a bouncy melody that could provide the soundtrack for children playing soldier.

The main lyrical motif of "Song for Children" continues into the following "Child Is Father of the Man." After a brooding instrumental opening, "Child Is Father of the Man" jumps back into its chipper titular refrain from the last song. The brooding music returns for the bridge, dispensing fatherly wisdom: Once you get "out of the wild," and "into what you can conceive," then "you'll achieve." It's hard not to hear this as Wilson giving his thirty-seven-year younger self some sage advice. Furthermore, SMiLE is a project that Wilson began as a kid but completed as an adult, making the child the father of this man. In this way, SMiLE becomes a journey within a journey, as Wilson travels back into his own youth to finish crafting a work in part about youth itself.

The final song of the childhood and aging movement is SMiLE's most legendary track, "Surf's Up." A sweeping ballad all about melody, "Surf's Up" tunnels through pulsing verses and soars into heartbreaking falsettos. The lyrics provide an abstract tour through something like the Gilded Age, filled with diamond necklaces and opera glasses, chandeliers and music halls. "Surf's Up" appeared on CBS News's 1967 special *Inside Pop: The Rock Revolution*. Wilson was filmed in late 1966, at home singing "Surf's Up" on piano. "Here's a new song, too complex to get all of, first time around . . ." explains a narrator over "Surf's

Up." "Poetic, beautiful even its obscurity, 'Surf's Up' is one aspect of new things happening in pop music today."[4] When the program aired on April 25, 1967—ten days after McCartney visited Wilson in the studio—*SMiLE* was weeks away from being abandoned. The 2004 *SMiLE* version of "Surf's Up" ends by reprising the "Child Is Father of the Man" theme in a slower and gentler tone. The children's song is love, the singer concludes, "and the children know the way," ending the second movement.

The third and final movement of *SMiLE* functions as two mini-movements—one about healthy living and one about the elements. The former begins with the three-song, two-minute medley "I'm in Great Shape/I Wanna Be Around/Workshop," which opens with a stately orchestral waltz like something from *The Lawrence Welk Show*. Suddenly, we hear a voice singing over chiming piano notes about how healthy he is—"Eggs and grits and lickety split." The orchestra subtly joins in before a saxophone picks up the melody and is cut off by "I Wanna Be Around," a pop standard from 1962. In his strange croon, Wilson sings about picking up the pieces of your broken heart over a lounge band at last call. We then hear whirring power drills, buzzing saws, and pounding hammers for a thirty-second tour of a workshop, grounded by vibes and low strings. In case this last transition was unclear, Wilson sometimes called out things like "Now, let's fix some hearts!" between the two songs when performing them live. You can still hear some hammers and saws as the movement transitions to the similarly clip-cloppy "Vege-Tables." It would play as a novelty song if it weren't so earnest—this is the song of a man who simply loves his vegetables. When the singer asks you to send in the name of your favorite vegetable over crunching bites, it only adds to its strange charm as the healthy living movement closes.

Since he began work on *SMiLE* in the 1960s, Brian Wilson intended there to be a four-movement suite about the elements: Earth, Wind, Fire, and Water. Where Jimi Hendrix did this organically on *Electric Ladyland*, Wilson set out to make an elements suite as part of *SMiLE*. "On a Holiday" appears to correspond with "Earth." Even though it's a bouncy pirate's sea shanty, there are lots of reference to land—a reprise of the "Roll Plymouth Rock" theme, followed by a landing in a Waikiki shanty town. "On a Holiday" concludes on a quieter note, with a prelude for the following "Wind Chimes." Representing "Wind," "Wind Chimes" begins as a hushed, twinkling ballad over xylophones and light percussion, telling of a man who loves his windchimes so much, they make him weep. The song then fluctuates between bursts of a giant full-band orchestra and a gentle toy piano and harpsichord. A whistle ignites the roller-coaster opening of "Mrs. O'Leary's Cow (Fire)." The piano leads the music up and down, until drums thunder in and start a huge fire of dissonant high chords held on keyboards, strings blurring into woodwinds blurring into horns blurring back into strings, sirens blaring, wordless vocal harmonies adding tension, all while a low fuzz guitar churns a sinister riff underneath. "Is it hot as hell in here or is it me?" the singer asks at the beginning of "In Blue Hawaii," the "Water" section of the suite. Paraphrasing the children's bedtime prayer "Now I Lay Me Down to Sleep," he asks for a drop of water and gets an entire state surrounded by it. The song springs along before going into its "A wah ha wah—Hawaii" chant—words evoke both water and the word Hawaii itself. "Aloha nui means goodbye," the singer tells us at the end of the song. The music then reprises the instrumental bridge of "Wind Chimes," and then closes with a heartfelt blessing of "Our Prayer."

The final song on the album is "Good Vibrations," stands alone. It was the seed that held the structure of SMiLE, allowing the work to come full circle. When "Good Vibrations" was originally written in 1966, Brian Wilson was inspired by people sensing emotion based on vibrations given out by others. He wrote the song around this idea with lyricist Tony Asher, until Beach Boys singer Mike Love stepped in and rewrote the lyrics to make it more about girls. On SMiLE, Wilson replaces some of Love's lyrics with Asher's original ones; Asher's lines like "she's already working on my brain" and "I wonder what she's pickin' up on me?" make it more existential. And except for Wilson's cry of "And I'm pickin' up—!" before the refrain, everything else remains identical to the Beach Boys' original version—the verses, pulsing with organ as bass slithers underneath; the refrain of voices layering in sound and variety, until they become a beautiful, shimmering tower, with the theremin's high wail darting all around. It was an obvious close for SMiLE, and an appropriate one as well.

On September 28, 2004, something happened that few could have predicted even a couple of years earlier: Brian Wilson released SMiLE. "Anchored by deft quotes and thematic repetitions, SMiLE is beautiful and funny, goofily grand," Robert Christgau raved in *Rolling Stone*, giving the album a rare five-star rating. "It's looser and messier than *Sgt. Pepper* and, one suspects, always would have been. But its *sui generis* Americanism counterbalances its paucity of classic pop songs."[5] Even before SMiLE was completed, *Sgt. Pepper* was seen as its rival, the two albums creating an equilibrium that the rest of the 1960s orbited around. So, the question remains, had it been released in the 1960s, would've SMiLE beaten *Sgt. Pepper*? I believe that if SMiLE had been released after *Sgt. Pepper*, it would've been the American *Sgt. Pepper* that outdid the Beatles and changed the 1960s landscape. And if *SMiLE* had come out when it was first supposed to—some six months before *Sgt. Pepper*—it would have changed the entire trajectory of rock and roll history by being rock's first major concept album and cementing the Beach Boys among the most innovative and influential artists in rock history.

Unlike *Sgt. Pepper*, *SMiLE* is a vast, unfinished, landscape—just like the country that inspired it. The music of *SMiLE* is a melting pot of American musical styles—rock, pop standards, country music, folk ballads, doo-wop, sea shanties, schmaltz, novelty tunes, children's songs, spirituals, marches, waltzes, and parlor music, with touches of classical and jazz here and there. Over the course of *SMiLE*, Pilgrims land at Plymouth Rock and pirates land in a Waikiki shanty town; a ribbon of concrete chases the American Indian and water flows through the Grand Coulee Dam; the transcontinental railroad goes up and Chicago burns down; the barnyard chickens cluck and the vegetables make crunching noises; carpenters clatter away in the workshop and windchimes softly knell in the breeze; good vibrations are picked up and the music all is lost for now.

A few weeks after Brian's Wilson's *SMiLE* came out in the fall of 2004, I saw him perform it at the Boston Orpheum. Wilson was the eye of the storm, sitting at his keyboard and leading the band like they were simply an extension of the music in his mind. The backing band exuded pure joy as they resurrected the beautiful harmonies of "Our Prayer," passed vegetables back and forth during "Vege-Tables," and donned red plastic fire hats for "Mrs. O'Leary's Cow." And then, at the very end of the show, as the band was holding out their triumphant final note, Wilson simply got up from his keyboard and walked away. Someone had to lead him back out from the side to receive his standing ovation, but his eyes were blank and he seemed unaware of what he had been doing for the past forty-five minutes. *SMiLE* may have been found, but seemingly at the price of its creator being lost.

Notes

1 Heylin, 532.
2 Wilson, 190.
3 Simmons.
4 "Inside Pop – The Rock Revolution."
5 Christgau.

22

All Across the Alien Nation: *American Idiot*

"Concept album sounds a little light in the loafers," Green Day drummer Tré Cool mused in an interview about his band's recently released album in the fall of 2004. He used an insensitive euphemism to convey the concept album's reputation as an overly pretentious endeavor that often felt closer to Times Square and Broadway than to the East Village's CBGB. "Punk-opera sounds more important, and this record's a monster." The interviewer remained skeptical: "Those reared on the Clash, though, may not be so forgiving toward the whole idea, no matter what it's called."[1] This was relatively uncharted territory of whether a punk band like Green Day could release a concept album while still being considered punk rock. And the fact that it then went on to be the basis of a multiple Tony Award-winning Broadway musical makes Tré Cool's initial assessment that much more ironic.

"It started out as a joke," Armstrong explained to *SPIN* magazine shortly before the album came out. "[Green Day bassist] Mike [Dirnt] was alone in the studio and called me and said, 'What am I going to do here?' I said, 'Why don't you write a thirty-second song?' So he did, and it was really good. I connected another thirty-second song, then Cool did, and all of a sudden it started taking on the characteristics of a rock opera. You have to keep your sense of humor when you do something like this, because you don't want it to sound pretentious. I like [the Who's] *Tommy*, but it's so literal. I didn't want to write, [*sings*] 'Here I am, walking down the stairs, preparing some food.'"[2] He confided to Dirnt and Cool that he wanted to make "the 'Bohemian Rhapsody' of the future,"[3] and informed *Rolling Stone* of the band's intent to make a "punk rock opera."[4] It would eventually be released as *American Idiot*.

So, is "punk rock opera" a contradiction of terms? "Well, you know, for me punk has always been about doing things your own way," Armstrong said shortly after *American Idiot* was released. "What it represents for me is an ultimate freedom and sense of individuality. Which basically becomes a metaphor for life and the way you want to live it. So as far as Green Day is concerned, I really want the band to form into its own thing and not just try to represent all of what punk rock is, because you then alienate people and you also alienate yourself. It's about remaining passionate in punk rock but at the same time just really doing your own thing so it's not just about writing punk rock music, but writing Green Day music."[5]

Like so many other concept albums, *American Idiot* is a journey. It plays like an echo of *Zen Arcade*, depicting a troubled punk protagonist ditching his small town for the big city, only to return to the small town at the end. With *American Idiot*, Green Day followed their punk muse into conceptual rock and roll and let out their grievances—about their country, about their president, about themselves—and people listened. And helped make the band into superstars.

The title track of *American Idiot* is a state of the union and a call to arms. It's also a tailormade three-minute single and killer start to an album. Built on the raw punk chords of Green Day's classic songs, the verses are a call-and-response between the singer and drums and the full band answering them with fury. The chorus has the tunefulness of a vintage Ramones' song and the subtlety of a Sherman tank. The thickness of the sound is matched by the density of the lyrics. "American Idiot" is a portrait of a twenty-first-century American wasteland, controlled by media, courting hysteria, and filled with tension. "Well, maybe I'm the faggot, America" the singer declares at one point. In an article exploring the censorship of the word "faggot," *The Advocate* wrote, "When Green Day sing that they are the 'faggot America' in their hit single 'American Idiot,' they are rejecting the 'redneck agenda' and 'paranoia' that in their view are sweeping the nation. So there is some irony in the fact that the word 'faggot' has been bleeped out of the song on a number of radio stations across the country, presumably because of its indecent nature."[6] In short, the title track of *American Idiot* draws line between "The Faggot America" and "The Redneck America," with the 2000 election still stinging as the 2004 election loomed on the horizon.

The nine-minute, five-section mini-rock opera "Jesus of Suburbia" comes next, throwing down the gauntlet that yes, this will be an artistically ambitious work. *American Idiot* was co-produced by Green Day with their longtime collaborator Rob Cavallo, and it is a perfectly produced album. There is not a piano note out of place or a guitar not ready to catch you when a song shift gears. Its glossy, pristine edges seem to belie its punk aesthetic, so that it's almost less like a Billie Joe punk rock opera than a Billy Joel punk rock opera. (Think "Scenes from an Italian Restaurant" with distorted guitars.) Which is by no means a bad thing. It's another way of saying that Green Day has decided to focus on songcraft and the album's overall shape and flow instead of fitting their vision into fourteen three-minute songs. "It's a lot of material," Armstrong told *Rolling Stone* in their first piece about the album. "We're trying to get one theme throughout the album, because we're in the album business, not in the business of making singles."[7]

More than any other song from *American Idiot*, "Jesus of Suburbia" is an album song (even though an edited version was eventually released as a single). The song fluctuates between rock, pop, and punk with all of the right musical touches—a piano here, an acoustic guitar there, 1960s backing vocals over here, maybe some bells—landing with precision. "Part I: Jesus of Suburbia" introduces the lead character of *American Idiot*, an apathetic teen living on "soda-pop and Ritalin" making his way through "a land of make-believe" that doesn't believe in him. "Part II: City of the Damned" switches tempo and adds piano as Jesus describes his world, hanging around 7-Eleven, reading bathroom graffiti, and the "holy scriptures of the shopping mall." The refrain lifts the melody of Bryan Adams' "Summer of '69," but somehow this only adds to its impact, mapping Armstrong's city of the dead onto Adams' nostalgic daydream. "Part III: I Don't Care" finds Armstrong turning into Johnny Rotten, spitting out words like nails. "Hearts recycled, but never saved," he declares, before Armstrong's voice returns for a punk chorus dismissing everything: "I don't care!" "Part IV: Dearly Beloved" starts out as pop-punk song about the space "in between insane and insecure," before shifting to power pop, complete with falsetto backing vocals and bells. Dirnt's one-note bass lick kick things back up for "Part V: Tales of Another Broken Home," which ends "Jesus of Suburbia" on a punk-rock high. "There's this Jesus of Suburbia character and he's pretty disenfranchised," Armstrong once elaborated. "He hates his town. Hates his family. Hates his friends. He needs to get out, so he leaves and goes into the city. He starts dealing with what true rebellion means. Rebellion could be disguised as self-destruction. You get involved with drugs or self-mutilation. Or it could mean you end up following your own beliefs and ethics. He's sort of torn."[8]

Jesus decides to take "Holiday" to the city. It is the album's finest moment, showing off Green Day's effortless ear for melody. The song pumps you up like a political rally, its lyrics riding up and down the tune, seeming to resolve before building tension to the next line. The singer wanders through an apocalyptic wasteland, filled with war, money, wrapped flags and plastic bags. But where the first two verses rely on cryptic imagery to suggest the big picture, the third goes in for the kill. "*The representative from California has the floor,*" a voice announces, and we hear Armstrong's voice through a distorted microphone calling out, "Sieg Heil to the president Gasman!" This is a not-too-subtle swipe at President George W. Bush, freely mixing images of the Iraq War with the Nazi fascism of the Second World War. Despite it being their most political song, Green Day wisely don't name their target. "We always wanted our music to be timeless," Armstrong told *SPIN* in late 2004. "Even the political stuff that we're doing now. I would never think of 'American Idiot' as being about the Bush administration specifically. It's about the confusion of where we're at right now."[9] In an earlier interview, Cool said it all: "This not about the Bush administration—although he is a perfect example of an American idiot."[10] For Green Day, Bush is the symptom, not the disease.

The most famous song on the album, "Boulevard of Broken Dreams," is Green Day's biggest US hit to date—reaching #2 on the *Billboard* Hot 100—as well as winning the 2006 Grammy winner for Record of the Year for its flawless production. Green Day considered it a hangover after the high of "Holiday," and indeed, "Boulevard" crawls out of "Holiday" with a reverberating synthesizer like a fuzzy brain behind bleary eyes. For such a central song on such a complex album, "Boulevard of Broken Dreams" is notable for its lyrical simplicity. It takes one of the most haunting modern landscapes—empty city streets—and watches Jesus make his way down his lonely road. With only his shadow walking beside him, Jesus wishes for someone to find him, but "'Til then I walk alone." By mixing the *Who's Next*-era synthesizers with the old Pixies/Nirvana quiet-verse/loud-refrain trick, Green Day make the whole thing work with their sense of melody and economy. Simple chord progressions and catchy melodies are the backbone of punk rock; Green Day just pulled off the noise and let them stand as pop.

"Are We the Waiting" slows things down, as Jesus waits for something to happen on these city streets. The song is anchored by an anthemic chorus that would make Joe Strummer proud—"Are we, we are, are we, we are, the waiting"—custom-built to be hollered as live shows. The song is an instant anthem but hidden within it is a key line from the Jesus of Suburbia about how "rage and love" are "the story of my life." Someone finally arrives for Jesus in the form of "St. Jimmy," the self-proclaimed "patron saint of the denial" with an angel face and proclivity for suicide. To introduce this punk character, Green Day reaches back into their older punk sound, pummeling through the song at full blast like a trashcan barreling down a flight of stairs. It's only in the final verse that they throw in a curveball, as the "ooh, St. Jimmy" backing vocals nearly turn the song into a Beach Boys pastiche.

Next up is the power-punk ballad "Give Me Novacaine," in which Jesus turns to St. Jimmy for a drug that will quell his stress. There is a sense of apathy that permeates this album, as Jesus's transition from his dead hometown to the empty city streets has left him wanting to feel better by feeling nothing at all. Cue the story's love interest, Whatsername, who is introduced as a rebel, saint, and vigilante in the thundering two-minute rocker "She's a Rebel." Jesus sees her as the embodiment of resistance—"and she's holding on my heart like hand grenade." Since Whatsername was likely based in part on women that Armstrong knew from his early punk days, it only makes sense that "She's a Rebel" is the purest punk heard so far on the album. Coming at the exact center of the album, it's what gives the work its heart (or rather, hand grenade), inspiring the album's iconic cover. How all of this will play out remains to be seen, but at least for the moment, Jesus finally *feels* something.

After a bizarre wooden drum interlude, "Extraordinary Girl" chronicles the rise and fall of the Jesus and Whatsername's brief courtship in a stomping punk song with layered guitars swinging on an oscillating riff. It's pretty bleak stuff—he feels like dying, she's sick of crying—and by the end, they admit it's not worth trying anymore. The opening schoolyard taunt of "Nobody likes you, everyone's left you," sung by Kathleen Hanna (leader of Bikini Kill and Le Tigre), begins "Letterbomb." The song starts with a soaring melody, before quickly retreating into a claustrophobic punk rattle that burns like a bridge doused in gasoline. We learn that the singer is not the Jesus of Suburbia and that St. Jimmy is a fiction created by the singer's rage (from his father) and love (from his mother), which makes him "the idiot America"; meanwhile, we also learn that Whatsername is fed up with the city too and is leaving Jesus. Throughout is the first line of the chorus—"It's not over 'til you're underground"—which at once seems to address the survival in an apocalyptic city, the finality of death, and a nod to the "underground" punk scene to which Green Day can never return because of their mainstream success. But what exactly is going on here? A narrative album losing its way.

The acoustic guitar of "Wake Me Up When September Ends" further defies any clear punk rock narratives. The song is an anomaly on *American Idiot*, perhaps the only song unrelated to the album's story. Armstrong wrote the song about his father's death from esophageal cancer when he was ten. Not coincidentally, this is the moment where everything falls apart in *American Idiot*, as Jesus finds that by settling in the city, he is still as alone as he was when he left home. "Wake Me Up When September Ends" plays like the depression that now weighs down the singer at his lowest point. And yet, it was released as a single and registered with people, reaching #6 on the *Billboard* Hot 100, making it the album's second-biggest hit (after the similarly alienated-in-the-street "Boulevard of Broken Dreams").

Just like the second track on the album, "Jesus of Suburbia," the second-to-last track on the album, is another nine-minute, five-part mini-rock opera called "Homecoming." It marks a rare time that the band's ambition extends beyond their reach. "Part 1: The Death of St. Jimmy" finds St. Jimmy telling Jesus that "We're fucked up but we're not the same," before blowing his brains out into the bay. "Part 2: East 12th St." begins with a "Nobody cares" riff that sounds like a punk rock version of Gary Numan's 1979 new wave hit "Cars." The lyrics are obscure, with Jesus filling out paperwork at an East 12th Street facility, but we don't learn why since his instinct is to stress out and run. "I just wanna be free," he says. "This life-like dream ain't for me!" In "Part 3: Nobody Likes You," Dirnt takes the lead, extending on the "Nobody likes you" theme introduced earlier in the album. Cool's "Part 4: Rock and Roll Girlfriend" a 1950s-style throw-back rocker that sounds more like Elton John trying to emulate early rock in "Crocodile Rock" than actual vintage rock. Armstrong returns for the finale of "Part 5: We're Coming Home Again," which plays to Green Day's pop-punk abilities, imagining Jesus going back home to his small town like it was a victory march. And then, the song parts for a "Boom. Ba-Boom. BOOM!" drum riff most famously heard in the Ronettes' eternal "Be My Baby" (and also Billy Joel's "Say Goodbye to Hollywood"). This brings a grand rock and roll sweep to the proceedings, giving the "Homecoming" suite a better ending than it deserves. In truth, only the fifth part of the work needed to be included on the album. And after one more "Nobody likes you" refrain, we are on to the album's finale.

After the debacle of "Homecoming," "Whatsername" ends the album where it should—Jesus still lovelorn over Whatsername even though they have gone their separate ways. In its own way, it's as stark of an I-wonder-where-is-she-now statement as "Caroline, No" at the end of the Beach Boys' *Pet Sounds*. "I made a point to burn all of the photographs," the singer admits in one of the finest lines of the album. The haunting melody (which invokes Jackson Browne's 1974 ballad "Fountain of Sorrow," of all things) brings out pathos in the singer's words while the song's musical textures shift from near-emo to the pulsing intensity of *The Joshua Tree*-era U2 to arena-ready rock, before working back down again into a simple finish. The singer's final words declare that in his darkest night, his memory will never turn back time—"Forgetting you, but not the time." And finally, the singer finds peace, or something as close as he'll ever get to it.

Green Day's *American Idiot* begins with the intent of a single narrative but loses focus partway through. It doesn't help that the album's best (and most lyrically cohesive) songs are the first four on the album, frontloading it with great promise that it cannot see through. The result is a bit of a mess. "*American Idiot* could have been a mess; in fact, it is a mess," wrote Rob Sheffield in his mostly-positive review in *Rolling Stone*.[11] "While messy in parts—an endearing aspect of the record—the biggest hoodwink is that beneath all its heartfelt rhetoric is a collection of excellent rock songs," Andrew Murfett stated in Melbourne's *The Age*.[12] "The album's opposing poles are its two, nine-minute, five-part song suites . . ." wrote Dorian Lynskey in *The Guardian*. "Between the two, *American Idiot* is a mess—but a vivid, splashy, even courageous mess."[13] Like the Beatles' "White Album" or the Clash's *London Calling*, *American Idiot* has a sprawl that you can get lost in, which makes the album that much more intriguing. It has all the puzzle pieces laid out for you, but it's up to you to put it all together. (A *London Times* critic suggested that it "doesn't follow a structured narrative, preferring to offer snapshots.")[14] Also, as a portrait of a disjointed country that's a media-obsessed, anxious mess, it's only appropriate that the music is too. It is a broken story of a broken country.

The pieces were finally assembled when Billie Joe Armstrong and director Michael Mayer created a Broadway musical version of *American Idiot* in 2009. They expanded the narrative by adding two more male protagonists, as well as songs from *American Idiot*'s follow-up album, *21st Century Breakdown*, which continued many themes of its predecessor. The show was a Tony-winning musical with a Grammy-winning cast album that ran for 422 performances and toured consistently for ten years between America and the UK. But Broadway was only one ending to this story that's still being written. And while some punk purists continue to scowl, Green Day has proven that punk is not a style, a fad, or a pose. It's not even a strict, easily-defined genre. For Green Day, it's something far more open. This is terrifying for some, but as Green Day has shown, it can be that much more of a tool for liberation—no matter what you're trying to escape.

Notes

1 Dixon.
2 Ganz.
3 Hendrickson.

4 Baltin.
5 Spitz, 181–2.
6 Goodridge.
7 Dansby.
8 Spitz, 163–4.
9 Pappademas.
10 Dixon.
11 Sheffield.
12 Murfett.
13 Lynskey.
14 Watson.

23

If You Want to Be Free: *The ArchAndroid*

In mid-May 2010, singer/songwriter Janelle Monáe was in New York City to promote her debut album, *The ArchAndroid*. It was an ambitious concept album about a futuristic society heavily influenced by Fritz Lang's 1927 silent sci-fi masterpiece, *Metropolis*. For decades, the film was only available in an incomplete print, but in 2008, an additional twenty-five minutes were found. Two years later, a near-complete version premiered at the New York Film Forum while Monáe and her producers were in town. "The coincidence seemed as if it was trying to tell us something," *Newsweek* journalist Jeremy McCarter wrote in his review of *The ArchAndroid*, "so *Newsweek* invited them all out to the movies. (Take that, boring record reviews!)"[1]

Metropolis tells the story of a dystopian world in which the wealthy live a life of leisure in skyscrapers, while the poor toil in deep underground factories that keep the rich utopia running. The city master's son, Freder, learns of the underworld and takes it upon himself to try to bridge the two worlds. A key plot point involves a mad scientist who creates the Maschinenmensch, a robot who looks like a beautiful woman. The film ends with Freder bringing together the hands of his father and the foreman of the underground workers. The film began with a message on the screen that reappears at the end: "THE MEDIATOR BETWEEN HEAD AND HANDS MUST BE THE HEART!"

As the credits rolled, Monáe turned to McCarter. "My mother was a janitor; I grew up working class," she said, before explaining that she then got a scholarship to study theater in Manhattan. "So I know about both sides of that struggle, between the haves and the have-nots." Monáe positions herself like Freder, a mediating heart between the working class and the elite. But as the title of *The ArchAndroid* implies, her debut album also saw her identifying with the Maschinenmensch, a female android from the future. Starting with her first EP in 2007, *Metropolis: Suite I (The Chase)*, Monáe introduced Cindi Mayweather, android number 57821 from the year 2719, who lives in a dystopian city called

Metropolis. Cindi is a famous android singer who is discriminated against by the oppressive government that restricts android rights. One of the most important laws is that androids cannot love humans. In the EP, Cindi falls for the human Sir Anthony Greendown and becomes a fugitive on the run, pursued by government agents and bounty hunters.

Monáe has further explained that Cindi's genetic code was cloned and that Monáe herself was one of Cindi's clones sent back in time; parts of this album came to her in dreams that were messages from Cindi. Like Parliament's *Mothership Connection*, Monáe's work followed in the tradition of Afrofuturism. For his 2010 article in *The Quietus*, "Janelle Monáe: A New Pioneer of Afrofuturism," journalist John Calvert spoke to Afrofuturist scholar Dr. Marlo David, who saw Monáe as a quintessential artist of Afrofuturistic music: "In the era of slavery, people of African descent were human enough to live and love and have culture, but were nonhuman to the extent that they were 'machines,' labor for capitalism." Dr. David believes this duality is central to Afrofuturism as "a cyborg identity, in resistance to that involuntary binary."[2] Monáe reflected this idea in a 2013 interview, describing androids as "a new form of the Other. Someone we can parallel the other to: African Americans, women, gays, lesbians, immigrants, and so on and so on. The minority . . . the one that does not have equal rights as [a] normal human being."[3]

Before coming out as a bisexual "free-ass motherfucker"[4] in 2018 and nonbinary ("I am everything")[5] in 2022, Monáe dodged questions about her sexuality. In 2010, she told *Rolling Stone*: "I only date androids. Nothing like an android—they don't cheat on you."[6] When Janelle Monáe released *The ArchAndroid* on May 18, 2010, she took these conflicting elements—including her experiences among the working class and the elite, the new world of Afrofuturism and the old world of silent film, machines and people, pop music and classical overtures—to create the next two installments of her "Metropolis" suite. Despite the seemingly overambitious scope of this project, the result was a triumph, where diverse genres, intense lyrics, and good-time music all flow naturally, intersecting through the mind and microphone of Janelle Monáe. As received through the intergalactic dispatches of Cindi Mayweather.

The ArchAndroid begins with its ambitions on its sleeve with the "Suite II Overture." The two-minute classical score packs in a lot—drum-powered flourishes, soaring violins, serene woodwinds, and layered strings—setting the stage for a moody work that will shift in sound and texture. The song ends with a wavy voice announcing: "It's your time, lead them back to one." The applause at the beginning and end of the track could imply a silent film screening with orchestral accompaniment, aligning with Monáe's vision of the album as an "emotion-picture."[7] The applause from the overture runs into the next track, "Dance or Die," as the music turns from a classical overture into modern dance music. "Cyborg. Android. D-boy. Decoy," intones poet Saul Williams before Monáe comes in with a relentless rap. Dancing is forbidden for androids in Metropolis, so android members of Cindi's fellow resistance dance in rebellion waiting "to find the one." For Monáe, dancing represents joy and freedom in a world run by the iron fist of the oppressive government, but until Cindi arrives, they remain underground—and dancing.

"Dance or Die" continues seamlessly into "Faster," hurried along by urgent drums and choppy electric guitar chords. It introduces Cindi Mayweather, trying to pull herself away from her forbidden affair with human Sir Anthony Greendown. Ironically, the place where it settles down—at least in performance, if not tempo—is the "Faster and faster I should run" refrain. "Locked Inside" further fleshes out Cindi's Metropolis, with a verse melody that interpolates Stevie Wonder's "Too High" and a disco-ready refrain that samples Michael Jackson's "Rock with You." Despite all the joy in the music, the lyrics paint a picture of the androids' bleak existence under the humans, in which "the man is always right." The swirling pre-chorus introduces the one thing that can keep her sane: Her love for Sir Greendown. The three tracks of "Dance or Die," "Faster," and "Locked Inside" are a "flawless introduction," wrote one contemporary reviewer in *Slant*, adding that "If *ArchAndroid* maintained that level of minute-for-minute consistency throughout, it would be nothing short of epochal."[8]

The smoky, mysterious "Sir Greendown" plays like an updated version of "Moon River" as sung in *Breakfast at Tiffany's* by Audrey Hepburn (who knew something about underclass oppression after living in German-occupied Holland as a young teenager). Yet "Sir Greendown" holds its own, as Cindi's sultry vocal invites Sir Greendown to leave with her in an hour. We then awake to the harsh realities of "Cold War," one of *The ArchAndroid*'s finest songs. It mixes a melodic, soaring vocal with lyrics of revolution, both of which tie in with the album's story without getting bogged down by pretensions. "If you want to be free," Cindi sings in the second verse, "Below the ground is the only place to be." The refrain grabs you by the collar—"Do you know what you're fighting for?"—bringing a life-or-death urgency to the song.

"Cold War" is followed by the first single released from the album, "Tightrope (feat. Big Boi)." In the context of *The ArchAndroid*, "Tightrope" plays like a national anthem, an infectiously catchy tune that features Cindi half-rapping over handclaps and funky bass, encouraging everyone to ignore haters who want to step on their dreams. The song blossoms with funky guitar and horns into a call to arms: "Whether you're high or low," Cindi sings, "You gotta tip on the tightrope." *The ArchAndroid* is an album about duality and contradiction with its portrayal of the human/android dichotomy. This is the ultimate balancing act, in which one must even out all the contradictory elements or else fall off the rope entirely—and Monáe stands above it all, high in the sky like a tightrope walker, making it look effortless.

The ninety-seven-second "Neon Gumbo" is a backwards recording of the "Closing Lullaby" movement of Monáe's 2007 song "Many Moons." It creates a psychedelic vibe that itself is as beautiful and disorienting as space itself. Rainfall at the end of "Neon Gumbo" leads us into "Oh, Maker," which begins with a clip-clop folk guitar and Cindi's voice singing like a twenty-eighth century Judy Collins. When the beat falls in after a few lines, it shifts the sound naturally from traditional to modern, leading to the song's unique palette. "Oh, Maker" expresses feelings in color from the once "rare, rare blue" of Sir Greendown's love to something that burns yellow to orange, then explodes from gray to black to "bloody wine." Everything builds to the rousing refrain in which Cindi confesses: "I really dared to love you, too." It speaks to a courage found in true love, even if you're not an android.

"Come Alive (War of the Roses)" starts with a bass riff that powers the entire song with a distinctively proto-punk rock sound. Cindi's android friends thinks that she's gone crazy, but she's content to dance inside her head. "THAT'S WHEN I COME ALIIIIIIIIVE!" she erupts like a punk rock *The Rocky Horror Picture Show*. Ever the shapeshifter, the song's instrumental bridge goes into a lovely, haunting section that drives punk into its kinder, gentler protégé new wave like a spear. The rocker returns, asking to "Take me six feet under" like a demon. And then, she totally loses it. Cindi starts screaming her lyrics like a possessed Sid Vicious, with any concern for pitch and precision gone out the window. For someone so in control, it thrills, both because it is so unexpected and yet fits in so naturally.

After the punk rock of "Come Alive," we get the psychedelic rock of "Mushrooms & Roses," with a laidback vibe like the layered wash of electric guitar like Jimi Hendrix's *Electric Ladyland*. The song itself tells of a paradise in which "lonely droids and lovers have their wildest dreams." The title embraces duality on two levels, referring both to the male anatomy (mushrooms) and female anatomy (roses), as well as downers (psychedelic mushrooms) and uppers ("roses" as slang for Adderall and Ritalin). As the closing song of *Metropolis: Suite II*, it ends the story in a happy place, while setting the scene for the love songs that will dominate the third suite.

The "Suite III Overture" begins with wistful strings as Cindi invites Sir Greendown to Wonderland, a place where are free to love. The music shifts to 1960s-era spy music that segues directly into "Neon Valley Street." The song plays like a beacon from Cindi to Sir Greendown, its lush strings and impassioned vocals held in place by the song's steady backbeat. The mood shifts to a rapped flashback, in which Cindi compares herself to Harriet Tubman, calling herself "An outlaw outrunning the law." "May this song journey on to you," she sings after the music shifts back into a ballad, using her song as a journey in and of itself—all within the larger journey of *The ArchAndroid*. The song ends with a fuzzy voice cryptically saying, "I hear the riot community approaching. Take my hand, Jane, let's go talk to them."

The voice belongs to Kevin Barnes, the leader, singer, and songwriter from the group Of Montreal, a psychedelic indie band from Athens, Georgia. His full band is featured with Monáe on the following track, "Make the Bus," a *Scary Monsters*-era David Bowie-style song about obsessing over "a terrible fixation" that should be kept "in the realm of fantasy." Barnes primarily wrote the song by himself, but then collaborated with Monáe on it. While Monáe spoke of how "we're inspired by each other's music," critics were less impressed with the song, which many heard as a weak spot on the album. One contemporary reviewer called it "an ill-considered invite," noting that the song "sounds like it was as much fun to make as it isn't to listen to."[9]

"Wondaland" comes next, a thumping disco groove where Cindi sounds like a little girl before pulling her voice into a sultry coo, like an innocent yet seductive Donna Summer. The playful, winking song is so infectiously catchy, it could be a bubblegum jingle that remains stuck in your head years after the commercial stops airing. Cindi makes sure that everyone understands this is a secret land where people are free to love, dance, create art, and compose music. It further alludes to the Wondaland Arts Society, a collective that Monáe co-founded to support artists, musicians, writers, poets, and filmmakers in Atlanta. As Monáe once explained about the real-life Wondaland: "It's a place where people can be themselves."[10] For both Monáe and Cindi, individualism is key.

The following "57821"—named for Cindi Mayweather's ID number—plays like a vision quest as Sir Greendown searches for Cindi with a hologram photo and a lock of her hair. The music is mysterious and graceful, hanging delicate in the air until it becomes a holy chant for a sacred crusade. "Say You'll Go" is Cindi's response to Greendown, a lovely ballad with a melody that evokes Stevie Wonder in its climb and sprawl. Like "57821," there is a sense of the spiritual, this time being invocation of the Eastern beliefs of Buddhism—the life cycle of Samsara, the holy book of Dhammapada, and the quest to reach nirvana—in order to "write our name in fire on each other's hearts." The song ends with a lovely rendition of Claude Debussy's "Clair De Lune." Cindi is coming to terms with being the ArchAndroid, as well as her love with Sir Greendown.

The nearly nine-minute, three-part closer "BabopbyeYa," ends the album in epic form. Beginning with dramatic symphony flourishes like a Hitchcock film, the music melts down into a sultry, late-night jazz club, with Cindi sounding remarkably like Ella Fitzgerald over music pitched between a torch song and a James Bond theme. "My BaBopByeYa—can you hear me calling?" she croons magnificently. "She is calling out to Anthony Greendown, who is her BaBopByeYa," Monáe explained in an interview. "There's a special call for him, and a special call for her. And when they hear that, they immediately know that they're safe and everything's okay."[11] More Hollywood string flourishes kick the song into a bossa-nova groove for the song's second movement, in which Cindi declares, "You have made a home in my memory" where Sir Greendown "will abide forever." Another flurry of strings clears the way for the song's third and final movement, in which the strings pull back against the music like a 1960s spy soundtrack while Cindi speaks her words as a poem. There is a defiance that powers the song: "This time I shall be unafraid," Cindi announces, promising that "violence will not move me." Cindi can see beyond tomorrow and declares, "My freedom calls and I must go—" hanging onto those last words like Aretha Franklin on a mountaintop. Brooding strings and smoky jazz piano close the album out with elegance.

For both Cindi Mayweather and Janelle Monáe, freedom is everything. In 2016, Monáe said: "I owe it to myself, and those who fought for my freedom, to be free. As much as I can." Three years earlier, Monáe was asked if she felt encouraged to bury her individualism and conform to set standards at the beginning of her career. "I never take those things personally and I am not a victim," She answered diplomatically. "But I had to make sure that I stood up for the things that I believed in: the right to wear a tuxedo, the right to have a concept album. When you feel like your rights are being taken away from you, you start to rebel—which has really worked for my career."[12]

The right to have a concept album. These words stopped me cold. Concept albums have long been the cliché domain of white male rockers. As a Black female performer in 2010, Monáe still felt like she had to fight for her right to have a concept album three decades after Donna Summer helped pave the way. This form, which was founded on the music breaking free of the record, is now something that must be fought for as a freedom. "If you listen to the album from the beginning to the end without skipping, you will hear that there is a story—and we like to think of the music as transformative because it is very diverse," Janelle Monáe once said about *The ArchAndroid*. "I mean, in terms of influence it encompasses all the things I love ... Plus, I do consider it genre-less, because I feel the music itself is so much bigger than labels and categories."[13]

Commercially, it was not the easiest sell. Despite near-universal critical acclaim and a Grammy nomination for Album of the Year, *The ArchAndroid* was only a modest seller, debuting and peaking at #17 on the *Billboard* 200 (it fared better on the Top R&B/Hip-Hop Albums chart, reaching #4). Neither "Tightrope" nor "Cold War" made the *Billboard* Hot 100 (astonishingly, she's yet to have a hit higher than #79 on the Hot 100 to date). None of her albums have gone Gold yet, although the single for "Tightrope" has. In terms of sales, it's likely that more people heard her small feature in fun.'s #1 smash hit "We Are Young" than in all of her own music combined. This is not only an injustice, but also kind of depressing.

While Monáe's next release, *The Electric Lady* in 2013, contained the fourth and fifth parts of the Metropolis suite, she took five years before releasing 2018's *Dirty Computer*, her first album that didn't feature her ongoing Metropolis narrative. "This project is about my freedom and challenging myself to live in the present and not in 2719 through Cindi," Monáe explained in a 2018 interview. "I feel like I can contribute to the present day and that I should contribute ... I want to honor those living on the outskirts of society due to their sexuality or gender identity ... waking up as an American who cares deeply about the American dream and the rights of all people to it, I feel there is too much at stake to be quiet and to mince my words on specific issues."[14] True to her word, Monáe spent the past few years advocating for the LBGTQIA+ community, as well as for African Americans in the era of Black Lives Matter. In other words, she has taken the dystopian fantasy lessons of albums like *The ArchAndroid* and applied them to an even scarier place: the here and now.

Notes

1 McCarter.
2 Calvert.
3 Favreau, 93.
4 Spanos.
5 Street.
6 Hoard.
7 Kot.
8 Cole.
9 Ibid.
10 Kot.
11 Favreau, 119.
12 Mossman.
13 Lewis.
14 *Fault Magazine*.

24

The One in Front of the Gun Lives Forever: *good kid, m.A.A.d city*

Kendrick Lamar was born and raised in the epicenter of gangsta rap just as the new genre took hold: Compton. In November 1995, when Lamar was eight, his father took him to the Slauson swap-meet two blocks from their home, where Tupac Shakur and Dr. Dre were filming a video for Tupac's "California Love." As Lamar sat on his father's shoulders to watch these hip-hop icons, one wonders if there was some sort of connection made between the present and future of the music. Tupac, who would die ten months after Lamar saw him in person, left a mark on the young artist to-be, and remained Lamar's favorite rapper for life.

Then, on September 13, 2010—the fourteenth anniversary of Tupac's death—the late rapper appeared to Lamar in a dream. Tupac told him: "Keep doing what you're doing; don't let my music die."[1] The following day, Lamar released his fourth solo mixtape, *Overly Dedicated*. The mixtape made the *Billboard* charts, eventually catching the attention of Dr. Dre. By the end of the year, Lamar signed a deal with Dre's label, Aftermath Entertainment, which set the stage for his major label debut the following year. With Tupac as his patron saint and Dr. Dre as his patron of the arts, Lamar would take the notion of "California Love" and deconstruct it, crafting a portrait of growing up in Compton that was as singular and nuanced as Tupac's hit was unifying and mythic.

"Talk about Kendrick Lamar's musical lineage and Tupac Shakur is his most obvious forefather...," writes Miles Marshall Lewis in his masterful study *Promise That You Will Sing About Me: The Power and Poetry of Kendrick Lamar*. "But Kendrick's artistry deserves an evaluation that considers him in the context of ... other singer-songwriters who addressed freedom, equality, and Afro-pessimism in their work. His work shares as much of its sensibilities with Marvin Gaye's discography as any rapper he ever put on a pedestal, starting with the idea of the concept album." Arguably every album Lamar has released has been a concept album. Noting this, a *Rolling Stone* interviewer in 2017 asked Lamar if he ever rejected a song because it didn't fit in with his album's concept. "I've done that a lot," he answered. "I care about the body of work, not just the big single. I come from that era. I can't shake it, either; no matter how big streaming gets."² Five years earlier, Lamar proved that he was already operating under this philosophy when he released his major-label debut, the fascinating and complex *good kid, m.A.A.d city*.

From its polaroid cover of a boyhood Lamar sitting with his uncle and father (black bars over everyone's eyes except Kendrick's), *good kid, M.A.A.d city* sets the stage for something intimate, yet ominous. Written on the bottom of the polaroid is "GOOD KID MAAD CITY: A SHORT FILM BY KENDRICK LAMAR." Indeed, listening to the album is like watching an arthouse film, as if John Singleton's *Boyz in the Hood* was edited by Quentin Tarantino. "Each piece, I want to trigger certain points where you make a connection," Lamar explained about the album. "Almost like a *Pulp Fiction* feel—you have to listen to it more times to live with it and breathe with it."³ Like Compton itself, it's multilayered and complex, filled with good and bad, souls lost and found.

good kid, m.A.A.d city begins with a tape deck loading to play several young men reciting the Sinner's Prayer. The music rises with angelic holiness, making it easy to miss the snaking bass that begins the actual first song. "Sherane a.k.a Master Splinter's Daughter" introduces the protagonist's love interest, the sexy but mysterious Sherane (the title alludes to the Teenage Mutant Ninja Turtles' rat instructor—indicating she's a hoodrat). She's the match that lights the album's fuse for everything that follows. It's 2004, and the album's protagonist/stand-in for Kendrick Lamar is seventeen years old. He meets Sherane at a house party, they dance to Ciara's "1, 2 Step," and he gets her number. They text all summer as the singer's attraction grows. After the summer, he invites himself over to hookup. As he approaches, she comes out and waves. He smiles back until he sees two thugs in black hoodies approaching him. Then his phone rings—he lets it go to voicemail.

It's his mother. "Damn, I'm sittin' here waitin' on my van," she says. "You told me you was goin' be back in fifteen minutes." She says he better not be "out there messin' with them damn hoodrats out there, shit—'specially with that lil' crazy-ass girl Sherane." His father provides comic relief as he takes the phone with equal urgency: "Where my motherfuckin' dominoes at? This is the second time I asked you to bring my fuckin' dominoes!" Both parents are played by Lamar's parents, giving it an extra layer of realism. The following "Bitch Don't Kill My Vibe" steps away from the album's narrative to the current-day Lamar, calling out his rookie hip-hop peers for chasing fame instead of focusing on music. "You can see that my city found me, then put me on stages," the singer raps, before returning to humility: "I am a sinner who's probably gonna sin again. Lord forgive me." At the end of "Bitch Don't Kill My Vibe" is a short skit, in which his buddy tells him to "Get yo' freestyles ready!"

We flashback to "Backseat Freestyle," in which the album's protagonist is back in 2004 and freestyle rapping in his friend's car. Lamar sidelines his current sophisticated lyrical style in which for a more straightforward, juvenile style, such as when he prays that "my dick get big as the Eiffel Tower" so he can "fuck the world for seventy-two hours." In 2004, Lamar was rapping under the name K-Dot, which he dropped in 2010 in favor of his birth name. In 2017, Lamar was asked when he found his own style: "I think it was the day I said I was gonna go by my real name, Kendrick Lamar [instead of K-Dot]. Yeah. And really just tell my story. Once I did that, it was easier for me to find my own voice, because nobody can tell my story the way I tell it."[4] By using his own name, he takes more ownership for the work, or at least has one less layer between the artist and audience. And for an album so steeped in autobiography, this makes all the difference.

"Listen to this true motherfuckin' story told by Kenrick Lamar," the protagonist says at the beginning of "The Art of Peer Pressure," a study of the singer under the influence of his friends. Like Kendrick Lamar himself, the singer doesn't normally use drugs, but smokes a blunt to look cool. He and his crew end up robbing a house, only to find someone else there and the police on their tail. Meanwhile, the singer's blunt kicks in, which turns out to be laced with angel dust, disorienting him. During the singer's narrow escape, his mother calls—"Hello, what you doin'?" she asks; "Kickin' it" he says—as he barely avoids his first offense. His friends drop off the singer to sober up, knowing he has plans later with Sherane.

"Money Trees" recaps much of the story so far, including the break-in of "The Art of Peer Pressure" and the rapping of "Backseat Freestyle." More obscure is his apparent allusion to "Sherane," in which he says, "I fucked Sherane and went to tell my bros," but there is no other reference to them having been together since the party before the summer. It's a rare inconsistency in an album that otherwise appears completely tight. Either way, it's the foreboding refrain that makes the song: Everyone will respect the shooter, the singer explains, "But the one in front of the gun lives forever." Eight months before Lamar released this song, Trayvon Martin was shot and killed by George Zimmerman; after Zimmerman was acquitted in the summer of 2013, the #BlackLivesMatter movement began and reoriented public discussion about the killing of young minorities at the hands of law enforcement. As Lamar predicts, it's Trayvon's name that's already immortal. A skit at the end of the track features a new voicemail from the singer's mother—"Kendrick, just bring my car back, man ..."—with comic relief again provided by his father: "Did somebody say dominoes?"

"Poetic Justice" is the album's romantic slow-jam, which features Lamar's then-friend (and later-rival) Drake. Taking its title from John Singleton's 1993 film starring Tupac and Janet Jackson—and sampling Jackson's hit, "Anyplace, Anytime," from the film—"Poetic Justice" is a song that unmasks the feelings behind the love and lust in ways that are introspective and probing. "If you listen to 'Poetic Justice,' it's a song about a chick saying these legs are poems," Lamar once explained. "On the back end of that, is really the Sherane joint, so it's a dedication song for Sherane. And that's going into 'good kid' and 'm.A.A.d city' which completes the story."[5] That "Poetic Justice" correlates with the protagonist's thoughts about Sherane on his way over to seeing her in the album's first song is reinforced by the skit at the end, in which the two thugs described at the end of the earlier song confront him—the same scene shot from a different angle.

The following "good kid" picks up the story from after he is beaten down by the two thugs, presumably because of the gang territory he comes from. In real life, Lamar was never involved with a gang and had friends in both of the main rival gangs of Compton. The cops show up and harass him, even though he's done nothing wrong. One officer says, "Step on his neck as hard as your bullet-proof vest," eerily predicting Eric Garner's 2014 murder, during which he said "I can't breathe" eleven times as a police officer knelt on his throat. Coming between the deaths of Trayvon Martin and Eric Garner, *good kid, m.A.A.d city* plays from the center of America's racial crucible.

"m.A.A.d. city" continues the tale in two parts, the first using the thugs' questions as a refrain between which Lamar raps in a high-pitched nervous delivery. The song then becomes more defiant as gangsta rap legend MC Eiht helps set the scene of the mad streets of Compton. Lamar has explained that "m.A.A.d city" has two meanings: "My Angel on Angel Dust" and "My Angry Adolescence Divided."[6] The former refers to the laced weed in "The Art of Peer Pressure," while the latter speaks to being a good kid in a city of bad influences. To this end, Lamar has described himself as "Compton's Human Sacrifice." He's commented on how hard it was to do something positive coming out of Compton: "It was so easy for me to dabble in everything else that my homeboys was doing ... for me to come out of that and do something positive. The moment I made that decision to get in the studio and actually work and study the culture of hip-hop, then everything just started to open up and blossom for me."[7]

The following song, "Swimming Pools (Drank)," was chosen as the lead single for *good kid, m.A.A.d city*. Although it sounds like a party anthem, "Swimming Pools (Drank)" plays like a companion piece to "The Art of Peer Pressure," this time focusing on the effects of alcohol. "Some people wanna fit in the popular, that was my problem," the singer raps, as his friends encourage him to keep drinking. In the second verse, the singer's conscious speaks to him, warning that "if you do not hear me then you will be history, Kendrick." A hazy bridge provides an aural representation of a drunken state, as the singer calls out for Sherane—and then throws up. The song ends with a skit in which his friends plot revenge on the thugs who jumped the singer. They find the thugs and start a shootout, only to realize that Dave, the brother of one of the protagonist's crew, is killed in the crossfire. The fact we are given Dave's name—and not even his brother's—further reinforces the album's truism that the one in front of the gun lives forever.

The album turns to its centerpiece, the twelve-minute "Sing About Me, I'm Dying of Thirst." The one track is divided into two halves, "Sing About Me" and "I'm Dying of Thirst." "Sing About Me" is a composite of three portraits. The first is Dave's brother, who speaks to the protagonist until his words are cut off by three swift gunshots. The second verse is the sister of the subject of Lamar's 2011 song, "Keisha's Song," in which she berates Lamar for using her sister's name and story in his song. The third finds the singer contemplating his own mortality, with the hope that at least one person will sing about him after he's gone.

The second part of the song, "I'm Dying of Thirst," begins with a skit in the aftermath of Dave's killing, as Dave's brother loses it—"Fuck! I'm tired of this shit!"—that makes the singer see his sins closing in on him like a desert. He imagines the rapture and resolves to save himself through baptism. As Dave's brother continues to curse, an older woman (voiced by Maya Angelou) appears: "Why are you so angry? See, you men are dying of thirst ... That means you need water, holy water, you need to be baptized with the spirit of the Lord." She asks them to repeat the Sinner's Prayer that began the album, only now we hear her voice instead of their voices repeating it. "Alright now, remember this day," she concludes. "The start of a new life—your REAL life." This was based on a real event. "The same day [my homeboy got shot], I ran into an older lady ..." Lamar later explained. "and she breaks down the story of God, positivity, life, being free, and being real with yourself ... That song represents being baptized, the actual water, getting dipped in holy water. It represents when my whole spirit changed, when my life starts—my life that you know right now, that's when it starts."⁸ "Sing About Me, I'm Dying of Thirst" is the soul of *good kid, m.A.A.d city*. And it's real—Lamar is living testimony to the prophecy it foretells.

The next song, "Real," finds the protagonist coming to terms with the new world he now experiences after his baptism. He raps about all the things that you can love—fast cars, money, women, etc.—but finds emptiness in these delusions: "But what love got to do with it when you don't love yourself?" A final set of voicemails reveal the wisdom of his parents. His father consoles him for losing his friend, but tells him: "Any nigga can kill a man, that don't make you a real nigga. Real is responsibility. Real is taking care of your motherfucking family. Real is God, nigga." After the music ends, his mother says: "If I don't hear from you by tomorrow, I hope you come back and learn from your mistakes. Come back a man, tell your story to these black and brown kids in Compton. Let 'em know you was just like them, but you rose from that dark place of violence, becoming a better person." We hear a cassette tape being stopped and the main narrative beginning with "Sherane" is over and we are back from 2004 to present-day 2012.

The final song on *good kid, m.A.A.d city*, "Compton," marks the arrival of Kendrick Lamar. He celebrates his newfound faith and anoints himself king. His words are backed up by the presence of Dr. Dre, co-founder of N.W.A., who put Compton on the map with their timeless *Straight Outta Compton*, released when Lamar was a year old. It plays like a coronation, with Dr. Dre passing the Compton torch to a new generation. And then, right at the end, after the music stops, we hear five seconds of sound:

"Mom, I finna use the van real quick! Be back—fifteen minutes—!"

And the album fully reveals itself, ending with the very beginning.

If we put the album in chronological order, the protagonist meets Sherane at a party ("Sherane a.k.a Master Splinter's Daughter," first half). Summer passes; in fall, he has set up a date with Sherane, borrows the family van ("Compton" outro skit), and hangs out with his crew. They ask him to freestyle ("Bitch, Don't Kill My Vibe" outro skit), which he does ("Backstreet Freestyle"). He then smokes a laced joint and attempts to help rob a house, before his friends leave to him sober up ("The Art of Peer Pressure"). His thoughts turn to Sherane ("Poetic Justice") and he goes to see her, only to be approached by thugs as his mother calls asking where her van is ("Sherane," second half and outro skit).

The thugs jump him ("good kid"), he recoils from the violence of the city ("m.A.A.d city"), and turns to alcohol to feel better ("Swimming Pools (Drank)"). He recaps the story and realizes his friends' motivation is money, before his parents call about the van again ("Money Trees" outro skit). Meanwhile, his crew fight the thugs, and Dave dies in the firefight ("Swimming Pools" outro skit). The protagonist reflects on this death ("Sing About Me"), and his need for redemption, which is found with the older woman ("I'm Dying of Thirst"), as they repeat her words ("Sherane" opening skit). He celebrates his new life, reinforced by his parents' voice messages ("Real"). "Compton" is the finale, showing how far the protagonist has come. Only "Bitch, Don't Kill My Vibe" doesn't fit into the overall story, but it flows so well that you don't notice until you scrutinize its lyrics. So, that's the narrative of *good kid, m.A.A.d. city*. Or, at least, that's my version of it. Today. One of the most intriguing elements of this album is how it sets up a narrative that you can constantly ponder and shuffle to create the story.

good kid, m.A.A.d city was released to massive acclaim, debuting and peaking at #2 on the *Billboard* 200, and launching three Top 40 hits on the *Billboard* Hot 100: "Swimming Pools (Drank)," "Poetic Justice," and a remix of "Bitch Don't Kill My Vibe" featuring Jay-Z. In the world of hip-hop, Lamar had arrived as a new force. In 2022, *Rolling Stone* named *good kid* the #1 Best Concept Album of All-Time, despite the fact it was one of the newest titles on the list. Mosi Reeves writes about its placement: "The cover promises 'a short film by Kendrick Lamar,' and the rapper delivers with a coming-of-age opus, the cinematic scope of which has been rightfully compared to Scorsese and Tarantino."[9] And, one imagines, the creativity and precision of Tupac.

In an interview, Tupac once said: "I'm not saying I'm gonna change the world, but I guarantee that I will spark the brain that will change the world."[10] In terms of his ability to change the world, Kendrick Lamar defers to the opinion of his idol. "The idea of me sparking change? It's got to come from within," Lamar told a reporter a few weeks before *good kid, m.A.A.d city* was released. "I couldn't be saying I want Compton to change. You know, Compton is a beautiful place, but it's unpredictable. You just gotta keep your eyes open."[11]

Notes

1 Lewis, 140.
2 Hiatt.

3 Ahmed.
4 Hiatt.
5 Ahmed.
6 Ibid.
7 Badu.
8 Ahmed.
9 Reeves, et al.
10 Lewis, 217.
11 Hopper.

25

Won't Let My Freedom Rot in Hell: *Lemonade*

Fifty years after the Beatles released *Sgt. Pepper's Lonely Hearts Club Band* and helped usher in the album era for a music that previously had been song-focused, the tide shifted the other way, as individual songs (as nontangible downloads) drove much of the industry. Many artists who grew up with the record album fought against this trend, including arguably the biggest name in popular music, Beyoncé. "I feel like, right now, people experience music differently," she said about the release of her self-titled fifth album from 2013.

> I miss that immersive experience. Now people only listen to a few seconds of songs on the iPods and they don't really invest in a whole album. It's all about the single and the hype. So much gets between the music and the art and the fans. I felt like, I don't want anybody to give the message when my record is coming out. I just want this to come out when its ready and from me to my fans. I told my team I want to shoot a video for every song and put them out at the same time. Everyone thought I was crazy.[1]

She proved the crazies wrong. On December 13, 2013, the world awoke to find the new album *Beyoncé* for sale on iTunes. By the time physical copies were shipped the following week, the album had already gone Gold with over half a million copies sold in three days; a fortnight later, it went Platinum with over a million sold.

If Beyoncé was a pop sensation before her self-titled 2013 album, she was launched into the pop stratosphere afterwards. She proved she didn't have to play by the rules—she could now make her own. After 2014, she gave precious few extended interviews, one of the exceptions being an interview with *ELLE* in early April 2016. This came shortly after the release of a new single called "Formation," which would be the lead of her 2016 album, *Lemonade*. The interviewer asks Beyoncé what she wants to accomplish during the next phase of her career. "I hope I can create art that helps people heal," she responded. "Art that makes people feel proud of their struggle. Everyone experiences pain, but sometimes you need to be uncomfortable to transform. Pain is not pretty, but I wasn't able to hold my daughter in my arms until I experienced the pain of childbirth!"[2]

Nineteen days later, on April 23, 2016, a one-hour film by Beyoncé called *Lemonade* aired exclusively on HBO. After the film ended around 10:00 p.m., a new album called *Lemonade* appeared on Tidal for purchase. The following day, iTunes began selling it, too. Beyoncé had done it again—only this time, the vision was more cohesive, and the results were even better. Although the album was ostensibly about her husband Jay-Z's infidelities, it went beyond that. In its official statement about the album, Tidal called it a "conceptual project based on every woman's journey of self-knowledge and healing."[3] The fact that the company Tidal was owned by Jay-Z only adds the layers of complexity.

Here, we will only be looking at the album because the accompanying film (a cinematic journey through all of the album's songs) is out of this book's scope. Furthermore, the film edits some songs so that the fuller versions play on the album. But I still believe *Lemonade* doesn't fall into the category of a "soundtrack," since the music came before the film, as opposed to being created concurrently with it or after the fact. So even though the film was released first, I find the essential document of *Lemonade* to be the album. For someone so strict about keeping their personal life and public life separate, *Lemonade* is a revelation, a stunning rebirth of identity that fell into a grand conceptual tradition.

The first track on *Lemonade*, "Pray You Catch Me," is a prelude for the album, starting with the simple notes of a string bass (or a synthesizer imitating one) as Beyoncé sings wordless notes on top, layering her voice until it becomes a small sculpture of block chords. When the lyrics arrive, they cut right to the heart of the record: "You can taste the dishonesty," the singer intones. "It's all over your breath." The melody is sung like a confessional, as piano chords underpin the vocal line. In the refrain, the singer prays that she catches her lover whispering and that he catches her listening. She doesn't just want to catch him but for them both to be caught in the act at the same time, which ultimately frames the song—and in turn, the album—with a feeling of mutual standing; she wants the walls to come down between them so that they can see each other on the same level. The fact she's praying for this to happen adds a feeling of holiness, a plea for divine intervention that would allow them to be reborn and start anew. The song ends with a whisper: "*What are you doing, my love?*" The question hangs over the rest of the album as she seeks to find the answer.

A cymbal splash begins "Hold Up," before the ghostly plucked chords form its central riff. Although its use of off-beat sounds gives it a reggae feel—and, indeed, "Hold Up" is a very reggae-tinged song—it's actually a sample from easy listening crooner Andy Williams' song "Can't Get Used to Losing You" from his 1963 album *The Days of Wine and Roses*. When Beyoncé comes in, she sings the words with cool detachment and a sexy allure, her voice sliding down to unusual lower notes, giving the song a weird, hypnotic vibe. The song starts with the slinky chorus—"Hold up—they don't love you like I love you"—appropriating one of the central lines to the 2003 song "Maps" by the Yeah Yeah Yeahs. The song switches from the cool groove of the refrain to a rat-a-tat firing of the hip-hop-derived verses. "I don't wanna lose my pride," the singer offers, "but I'ma fuck me up a bitch"—and you believe her.

"Don't Hurt Yourself" is built around a drum groove, a reggae-style bass, and call-and-response organs and keyboards, giving Beyoncé a sparse foundation for her aggressive vocals. She shouts until she becomes distorted, twists words, hovers on the edge of going off-key, and cusses like a sailor. For someone so cautious about her musical refinement, this is Beyoncé singing punk rock. As she sings "Let it be, let it be, let it be" (a reference to the Beatles' great "divorce" album?), the drums, bass, and guitar come in behind her like a tidal wave, and the song turns into a thrashing rocker. "Don't Hurt Yourself" was co-written by the White Stripes' leader Jack White, who also plays rumbling bass on it and sings the refrain. It's a simple enough message—"When you hurt me, you hurt yourself"—and one that is carried by his offhanded delivery and effortless indie-rock swagger. "She took just sort of a sketch of a lyrical outline and turned into the most bodacious, vicious, incredible song," Jack White said of Beyoncé. "I don't even know what you'd classify it as—soul, rock and roll, whatever. 'Don't Hurt Yourself' is incredibly intense; I'm so amazed at what she did with it."[4]

After the raw intensity of "Don't Hurt Yourself," the following "Sorry" takes things back to a slower, laid-back R&B groove, while still holding on to its anger like a curse. It's a song about independence and feminism that flips the script on the typical masculine/feminine stereotypes. Now it's the female singer who tells the guy to "suck on my balls" and urges her female crew to raise their middle fingers; she depicts him as the one calling her on the phone crying. "I ain't thinking 'bout you," she snaps throughout the song, even if the Queen Bey doth protest too much, methinks. The closing section pulls the rug out from the rest of the song. The music shifts to a more robotic groove as the singer waits for her man to come home, leaves a note on the door, and walks out. The song's most famous line at the very end is when she imagines him wanting her once she's gone: "He better call Becky with the good hair," repeating the line a cappella to twist the knife. With "Becky" as code for a white girl, she created an instant catchphrase.

"6 Inch" is an ode to the hardworking woman, even including a stanza of "She work for the money," evoking Donna Summer's 1983 smash. The female lead in Beyoncé's song grinds from Monday to Friday and then works from Friday to Sunday, implying she's got (at least) two jobs. "We need men and women to understand the double standards that still exist in this world, and we need to have a real conversation so we can begin to make changes," Beyoncé explained a few weeks before *Lemonade* was released. "Ask anyone, man or woman, 'Do you want your daughter to have 75 cents when she deserves $1?' What do you think the answer would be? When we talk about equal rights, there are issues that face women disproportionately."[5] "6 Inch" further takes the image of the working woman and transforms her into a badass hero. No wonder the protagonist says after watching the woman with 6-inch heels walk into a club, "she murdered everyone and I was her witness."

The first half of *Lemonade* closes with one of its most intriguing songs, "Daddy Lessons." Beginning with a Dixieland jazz band, it transforms into a country/Americana song built around the acoustic guitar in a rustic ode to the singer's father. Beyoncé's father, Mathew Knowles, is a huge figure in her life. Before Beyoncé was a teenager, he courted financial ruin when he quit his job to become her full-time manager. This worked through her early solo career, but as she grew more confident, she pulled away from her father, eventually firing him. Mathew's own troubled marriage with Beyoncé's mother Tina, which found him engaging in countless affairs, added fuel to the fire, while Jay-Z's increasing influence replaced Mathew as a sounding board. All of which is to say that to have "Daddy Lessons" at the center of a pivotal album speaks volumes. In the song, the father tells the daughter that when trouble comes and "men like me come around," to shoot them. As Mathew's infidelities always haunted Beyoncé, learning that her own husband was unfaithful hit her deep. It's interesting in this context that the singer claims "Oh, my daddy said shoot." It at once tacitly acknowledges the father's misdeeds and gives her permission to shoot her lover if need be. After the song closes, we hear Beyoncé's young daughter saying, "Good job, Bey," carrying the song's message to a new generation.

"Love Drought" begins the second half of the album in transition. It's a slow song, but the beats and synthesizers behind it keep it mysterious yet grounded, like if a meteor shower appeared over New York City. The singer still holds on to her anger, but it's muted, as she tries to be fair to her man. "You're my lifeline," she sings, "are you tryna kill me?" But even when the verses begin to stray into cynicism, the refrain offers the first ray of hope in the album. "You and me could move a mountain," she sings, recognizing the good that she ultimately believes is underneath (and presumably stronger than) the bad. "Love Drought" sets the stage for the reconciliation that will play out across the album's second half.

"Sandcastles" is one of the most gorgeous songs on *Lemonade*—and simplest, too. Featuring only Beyoncé singing over a straightforward piano part, she sings three verses in three minutes, with the only additional sound being her radiant backing vocal in the third verse. While it takes its tradition from a torch song and is structured like a folksong, "Sandcastles" is ultimately steeped in gospel. The song paints quick but effective vignettes in the first two verses—him crying when she walks away; smashed dishes and pictures snatched from the frame—before resolving neatly in the third: "Show me your scars and I won't walk away." Beyoncé's vocal performance match each verse's mood perfectly. There's longing in the first verse, anger in the second, and passion in the third, as "Sandcastles" morphs from a tender ballad to a stunning kiss-off to a song of redemption. There's a famous adage that God answers all prayers, but sometimes the answer is no. "Sandcastles" plays like a secular version of this. For although the singer promised that she couldn't stay, "Every promise don't work out that way."

"Sandcastles" flows into "Forward," the most peculiar song on the album—an 80-second piano ballad sung almost entirely by British singer-songwriter James Blake. When Blake went into the studio, Beyoncé's team gave him her working version of the lyrics. "I've never sung anybody else's lyrics," Blake later explained. "So, I just assumed that's not I was going to be doing. So, I got my phone out and sang some of my own lyrics that were about something else and about somebody else. But it fit somehow into the song and it fit into the album, and I'm just honored that they used it."[6] The song fits into *Lemonade* because it is about moving forward, but one imagines Beyoncé was most touched by the final line, which is the only one she duets with Blake on: "Go back to sleep in your favorite spot just next to me." Like "Love Drought," it's a song about moving on, while still holding on to the hope of what used to be can still be.

The onslaught of drums and organ begins the mad rush of "Freedom," perhaps the finest track on *Lemonade*. The sound fills out into a full rock band, which is sampled from the song "Let Me Try" by the obscure psychedelic Latin American band Kaleidoscope. "Freedom" takes Kaleidoscope's funky rock build-up and overlays folk recording samples from a 1959 sermon and a 1947 prison song, giving the effect of garage rock funk filled with ghosts. The refrain ties it all together, as the Kaleidoscope sample is back with the modern beats on top of it; the build allows the song to transcend itself, as the singer proclaims her ability to break chains and not let freedom rot in hell. It's a thrilling moment, the sound of scaling a mountain and taking in the wisdom. The second verse wades through waters to connect the singer's plight to Harriet Tubman, another Black woman who, once finding her way to freedom, led others to freedom, too. Kendrick Lamar's rap on the third verse further builds the tension, a claustrophobic rush through city streets while calling for openings—of the mind, of the streets—while the song closes in around him. Beyoncé sings the final refrains, all ending with the singer declaring she'll keep running because "a winner don't quit on themselves." And then to illustrate the point, we hear the voice of Jay-Z's grandmother, Hattie White, on her ninetieth birthday: "I had my ups and downs, but I always find the inner strength to pull myself up. I was served lemons, but I made lemonade."

The penultimate "All Night" finds the singer reconciling with her mistreating lover over an edgy guitar riff, before the song washes over into a laidback, lush groove. The refrain is a work of beauty, as the singer sings dreams of making love all night long, her words punctuated by the sampled horns from OutKast's 1998 song "SpottieOttieDopaliscious." At the heart of "All Night" is redemption and rebirth, pushing secular love into sacred love. The singer wants her lover to baptize his tears and dry his eyes, says that true love brings her salvation, and that with every tear she found redemption. "All Night" is a rare song that sounds instantly familiar despite being wholly new. There are elements of rock, soul, R&B, and funk, all polished into perfect pop, until everything sounds like a classic dance song you never want to end. And then, at the end of the song itself, we hear a whisper, which closes the question posed at the end of "Pray You Catch Me": "*How I missed you, my love.*" And just like on *Sgt. Pepper*, the album's concept resolves on its penultimate song, before launching into its finale, "Formation."

The last song on *Lemonade* finds Beyoncé stepping forward from the relationship woes of the other album's other eleven songs to celebrate herself—and by extension, Black women worldwide. Beginning with two strings reverberating in a strange call-and-response with each other, it soon turns into a R&B dancefloor track. The singer describes a life of rare luxury and power, but also establishes her African American and Creole roots, promising that "they never take the country out me." After establishing her own determination in the refrain—"I dream it, work hard, I grind 'til I own it"—and saying that she slays *a lot* (the word "slay" is said in the song 49 times, counting backing vocals), she calls upon her ladies to get in formation. The idea of calling on the Black women of the world to follow her empowered lead echoes what *Lemonade* has been doing all along—getting what you know you deserve by exerting honest work and uncompromising strength.

The final lines of "Formation"—"Always stay gracious, best revenge is your paper"—could be written off as a badass brag, but it also hits at the root of the *Lemonade* project. The only reason Beyoncé was able to make and release *Lemonade* on her own terms was because she used her own money to do it. As a very private star who spent much of her career compartmentalizing her public and private lives, Beyoncé's *Lemonade* plays like a burst of freedom, throwing it all out there and letting the chips fall where they may.

When *Lemonade* was released (or rather, appeared), it rocketed to #1 in *Billboard*. Critics met it with great praise, as *Rolling Stone* gave it a perfect five stars and called it "her most powerful, ambitious statement yet"[7]; *Rolling Stone* was also among the many who crowned it the best album of the year, along with *The New York Times*, *The Los Angeles Times*, *Billboard*, and *Entertainment Weekly*, and countless others. *Lemonade* was nominated for three Grammys, including Album of the Year, while the songs "Formation," "Don't Hurt Yourself," and "Freedom," were nominated as well.

Although *Lemonade* lost Album of the Year to Adele's *25*, it did win Best Urban Contemporary Album. In her acceptance speech, Beyoncé said in part: "We all experience pain and loss, and often we become inaudible. My intention for the film and album was to create a body of work that would give a voice to our pain, our struggles, our darkness and our history. To confront issues that make us uncomfortable."[8] In the time of Black Lives Matter and polarizing politics, Beyoncé took her own struggles and mapped them onto our greater cultural history. She turned the personal into the political, the singular into the universal. And by releasing it the way she did, as a surprise film and album, she took the modern trends overpowering the album format—songs over albums, digital over physical, watching music videos over listening to music—and beat the game by reinventing it.

Notes

1 Taraborrrelli, 437.
2 Gottesman.
3 Spanos.
4 NPR Staff.
5 Gottesman.
6 Lozano.
7 Sheffield.
8 Russonello.

Conclusion: When Everybody Who Is Lonely Will Be Free

The rock concept album was born in a perfect storm of recording technology, psychedelic drugs, and rock music. By the late 1960s, advances in the music industry standards such as the use of stereo, multitrack layering of sounds, and the improvement of sound quality all led to a more vibrant, immersive sound. Meanwhile, the increasing popularity of LSD meant that users could experience a dense, almost religious reawakening that some saw as akin to a spiritual rebirth. As for the music, it was always free. Unlike fine art or writing, music is a strictly ephemeral phenomenon. The way in which we hear it is at once invisible and immediate, causing it to be a more intimate interactive experience. As technology improved music's lifelike qualities, psychedelic drugs like LSD enriched how the mind could experience it. With rock music in these crosshairs, it expanded the possibilities of what rock could do, what rock could say, and what rock could mean. In one of the Beatles' earliest and most influential acid songs, "Tomorrow Never Knows" from *Revolver* in 1966, John Lennon sings of playing the game of "existence to the end . . . of the beginning."

"Everybody says it's a dying, *death* experience," explained LSD advocate Timothy Leary as he approached his own death. "If you don't die, you didn't get your money's worth from your dealer. Dying was built right into it. Why do you think we were using the *Tibetan Book of the Dead* as our guiding text?"[1] Starting with the first major rock concept album, *Sgt. Pepper's Lonely Hearts Club Band*, the Beatles used the ultimate form of escape available to them, rock and roll, to break free from the ultimate dead-end road, death itself. To do so was nothing short of miraculous. "I declare that the Beatles are mutants," Leary said after *Sgt. Pepper*'s release. "Prototypes of evolutionary agents sent by God with a mysterious power to create a new species—a young race of laughing freemen . . ."[2]

The Beatles used the concept album to forge a path from death into freedom. Death looms large in the human psyche in part because it is so inevitable and so unknowable; it's the one trip in life that you must take alone. Freedom, on the other hand, implies an ability to go anywhere at any time, to ramble on your own terms. This too can be done alone, but in the 1960s, many of the most celebrated touchstones—the formation of the Haight-Ashbury scene in 1966, the Monterey Pop Festival in 1967, and Woodstock in 1969—functioned like a destination for a generation of wandering souls. With many young people painted as freaks and outcasts by their communities, these events provided a new community that promised everyone the freedom to be themselves.

In the year before she released *Blue*, Joni Mitchell captured the feeling of this in her song "Woodstock." The singer encounters a child of God going to the three-day festival to join in a rock and roll band. They plan to camp out on the land and try to set their soul free. As we have seen, Mitchell once defined freedom as follows: "Freedom implies a lot of loneliness you know, a lot of unfulfillment. It implies always the search for fulfillment, which sometimes is more exciting than the fulfillment itself."³ Mitchell is on to something here. Her words imply that loneliness and freedom is intrinsically linked. The opening song in *Blue*, "All I Want," gives the game away, as the singer begins on a lonely road traveling and looking for the key to set her free.

Once you start to dig around, freedom is everywhere. Many of the albums are about the freedom of escape—from one's self (*Sgt. Pepper*), from one's secular world (*What's Going On*), from one's modern-day angst (*The Dark Side of the Moon*), from one's planet (*Mothership Connection*), from societal gender roles (*Exile in Guyville*), or from sinful temptation (*good kid, m.A.A.d. city*). Many albums are about noble attempts made to escape that ultimately fail (*Seventh Son of a Seventh Son*, *The Downward Spiral*, *Ready to Die*, and, depending on how you hear it, *Ziggy Stardust* and *OK Computer*). Meanwhile, the Who's *Tommy* tells us that freedom tastes of reality, while Beyoncé refuses to let her freedom rot in hell in *Lemonade*. And in *The ArchAndroid*, Janelle Monáe tells us that if you want to free, underground is the only place to be.

The Mothers of Invention hit the nail on the head in their song "Take Your Clothes off When You Dance," which promises someday everyone who is lonely will be free (to sing, dance, and love). In mocking *Sgt. Pepper*, Zappa draws a more explicit line between loneliness and freedom than anything on *Sgt. Pepper* itself. And yet, loneliness has a way of hiding in plain sight. After all, the Beatles remade themselves into a *lonely* hearts club band. Jimi Hendrix sings about how "Loneliness is such a drag" in "Burning of the Midnight Lamp"; Ziggy Stardust breaks though to the audience by shouting, "Oh no love, you're not alone!" in

"Rock and Roll Suicide"; Donna Summer describes her protagonist as spending lonely days with no one on her side in "Once Upon a Time"; Hüsker Dü sing about a protagonist who would rather be alone in "Whatever"; Liz Phair sings about how preparing to spend the next year alone in "Fuck and Run"; and Green Day invoke Joni Mitchell's "All I Want" by walking a lonely road all alone in "Boulevard of Broken Dreams."

These concept albums are filled with freaks, loners, and outsiders who stand apart from society. The Beatles' Sgt. Pepper band evoke a smarmy music hall orchestra, thirty years out of time with its contemporary era. Jimi Hendrix celebrates a secret underwater future of mermen. The Who's Tommy is an autistic freak, Ziggy Stardust is an androgynous space alien, and the Seventh Son of a Seventh Son is a conflicted and feared clairvoyant. Pink Floyd and Radiohead craft albums about the estrangement caused by modern society and technology. Donna Summer's fairytale happens in an empty, dreamlike land where she appears to be the only distinct person—even her prince is oddly faceless. Hüsker Dü and Green Day both craft epics about a depressed teen who leaves his home only to run off to a city that's even more miserable. De La Soul put themselves up against the mainstream rap scene by casting themselves as misunderstood outsiders while Liz Phair declares war on the Guyville scene. Trent Reznor sings about a lost soul who is too trapped in misery to make any meaningful connection with another person, while Notorious B.I.G. paints himself as a criminal. Janelle Monáe tells the story of an android superstar from the future who lives underground to hide from her oppressive government. And of course, the Mothers of Invention create a safe haven for freaks—including those who don't realize they are.

The only albums that don't feature these kinds of antiheroes are either general narratives (the Moody Blues' *Days of Future Passed*, Marvin Gaye's *What's Going On*, Jethro Tull's *Thick as a Brick*, and Brian Wilson's *SMiLE*), or albums that speak of largely autobiographical journeys (Joni Mitchell's *Blue*, *The Miseducation of Lauryn Hill*, Kendrick Lamar's *good kid, m.A.A.d city*, and Beyoncé's *Lemonade*). But these albums are in the minority of the concept album. Even if they don't feature a lonely outcast as a central figure, they work in the real pain of loneliness into their grooves alongside the sheer relief of freedom.

Elvis Presley, who did so much to define rock and roll freedom in his early Sun records, also personified rock and roll loneliness on his first RCA hit: "Heartbreak Hotel." The song's stark lyrics and deep echo conjured a world where the singer is so lonely he could die. "The word is *lonely*," Nick Bromell posited in his study *Tomorrow Never Knows: Rock and Psychedelics in the 1960s*.

Elvis defines the new situation and names it as a new place in which the generation just coming of age will be forced to *dwell*. The home becomes a hotel; the private becomes public; surrounded by lonely other, one is jostled in one's loneliness. This is the place where the state of being alone is replaced by the state of being *lonely* ... It is the loneliness we would seek to overcome through shared music, through free sex, through the myth of a generation, through the pharmacology of Dr. Hofmann (inventor of LSD), and through the cult of love and connection musiked by the Beatles.[4]

The combination of rock and psychedelics, Bromell explains later in the book, "took the kids out of the conventional world structured by parents, away from the expectant gaze of others, but instead of delivering them into a void of loneliness, they dropped them in a world radiant with connections and community, saturated with significance."[5]

We can feel this with some of the early concept albums, where community is everything. Part of *Sgt. Pepper*'s genius was that it conjured a community that everyone could join by listening to the record. *Days of Future Passed*, *Electric Ladyland*, and *Tommy* all tapped into this feeling either in their all-inclusive themes or the cohesion of each record. Even *Tommy*, which was meant to prove in part that reaching the highest high required abstinence from drugs, created its own community within the album itself, as Tommy's followers grow in number. And while *We're Only in It for the Money* similarly eschewed drugs and openly mocked the counterculture, it too was a document of a community, only it unified a sort of counter-counterculture.

With the implosion of the 1960s, the community it fostered could only be found in pieces here and there. *Mothership Connection* took the LSD-fueled journey and set their spaceship towards the sky, while *3 Feet High and Rising* took on some of the trappings of psychedelic music such as bright colors, peace signs, and flowers to create a safe space for thinkers and dreamers everywhere (although the band members held firm that they were not hippies). *SMiLE* was the latter-day epilogue to the 1960s community, resurrecting a trippy, surreal country that had such a dizzying array of lyrics, genres, and voices, it leads to an endless world of possibilities that strives to include everyone in its greater tapestry.

But these community-based albums were the exception, not the rule. As the 1960s turned into the 1970s, the focus shifted from the greater community to the inner-self. *What's Going On* served as a transition work, as its sermon-like structure implied an audience listening to it—not to mention the ambient party crowd of the title track. But the album's theme of drugs focused on harder substances while its ecological warnings spoke of a world coming apart, as opposed to a vivid place to be reborn. So, the singer follows a crusade to God and seems to reach a spiritual resolution (if not freedom) but is brought back down by the loneliness of the inner city.

Blue was the blossoming of the self over the community. Indeed, the places that do appear in Mitchell's songs—her native California, her time in Greece, countries she passes through like France and Spain—are filtered through either one person (a former lover), or herself. It works because Mitchell is a brilliant songwriter, but it sets the stage for many less-talented songwriters to wallow in their own self-indulgent sagas. *Thick as a Brick* lampoons the over-the-top and too-self-serious concept albums by making a tongue-and-cheek epic. What seems at first like an idyllic pastoral community, complete with its own newspaper, is an entirely fictional satire. *The Rise and Fall of Ziggy Stardust and The Spiders from Mars* sets its sights beyond mere community to try to save the world (while attempting to become the biggest star in the world). Despite efforts to break through the wall to the listener, the weight of the central character overpowers anyone else in the narrative until they become a blur of fans, road managers, and groupies. The rock and roll suicide works at the end because Ziggy has been so isolated all along. *The Dark Side of the Moon* is a paean to isolation in the modern world; spiritually, it's the father to *OK Computer*. *Zen Arcade* follows an alienated teenager who leaves his miserable home to run off into the city, only to find lost love, drugs, and confusion, which not only solidifies the narrative in and of itself, but also provides a blueprint for *American Idiot* twenty years later. *Seventh Son of a Seventh Son* pits its protagonist against his community, while *Exile in Guyville* charts an escape from the Guyville community with a Rolling Stones' LP as its Vigil. *The Downward Spiral*, *Ready to Die*, and *The Miseducation of Lauryn Hill* are more or less semi-autobiographical tales following in the tradition of *Blue*.

The final three albums of this book stand together. *The Archandroid* walks a line, as the singer finds a secret underground community as she staves off the tyranny of the ruling mainstream community. *good kid, m.A.A.d city* is a semi-autobiographical work that tries to square his home community of Compton with his own moral code. And *Lemonade* is similarly based on real life, but the singer goes a step further by using her power to summon and empower Black women everywhere. After so many albums that focus on an individual, *Lemonade* makes a key pivot in its third act to beckon a community that has gone overlooked for far too long.

Against this backdrop, we have seen the album community itself change drastically over the years. Ever since Napster blew up the music industry around the turn of the millennium, people have been declaring the album's death for over two decades now. It seemed to be recorded music coming full-circle—after decades of the album being the centerpiece of the industry, everything was shifting back to the single song in a way that arguably it hadn't been since the Second World War era. The truth, as always, is not so simple, especially as time—and technology—marches forward.

In 2022, music consumption in the United States, as measured by album units, grew by 9.2 percent.[6] The catch is that these are album *units*, which includes not only traditional sales, but also track equivalent albums (in which ten downloads per album equals one album unit), and streaming equivalent albums (in which 1,250 premium streams or 3,750 free streams equals one album unit). This type of criteria doesn't bode well for the concept album, which is generally one creative unit and meant to be consumed all together and in order. Traditional album sales can still deliver that, but once you get into track equivalent albums and streaming equivalent albums, everything goes out the window. Meanwhile, even though the overall music consumption grew by 9.2 percent, this was a statistic *measured* in album units, but not a reflection of album sales itself. Total album sales (including physical and digital purchases) fell by 8.2 percent.[7] So even if overall music sales are up, album sales are falling as song-oriented streaming and playlists veer the narrative back to the single song.

And yet there's one trend that speaks right to the concept album's heart. For the second in a row, vinyl records outsold CDs in 2022.[8] Furthermore, 43 percent of all albums sold in the United States (including physical and digital) were vinyl records. And it's not only albums from the eras discussed in this book.[9] Last year, Taylor Swift led the vinyl revolution as one out of every twenty-five vinyl records sold were one of her titles. So even though vinyl is often seen as an aging retro-hipster fad, it's making a comeback as a listening vehicle for a new generation.[10] And with so much focus on the digital formats and streaming, it's refreshing to find one corner of the marketplace where things are going back to analog.

As albums like *Sgt. Pepper, Tommy, What's Going On, Ziggy Stardust,* and *The Dark Side of the Moon* reach and pass the half-century mark, their significance as monolithic obelisks only become more entrenched with age. And yet, their obelisks have become tombstones. While they pioneered the concept album as a form, it is the newer, unforeseen music—punk, hip-hop, and techno, among others—who have carried the torch. And of course, as Beyoncé—or Taylor Swift—could tell you, there's always room for great pop music in there too.

Even as the concept album is subject to change in the way it's sold and consumed, the art form remains persistent. Several of the most acclaimed concept albums in this book (*American Idiot*, *The Archandroid*, and *good kid, m.A.A.d city*) were released in the new millennium. In many ways, the new kinds of media formats have increased the concept album's capabilities. That's why closing with Beyoncé's *Lemonade* seemed so appropriate. She released her album as a multimedia extravaganza with a film of the album's songs, making a sort of visual equivalent to the concept album. Furthermore, as we have seen, artists like Beyoncé and Kendrick Lamar grew up with the album format and still think of their works as discrete albums as opposed to a bunch of songs put together. Perhaps the real question is how the concept album will fare as an increasing number of artists and consumers are born farther and farther away from the mainstream physical consumption of music. I imagine that some form of the album—and the concept album—will prevail because one major goal of an artist is to make a statement. And you can make a much better statement across a vinyl LP than on a four-minute pop song.

As the Beatles once said, "Nothing has changed, it's still the same." It came out on an album that then changed everything.

Notes

1 Gilmore, 397.
2 Norman, 293.
3 Valentine.
4 Bromell, 42.
5 Ibid., 74–5.
6 Caulfield.
7 Ibid.
8 Ibid.
9 Ibid.
10 Ibid.

Works Cited

Introduction: Ramblin' on my Mind

Badman, K. (2004), *The Beach Boys: The Definitive Diary of America's Greatest Band on Stage and in the Studio*, San Francisco: Backbeat Books.

Capitol Records, "Wild Is Love," advertisement, *Billboard*, September 5, 1960. Available online: https://worldradiohistory.com/Archive-All-Music/Billboard/60s/1960/Billboard%201960-09-05.pdf (accessed May 21, 2023).

Capitol Records, "Wild Is Love," advertisement, *Billboard*, September 5, 1960. Available online: https://worldradiohistory.com/Archive-All-Music/Billboard/60s/1960/Billboard%201960-09-12.pdf (accessed May 21, 2023).

CashBox Editors, "Another Old Way Out The Window," *CashBox*, May 20, 1967. Available online: https://worldradiohistory.com/Archive-All-Music/Cash-Box/60s/1967/CB-1967-05-20.pdf (accessed December 27, 2022).

Columbia Records, "Dealer-Jockey Report," advertisement, *Billboard*, February 25, 1956. Available online: https://worldradiohistory.com/Archive-All-Music/Billboard/50s/1956/Billboard%201956-02-25.pdf (accessed May 21, 2023).

"concept, n.". OED Online. March 2023. Oxford University Press. https://www.oed.com/view/Entry/38130?redirectedFrom=concept+album. Available online: https://www.oed.com/view/Entry/38130?redirectedFrom=concept+album#eid1121036060 (accessed May 26, 2023).

Malagaris, T. (1967), "Local Recording Company Enjoys Healthy Growth," *The Chicago Tribune*, November 19, 1967, Section 10A-13. Available online: https://www.newspapers.com/image/376633686 (accessed November 26, 2021).

Marcus, G. (1970), "Self Portrait," *Rolling Stone*, June 8, 1970. Available online: https://www.rollingstone.com/music/music-album-reviews/self-portrait-107056/ (accessed December 27, 2022).

Miller, J. (1999), *Flowers in the Dustbin: The Rise of Rock and Roll*, New York: Simon & Schuster.

"Music of the Danube," *Billboard*, September 9, 1957, 38. Available online: https://worldradiohistory.com/Archive-All-Music/Billboard/50s/1957/Billboard%201957-09-09.pdf (accessed May 21, 2023).

Nelson, P. "'Rock Is Too Serious,' Says the Who," *The New York Times*, June 2, 1968, 20D. Available online: https://timesmachine.nytimes.com/timesmachine/1968/06/02/90667380.html?pageNumber=157 (accessed May 21, 2023).

Record World, "New Stones LP 'Landmark,'" *Record World*, December 9, 1967, 22. Available online: https://worldradiohistory.com/hd2/IDX-Business/Music/Archive-Record-World-IDX/IDX/60s/67/RW-1967-12-09-OCR-Page-0022.pdf#search=%22concept%20album%22 (accessed December 28, 2022).

Variety (1961), "Korvette Mulls Own Indie Label," *Variety*, October 1, 1961, 49. Available online: https://archive.org/details/variety-1961-10/page/48/mode/2up (accessed December 27, 2022).

"Wild Is Love," *Billboard*, September 19, 1960, 47. Available online: https://worldradiohistory.com/Archive-All-Music/Billboard/60s/1960/Billboard%201960-09-19.pdf (accessed May 21, 2023).

Part 1: The Founding Era (1967–9)

Chapter 1: We Hope You Will Enjoy the Show: *Sgt. Pepper's Lonely Hearts Club Band* by the Beatles

Beatles, The, (2000), *The Beatles: Anthology*, San Francisco: Chronicle Books LLC.

MacDonald, I. (1994), *Revolution in the Head: The Beatles' Records and the Sixties*, New York: Henry Holt and Company.

Miller, J. (1999), *Flowers in the Dustbin: The Rise of Rock and Roll*, New York: Simon & Schuster.

White, C. (1984), *The Life and Times of Little Richard: The Quasar of Rock*, New York: Harmony Books.

Chapter 2: This Day Will Last a Thousand Years: *Days of Future Passed* by the Moody Blues

Barnes, M. (2020), *A New Day Yesterday: UK Progressive Rock & The 1970s*, New York: Omnibus Press.

Beard, D. (2012), "Revisit the Moody Blues' landmark album, 'Days of Future Passed,'" *Goldmine*, June 12, 2012. Available online: https://www.goldminemag.com/articles/revisit-the-moody-blues-landmark-album-days-of-future-passed (accessed 30 November 2021).

Cushman, M. (2017), *Long Distance Voyagers: The Story of the Moody Blues, Volume 1 (1965–1979)*, San Diego: Jacobs/Brown Press.

Davies, H. (2009), *The Beatles*, New York: W.W. Norton & Company.

Donnelly, D. (1968), "The Teen Beat," *Honolulu Star Bulletin*, March 16, 1968, B-3.

Goldstein, R. (1967), "We Still Need the Beatles, But. . .," *The New York Times*, June 18, 1967, p. 24D. Available online: https://timesmachine.nytimes.com/timesmachine/1967/06/18/89671145.html?pageNumber=104 (accessed December 31, 2022).

Powell, M. (2008), "The Moody Blues: Days of Future Passed" (CD Reissue Liner Notes), Decca Music Group Limited.

Runtagh, J. (2018), "The Moody Blues' 'Nights in White Satin': An Oral History," *Rolling Stone*, April 9, 2018. Available online: https://www.rollingstone.com/music/music-features/the-moody-blues-nights-in-white-satin-an-oral-history-630219/ (accessed December 6, 2021).

Uncut (2014), "The Making Of... The Moody Blues' Nights in White Satin," *Uncut*, November 21, 2014. Available online: https://www.uncut.co.uk/features/the-making-of-the-moody-blues-nights-in-white-satin-1699/ (accessed December 4, 2021).

Chapter 3: We Are the Other People: *We're Only in It for the Money* by the Mothers of Invention

Gray, M. (1985), *Zappa*, New York: Proteus Books.

Giuliano, G. (1997), *Dark Horse: The Life and Art of George Harrison*, New York: Da Capo Press.

Lammle, R. (2014), "Maryland's Amazing 'Half-Boy,'" *Mental Floss*, April 28, 2014, https://www.mentalfloss.com/article/56400/strange-states-marylands-amazing-half-boy.

MacDonald, I. (1994), *Revolution in the Head: The Beatles' Records and the Sixties*, New York: Henry Holt and Company.

Miles, B. (2004), *Zappa: A Biography*, New York: Grove Press.

Rolling Stone (1987), "The Top 100 Albums of the Last 20 Years," *Rolling Stone*, August 27, 1987.

Walley, D. (1996), *No Commercial Potential: The Saga of Frank Zappa*, New York: Da Capo Press.

Chapter 4: The One That Rambles on a Million Miles: *Electric Ladyland* by the Jimi Hendrix Experience

Cannon, G. (1968), "Jimi Hendrix: Electric Ladyland (Polydor), *The Guardian*, November 5, 1968. Available online: https://www.theguardian.com/music/2018/nov/05/jimi-hendrix-electric-ladyland-review-1968 (accessed December 15, 2022).

Cross, C.R. (2005), *Room Full of Mirrors: A Biography of Jimi Hendrix*, New York: Hyperion.

Fairchild, M. (1993), "Electric Ladyland." Liner notes for *Electric Ladyland* by the Jimi Hendrix Experience—MCAD-10895, 1993, compact disc.

Genovese, E.D. (1976), *Roll, Jordan, Roll: The World the Slaves Made*, New York: Vintage Books.

Glover, T. (1968), "Electric Ladyland," *Rolling Stone*, November 9, 1968. Available online: https://www.rollingstone.com/music/music-album-reviews/electric-ladyland-183197/ (accessed December 31, 2022).

Hansen, B. (1969), "Jimi Hendrix in Electric Ladyland," *Hit Parader*, April 1969. https://www.jimihendrixcollector.com/magazine-1969-1 (accessed December 18, 2022).

Melody Maker (1968), "Cover Girls Are Not Amused," *Melody Maker*, November 9, 1968.

Perry, J. (2004) *Electric Ladyland*, New York: Continuum.

Potash, C. (ed.), (1996), *The Jimi Hendrix Companion: Three Decades of Commentary*, New York: Schirmer Books.

Chapter 5: Amazing Journey: *Tommy* by the Who

Barnes, R. (1996), "Deaf, Dumb and Blind Boy." Liner notes for *Tommy* by the Who, MCA Records—MCAD-11417, 1996, compact disc.

Cohn, N. (1969), "'Tommy,' The Who's Pinball Opera," *The New York Times*, May 18, 1969.

Daltrey, R. (2018), *Thanks a Lot Mr. Kibblewhite: My Story*, New York: Henry Holt and Company.

Fricke, D., et al. (1987), "The Rolling Stone 20th Anniversary Interview: Pete Townshend," *Rolling Stone*, November–December 1987.

Green, R. (1969) "The Who: Tommy," *New Musical Express*, May 24, 1969. Available online: https://www.rocksbackpages.com/Library/Article/the-who-itommyi-track-stereo-613-0134-76s-1d (accessed November 4, 2022).

Marsh, D. (1983), *Before I Get Old: The Story of the Who*, London: Plexus.

Miles (1969), "The Who: Tommy (Track)," *International Times*, May 9, 1969. Available online: https://www.rocksbackpages.com/Library/Article/the-who-itommyi-track (accessed November 8, 2022).

Townshend, P. (2012), *Who I Am: Pete Townshend*, New York: Harper Perennial.

Wenner, J.S. (1968), "Pete Townshend Talks Mods, Recording, and Smashing Guitars," *Rolling Stone*, September 14, 1968.

Part 2: The Golden Era (1970-1974)

Chapter 6: God Knows Where We're Heading: Marvin Gaye's *What's Going On*

Aletti, V. (1971), "What's Going On," *Rolling Stone*, August 5, 1971.

Du Bois, W.E.B. (1999), *The Souls of Black Folk*, W.W. Norton & Company: New York.

Dyson, M.E. (2005), *Mercy, Mercy Me: The Art, Loves and Demons of Marvin Gaye*, Basic Civitas Books: New York.

Fong-Torres, B. (1972), "Honor Thy Brother-in-Law: A Visit with Marvin Gaye," *Rolling Stone*, April 27, 1972. Available online: https://www.rollingstone.com/music/music-news/honor-thy-brother-in-law-a-visit-with-marvin-gaye-244223/ (accessed October 19, 2022).

Jones, L. (1999), *Blues People: Negro Music in White America*, Quill: New York.

"Marvin Gaye on The Making of What's Going On (Interview)." FunkSoulTV, November 18, 2021. Video, https://www.youtube.com/watch?v=TjvINi0A_PY&t=18s.

Ritz, D. (1991), *Divided Soul: The Life of Marvin Gaye*, New York: Da Capo.

Robinson, S. (2000), "What's Going On." Liner Notes for *What's Going On* by Marvin Gaye, Motown—440 013 404-2, 2001, compact disc.

Warner, M., ed. (1999) *American Sermons: The Pilgrims to Martin Luther King Jr.*, New York: Library of America.

Chapter 7: I Am on a Lonely Road and I Am Traveling: Joni Mitchell's *Blue*

Crouse, T. (1971), "Blue," *Rolling Stone*, August 5, 1971. Available online: https://www.rollingstone.com/music/music-album-reviews/blue-104415/ (accessed January 10, 2023).

Crowe, C. (1979), "Joni Mitchell: The Rolling Stone Interview," *Rolling Stone*, July 26, 1979. Available online: https://jonimitchell.com/library/view.cfm?id=300 (accessed October 13, 2022).

Crowe, C. (2021), "Mitchell Opens up to Cameron Crowe about Singing Again, Lost Loves and 50 Years of 'Blue,'" *The Los Angeles Times*, June 20, 2021. Available online: https://www.latimes.com/entertainment-arts/music/story/2021-06-20/joni-mitchell-cameron-crowe-50th-anniversary-blue (accessed October 13, 2022).

Marom, M. (1974), "Face to Face," *McLean's*, June 1, 1974. Available online: https://jonimitchell.com/library/view.cfm?id=434 (accessed October 13, 2022).

Mossman, K. (2021), "'I Didn't Want Anyone to Know It Was Me': On Being Joni Mitchell's 'Carey,'" *The New Statesman*, December 17, 2021. Available online: https://www.newstatesman.com/katemossmaninterview/2021/12/joni-mitchell-carey-california-blue-lyrics-cary-raditz-interview (accessed October 13, 2022).

Rudis, A. (1971), "Joni's Album a Personal Statement," *The Cincinnati Enquirer*, August 15, 1971. Available online: https://jonimitchell.com/library/view.cfm?id=3482 (accessed October 14, 2022).

Valentine, P. (1972), "Joni Mitchell Interview," *Sounds Magazine*, June 3, 1972. Available online: https://jonimitchell.com/library/view.cfm?id=344 (accessed October 13, 2022).

Watts, M. (1983), "Joni Mitchell: The Public Life of a Private Property," *The Sunday Times*, April 17, 1983. Available online: https://jonimitchell.com/library/view.cfm?id=1629 (accessed October 14, 2022).

Willis, E. (1973), "Still Travelling: Joni Mitchell's 'Blue,'" *The New Yorker*, February 24, 1973. Available online: https://www.newyorker.com/magazine/1973/03/03/joni-mitchell-still-travelling (accessed October 14, 2022).

Yaffe, D. (2018), *Reckless Daughter: A Portrait of Joni Mitchell*, New York: Sarah Crichton Books.

Chapter 8: We'll Have Superman for President: Jethro Tull's *Thick as a Brick*

Eisen, B. (2012), Q&A: Jethro Tull's Ian Anderson on His 'Thick as a Brick' Sequel," Rolling Stone, April 4, 2012. Available online: https://www.rollingstone.com/music/music-news/qa-jethro-tulls-ian-anderson-on-his-thick-as-a-brick-sequel-58908/ (accessed November 15, 2022).

Gerson, B. (1972), "Thick as a Brick," *Rolling Stone*, June 22, 1972. Available online: https://www.rollingstone.com/music/music-album-reviews/thick-as-a-brick-248763/ (accessed January 19, 2022).

Jethro Tull, *Thick as a Brick (25th Anniversary Edition)*. Chrysalis Records Ltd.—7243 8 57705 2 4, 1998, compact disc, track 4.

Marsh, D. (1972), "Jethro Tull: Thick as a Brick," *Creem*, August 1972. Available online: https://www.rocksbackpages.com/Library/Article/jethro-tull-thick-as-a-brick (accessed January 19, 2022).

Welch, C. (1972), "Tull's 'Tommy'?" *Melody Maker*, March 11, 1972. Available online: http://www.tullpress.com/mm11mar72.htm (accessed December 31, 2022).

Chapter 9: Like a Regular Super Star: David Bowie's *The Rise and Fall of Ziggy Stardust and the Spiders from Mars*

Edwards, H., and T. Zanetta (1986), *Stardust: The David Bowie Story*, New York: McGraw-Hill Book Company.

Far Out staff, "Enter, Ziggy Stardust: David Bowie Introduces His Alien Rock Star in a Rare 1972 Radio Interview," *Far Out Magazine*, September 20, 2020. Available online: https://faroutmagazine.co.uk/david-bowie-ziggy-stardust-rare-interview-audio-1972/ (accessed May 25, 2023).

Miller, J. (1999), *Flowers in the Dustbin: The Rise of of Rock and Roll, 1947–1977*, New York: Simon & Schuster.

Chapter 10: And If the Band You're in Starts Playing Different Tunes: Pink Floyd's *The Dark Side of the Moon*

Harris, J. (2006), *The Dark Side of the Moon*, New York: Harper Perennial.

Mason, N. (2017), *Inside Out: A Personal History of Pink Floyd*, San Francisco: Chronicle Books.

Part 3: The Modern Era (1975–89)

Chapter 11: Tear the Roof off the Sucker: Parliament's *Mothership Connection*

Clinton, G., with B. Greenman (2014), *Brothas Be, Yo Like George, Ain't That Funkin' Kinda Hard on You?* New York: Atria Books.

Dery, M. (ed.) (1994), *Flame Wars: The Discourse of Cyberculture*, Durham: Duke University Press.
Mills, D., L. Alexander, T. Stanley and A. Wilson (1998), *For the Record: George Clinton and P-Funk: An Oral History*, New York: Avan Books.
Needs, K. (2014), *George Clinton & The Cosmic Odyssey of the P-Funk Empire*, New York: Omnibus Press.
Patoski, N. (1976), "The Bizarre World of George Clinton (Parliament/Funkadelic Drop the Funk Bomb on America)," *Phonograph Record*, December 1976.

Chapter 12: Fairy Tale High: Donna Summer's *Once Upon a Time. . .*

Aletti, V. (1977), "Disco File," *Record World*, November 12, 1977.
Jeffery, A. (2021), *Once Upon a Time*, New York: Bloomsbury.
Summer, D. (2003), *Ordinary Girl: The Journey*, New York: Villard.

Chapter 13: There's No Returning on This Chartered Trip Away: Hüsker Dü's *Zen Arcade*

Azerrad, M. (2002), *Our Band Could Be Your Life: Scenes from the American Indie Underground, 1981–1991*, New York: Little, Brown and Company/Back Bay Books.
Fricke, D. (1985), Zen Arcade, *Rolling Stone*, February 14, 1985. Available online: https://www.rollingstone.com/music/music-album-reviews/zen-arcade-205974/ (accessed July 22, 2022).
Fricke, D. (1985), "The Time Lords," *Melody Maker*, May 11, 1985. Available online: http://www.mmmm.eclipse.co.uk/press/HuskerDu-MM5-85.htm (accessed July 25, 2022).
Lee, C. (1984), "Hüsker Dü a Product of Minneapolis' Rock Scene," *The Los Angeles Times*, December 15, 1984. Available online: http://www.thirdav.com/zinestuff/lat1284.html (accessed July 22, 2022).
Mould, B., with M. Azerrad (2011), *See a Little Light: The Trail of Rage and Melody*, New York: Little, Brown and Company.
Rolling Stone, (1989), "100 Best Albums of the Eighties," *Rolling Stone*, November 16, 1989. Available online: https://www.rollingstone.com/music/music-lists/100-best-albums-of-the-eighties-150477/u2-war-68850 (accessed July 25, 2022).

Chapter 14: As Soon as You're Born You're Dying: Iron Maiden's *Seventh Son of the Seventh Son*

Dickinson, B. (2018), *What Does This Button Do?: Bruce Dickinson: An Autobiography*, New York: Dey Street.
Lawson, D. (2019), "How *Seventh Son of a Seventh Son* Lifted Iron Maiden to Heavy Metal Immortality, *Metal Hammer*, January 28, 2019. Available online: https://www.

loudersound.com/features/how-seventh-son-of-a-seventh-son-lifted-iron-maiden-to-heavy-metal-immortality (accessed March 9, 2022).

Ruskell, N. (2020), "Iron Maiden's *Seventh Son of a Seventh Son* Remains an Unimpeachably Perfect Album," *Kerrang!* November 23, 2020. Available online: https://www.kerrang.com/iron-maidens-seventh-son-of-a-seventh-son-remains-an-unimpeachably-perfect-album (accessed March 12, 2022).

Witter, S. (1988), "Welcome to the Machine: Iron Maiden," *New Musical Express*, March 12, 1988. Available online: https://www.rocksbackpages.com/Library/Article/welcome-to-the-machine-iron-maiden (accessed March 9, 2022).

Chapter 15: This Is a Recording: De La Soul's *3 Feet High and Rising*

Bellware, K. (2023), "De La Soul Finally Streams, a Scream for Beloved Hip-Hop Trio's Fans," *The Washington Post*, January 5, 2023. Available online: https://www.washingtonpost.com/lifestyle/2023/01/05/de-la-soul-streaming/ (accessed January 15, 2023).

CashBox, (1968), "The Turtles Present the Battle of the Bands," *CashBox*, November 26, 1968. Available online: https://worldradiohistory.com/hd2/IDX-Business/Music/Archive-Cash-Box-IDX/60s/1968/CB-1968-10-26-OCR-Page-0034.pdf#search=%22concept%20album%22 (accessed December 29, 2022).

Cohen, F. (2016), "De La Soul's Legacy Is Trapped in Digital Limbo," *The New York Times*, August 9, 2016. Available online: https://www.nytimes.com/2016/08/14/arts/music/de-la-soul-digital-albums.html (accessed May 4, 2022).

Coleman, B. (2007), *Check the Technique: Liner Notes for Hip-Hop Junkies*, New York: Villard Books.

O'Hagan, S. (1989), "De La Soul: Brothers from Another Planet," *New Musical Express*, October 21, 1989. Available online: https://www.rocksbackpages.com/Library/Article/de-la-soul-brothers-from-another-planet (accessed April 22, 2022).

Owen, F. (1989), "Sampling: Bite This," *SPIN*, November 1989. Available online: https://www.rocksbackpages.com/Library/Article/sampling-bite-this (accessed April 22, 2022).

Push, (1989), "De La Soul: 3 Feet High and Rising (Tommy Boy/Big Life)," *Melody Maker*, March 18, 1989. Available online: https://www.rocksbackpages.com/Library/Article/de-la-soul-i3-feet-high-and-risingi-tommy-boybig-life (accessed April 22, 2022).

Push, (1989), "De La Soul: Space Cadets," *Melody Maker*, April 8, 1989. Available online: https://www.rocksbackpages.com/Library/Article/de-la-soul-space-cadets (accessed April 22, 2022).

Serpick, E. (2009), "'3 Feet High and Rising': De La Soul's Track by Track Guide to Groundbreaking 1989 LP," Rolling Stone, June 3, 2009. Available online: https://www.rollingstone.com/feature/de-la-soul-1989-lp-3-feet-high-rising-track-by-track-guide-69292/amp/ (accessed May 2, 2022).

Weingarten, C.R. (2014), *It Takes a Nation of Millions to Hold Us Back*, New York: Bloomsbury.

Part 4: The Postmodern Era (1990–9)

Chapter 16: I Wanna Be Mesmerizing Too: Liz Phair's *Exile in Guyville*

Arnold, G. (2018), *Exile in Guyville*, New York: Bloomsbury.

Cummings, S. (1993), "Liz Phair Explodes the Canon," *LA Weekly*, July 16, 1993. Available online: https://www.lizphair.net/press/1993/liz-phair-explodes-the-canon/ (accessed July 30, 2022).

Ganz, C. (2010), "He Said, She Said: How Liz Phair Took the Rolling Stones to Guyville," *Rolling Stone*, May 21, 2010. Available online: https://www.rollingstone.com/music/music-news/he-said-she-said-how-liz-phair-took-the-rolling-stones-to-guyville-73618/ (accessed August 1, 2022).

Hopper, J. (2013), "Girly Show: The Oral History of Liz Phair's 'Exile in Guyville,'" *SPIN*, June 24, 2013. Available online: https://www.spin.com/2013/06/liz-phair-exile-in-guyville-oral-history-best-1993/2/ (accessed July 30, 2022).

"Liz Phair Interview plus Video and Live Performance." Lovers of 120 Minutes on MTV. May 18, 2023. Video, https://www.youtube.com/watch?v=DjAeCQmU7aM&t=183s

Marcus, G. (2014), "Real Life Rock Top Ten—June 2014," *The Believer*, June 1, 2014. Available online: https://www.thebeliever.net/real-life-rock-top-ten-52/ (accessed July 31, 2022).

Ozzi, D. (2018), "After 25 Years in Guyville, Liz Phair Is Glad to Be in Woman-World," *Vice*, April 30, 2018. Available online: https://www.vice.com/en/article/8xkp8z/after-25-years-in-guyville-liz-phair-is-glad-to-be-in-woman-world (accessed July 31, 2022).

Spanos, B. (2018), "Liz Phair Breaks Down 'Exile in Guyville,' Track by Track," *Rolling Stone*, May 4, 2018. Available online: https://www.rollingstone.com/music/music-features/liz-phair-breaks-down-exile-in-guyville-track-by-track-628853/ (accessed July 31, 2022).

Trucks, R. (2008), "Exile in Guyville: The Oral History," *The Village Voice*, June 17, 2008. Available online: https://www.villagevoice.com/2008/06/17/exile-in-guyville-the-oral-history/ (accessed August 5, 2022).

Chapter 17: I Am the Silencing Machine: Nine Inch Nails' *The Downward Spiral*

Chirazi, S. (1994), "Nine Inch Nails: Techno Fear!" *Kerrang!*, April 1994. Available online: https://www.rocksbackpages.com/Library/Article/nine-inch-nails-techno-fear (accessed September 6, 2022).

Garbarini (1994), "Pretty Hate Machinery—Trent Reznor Nails It Down," *Musician*, March 1994. Available online: http://www.nin-pages.de/1994_Musician_Maerz_english.htm (accessed September 15, 2022).

Gold, J. (1994), "Nine Inch Nails: Love It to Death," *Rolling Stone*, September 8, 1994. Available online: https://www.rollingstone.com/music/music-news/nine-inch-nails-love-it-to-death-2-96265/ (accessed September 6, 2022).

Hilburn, R. (1994), "Album Review: Nine Inch Nails, 'The Downward Spiral,'" *The Los Angeles Times*, March 6, 1994. Available online: https://www.latimes.com/archives/la-xpm-1994-03-06-ca-30539-story.html (accessed September 7, 2022).

Kott, G. (1994), "Nine Inch Nails, The Downward Spiral," The Chicago Tribune, March 6, 1994. Available online: https://www.chicagotribune.com/news/ct-xpm-1994-03-06-9403060310-story.html (accessed September 7, 2022).

O'Dair, B. (ed.) (1997), *Trouble Girls: The* Rolling Stone *Book of Women in Rock*, New York: Rolling Stone Press.

Rickly, G. (2004), "Geoff Rickly Interviews Trent Reznor, *Alternative Press*, June 26, 2004. Available online: https://www.theninhotline.com/archives/articles/manager/display_article.php?id=11 (accessed September 24, 2022).

Steinke, D. (1994), "This Little Piggie Went Argo," *SPIN*, July 1994. Available online: http://www.nin-pages.de/1994_Spin_Juli_english.htm (accessed September 15, 2022).

Weisbard, E. (1996), "Trent Reznor: Sympathy for the Devil," *SPIN*, February 1996. Available online: https://www.rocksbackpages.com/Library/Article/trent-reznor-sympathy-for-the-devil (accessed September 6, 2022).

Wilde, L. (1994), "Wigged Out!" *Melody Maker*, June 11, 1994. Available online: http://www.nin-pages.de/1994_Melody_Maker_Juni.htm (accessed September 15, 2022).

Wiederhorn, J. (1994), "Going Down with Trent Reznor," *Circus*, May 1, 1994. Available online: https://www.theninhotline.com/archives/articles/manager/display_article.php?id=568 (accessed September 23, 2022).

Chapter 18: I Feel Like Death Is Fuckin' Callin' Me: Notorious B.I.G.'s *Ready to Die*

Fernando, Jr., S.H. (1995), "The Notorious B.I.G. Is Living Large," *Rolling Stone*, June 1, 1995. Available online: https://www.rollingstone.com/music/music-news/the-notorious-b-i-g-is-living-large-193171/ (accessed May 29, 2022).

Michael, S. (1997), "Last Exit from Brooklyn: The Notorious B.I.G.," *SPIN*, May 1, 1997.

Nelson, H. (1994), "Hitting the B.I.G. Time," *Billboard*, September 17, 1994, p. 30.

Shortie, (1994), "The Notorious B.I.G.: Ready to Die," *The Source*, October 1994, p. 79. Available online: https://pressrewind.files.wordpress.com/2007/03/biggie_source1094.jpg (accessed May 31, 2022).

Tinsley, J. (2022), *It Was All A Dream: Biggie and the World That Made Him*, New York: Abrams Press.

Touré, (1994), "Biggie Smalls, Rap's Man of the Moment," *The New York Times*, December 18, 1994, p. 42. Available online: https://www.nytimes.com/1994/12/18/arts/pop-music-biggie-smalls-rap-s-man-of-the-moment.html?searchResultPosition=2 (accessed June 4, 2022).

Chapter 19: A Handshake of Carbon Monoxide: Radiohead's *OK Computer*

Aizlewood, J. (2022), *Radiohead: Life in a Glasshouse*, London: Palazzo Editions Ltd.

Footman, T. (2007), *Radiohead: Welcome to the Machine: OK Computer and the Death of the Classic Album*, Surrey: Chrome Dreams.

Greene, A. (2017), "Radiohead's 'OK Computer': An Oral History," *Rolling Stone*, June 15, 2017. https://www.rollingstone.com/music/music-features/radioheads-ok-computer-an-oral-history-196156/ (accessed July 10, 2022).

Kemp, M. (1997), "Radiohead: *OK Computer* (Capitol)," *Rolling Stone*, July 10, 1997. Available online: https://www.rocksbackpages.com/Library/Article/radiohead-iok-computeri-capitol- (accessed July 10, 2022).

Oldham, J. (1998), Radiohead: "OK Computer (Parlophone)," *NME*, January 1, 1998. Available online: https://web.archive.org/web/20000817181703/http://www.nme.com/reviews/reviews/19980101000014reviews.html (accessed July 10, 2022).

Petrusich, A. (2017), "The Whispered Warnings of Radiohead's 'OK Computer' Have Come True," *The New Yorker*, June 23, 2017. Available online: https://www.newyorker.com/culture/culture-desk/the-whispered-warnings-of-radioheads-ok-computer-have-come-true (accessed July 10, 2022).

Randall, M. (1998), "The Golden Age of Radiohead," *Guitar World*, April 1, 1998. Available online: https://www.rocksbackpages.com/Library/Article/the-golden-age-of-radiohead (accessed July 10, 2022).

SPIN (1998), "The 20 Best Albums of '97," *SPIN*, Volume 14, Number 1, January 1998, p. 86.

Chapter 20: I Chose to Use My Heart: Lauryn Hill's *The Miseducation of Lauryn Hill*

Farley, C.J. (1999), "Music: Rhythm Nation: Lauryn Hill," *TIME*, February 8, 1999. Available online: https://content.time.com/time/subscriber/article/0,33009,990180,00.html (accessed June 13, 2022).

Furman, L., and Furman, E. (1999), *Heart of Soul: The Lauryn Hill Story*, Ballantine Books: New York.

Morgan, J. (2018), *She Begat This: 20 Years of* The Miseducation of Lauryn Hill, New York: Atria Books.

Woodson, C.G. (1933), *The Mis-Education of the Negro*, Dover Publications, Inc.: New York.

Part 5: The New Millennium (2000-2016)

Chapter 21: I Been Taken for Lost and Gone and Unknown for a Long, Long Time: *Brian Wilson Presents SMiLE*

Christgau, R. (2004), "Smile," *Rolling Stone*, October 14, 2004. Available online: https://www.rollingstone.com/music/music-album-reviews/smile-103518/ (accessed August 12, 2022).

Heylin, C. (ed.) (2000), *The Da Capo Book of Rock & Roll Writing*, New York: Da Capo Press.

"Inside Pop – The Rock Revolution," Drksrfr, March 16, 2012. Video, 45:07:00, https://www.youtube.com/watch?v=afU76JJcquI

Simmons, S. (2004), "Brian Wilson: Smile? Don't Mind if I Do. . .," *Mojo*, March 2004. Available online: https://www.rocksbackpages.com/Library/Article/brian-wilson-smile-dont-mind-if-i-do (accessed August 12, 2022).

Wilson, B. (2016), *I Am Brian Wilson*, New York: Da Capo Press.

Chapter 22: All Across the Alien Nation: Green Day's *American Idiot*

Baltin, S. (2004), "Green Day Craft Punk Opera," *Rolling Stone*, May 26, 2004. Available online: https://www.rollingstone.com/music/music-news/green-day-craft-punk-opera-252158/ (accessed June 19, 2022).

Dansby, A. (2004), "Green Day Ready 'Idiot,'" *Rolling Stone*, May 14, 2004. Available online: https://www.rollingstone.com/music/music-news/green-day-ready-idiot-233754/ (accessed June 19, 2022).

Dixon, G. (2004), "Still Punk After All These Years," *Globe & Mail*, September 27, 2004. Available online: https://go.gale.com/ps/retrieve.do?tabID=T004&resultListType=RESULT_LIST&searchResultsType=SingleTab&hitCount=19&searchType=AdvancedSearchForm&currentPosition=1&docId=GALE%7CA122539381&docType=Article&sort=Pub+Date+Forward+Chron&contentSegment=ZONE-Exclude-FT&prodId=AONE&pageNum=1&contentSet=GALE%7CA122539381&searchId=R6&userGroupName=loc_main&inPS=true (accessed June 19, 2022).

Ganz, C. (2004), "Intimate Portrait: Billie Joe Armstrong," *SPIN*, September 10, 2004. Available online: https://www.spin.com/2004/09/intimate-portrait-billie-joe-armstrong/ (accessed June 19, 2022).

Goodridge, M. (2004), "'Faggot' Phobia," *The Advocate*, November 23, 2004. Available online: https://go.gale.com/ps/retrieve.do?tabID=T003&resultListType=RESULT_LIST&searchResultsType=SingleTab&hitCount=319&searchType=AdvancedSearchForm&currentPosition=77&docId=GALE%7CA126164503&docType=Article&sort=Pub+Date+Forward+Chron&contentSegment=ZONE-Exclude-FT&prodId=AONE&pageNum=4&contentSet=GALE%7CA126164503&searchId=R3&userGroupName=loc_main&inPS=true (accessed June 19, 2022).

Hendrickson, M. (2005), "Green Day and the Palace of Wisdom," *Rolling Stone*, February 24, 2005. Available online: https://www.rollingstone.com/music/music-news/green-day-and-the-palace-of-wisdom-245640/ (accessed June 19, 2022).

Lynskey, D. (2004), "Green Day, American Idiot," *The Guardian*, September 17, 2004. Available online: https://web.archive.org/web/20140118223141/http://www.theguardian.com/music/2004/sep/17/popandrock.shopping2 (accessed June 19, 2022).

Murfett, A. (2004), "American Idiot," *The Age*, October 1, 2004. Available online: https://go.gale.com/ps/retrieve.do?tabID=T004&resultListType=RESULT_LIST&searchResultsType=SingleTab&hitCount=396&searchType=AdvancedSearchForm&currentPosition=16&docId=GALE%7CA285009424&docType=Brief+article&sort=Pub+Date+Forward+Chron&contentSegment=ZONE-Exclude-FT&prodId=AONE&pageNum=1&contentSet=GALE%7CA285009424&searchId=R8&userGroupName=loc_main&inPS=true (accessed June 19, 2022).

Papademas, A. (2004), "Green Day: P*ssd Off and Better Than Ever," *SPIN*, November 2004 Available online: https://www.spin.com/2004/11/green-day-pssed-and-better-ever/ (accessed June 19, 2022).

Sheffield, R. (2004), "American Idiot," *Rolling Stone*, September 30, 2004. Available online: https://www.rollingstone.com/music/music-album-reviews/american-idiot-184555/ (accessed June 19, 2022).

Spitz, M. (2006), *Nobody Likes You: Inside the Turbulent Life, Times, and Music of Green Day*, New York: Hyperion.

Watson, I. (2004), "Green Day: American Idiot (Reprise)," *The Times*, September 18, 2004. Available online: https://go.gale.com/ps/retrieve.do?tabID=T004&resultListType=RESULT_LIST&searchResultsType=SingleTab&hitCount=396&searchType=AdvancedSearchForm&currentPosition=8&docId=GALE%7CA122387567&docType=Brief+article&sort=Pub+Date+Forward+Chron&contentSegment=ZONE-Exclude-FT&prodId=AONE&pageNum=1&contentSet=GALE%7CA122387567&searchId=R5&userGroupName=loc_main&inPS=true (accessed June 19, 2022).

Chapter 23: If You Want to Be Free: Janelle Monáe's *The ArchAndroid*

Calvert, J. (2010), "Janelle Monáe: A New Pioneer of Afrofuturism," *The Quietus*, September 2, 2010. Available online: https://www.rocksbackpages.com/Library/Article/janelle-mone-a-new-pioneer-of-afrofuturism (accessed July 3, 2022).

Cole, M. (2010), "Janelle Monáe: The ArchAndroid (Suites II and III of IV)," *Slant*, May 18, 2010. Available online: https://web.archive.org/web/20141014073929/http://www.slantmagazine.com/music/review/janelle-mon%c3%a1e-the-archandroid-suites-ii-and-iii-of-iv (accessed July 4, 2022).

Fault Magazine, "Janelle Monáe: This Is Your Fault," *Fault Magazine*, April 23, 2018. Available online: https://fault-magazine.com/2018/04/janelle-monae-covers-fault-magazine-issue-28/ (accessed July 3, 2022).

Favreau, A. (2021), *The ArchAndroid*, New York: Bloomsbury Academic.

Hoard, C. (2010), "Artist of the Week: Janelle Monáe," *Rolling Stone*, June 30, 2010. Available online: https://www.rollingstone.com/music/music-news/artist-of-the-week-janelle-monae-186564/ (accessed July 3, 2022).

Kot, G. (2010), "Janelle Monáe: The Interview: I Identify with Androids," The Chicago *Tribune*, May 26, 2010. Available online: https://web.archive.org/web/20131020021441/http://leisureblogs.chicagotribune.com/turn_it_up/2010/05/janelle-monae-the-interview-i-identify-with-androids.html (accessed July 4, 2022).

Lewis, P. (2010), "Janelle Monáe: Funky Sensation," *Blues and Soul*, October 9, 2010. Available online: https://web.archive.org/web/20101009211134/http://www.bluesandsoul.com/feature/554/janelle_monae_funky_sensation (accessed July 4, 2022).

McCarter, J. (2010), "Pop Goes the Art House," *Newsweek*, June 7, 2010. Available online: https://web.p.ebscohost.com/ehost/detail/detail?vid=15&sid=b6bd2f12-e040-4ef0-a73c-8134468b399e%40redis&bdata=JkF1dGhUeXBlPWlwLGNvb2tpZSx1cmwsd WlkJnNpdGU9ZWhvc3QtbGl2ZSZzY29wZT1zaXRl#AN=504440529&db=brd (accessed July 3, 2022).

Mossman, K. (2013), "Janelle Monáe: 'I'm a Time Traveler. I Have Been to Lots of Diffeeent Places," *The Guardian*, June 29, 2013. Available online: https://www.theguardian.com/music/2013/jun/30/janelle-monae-electric-lady-album-interview (accessed July 7, 2022).

Spanos, B. (2018), "Janelle Monáe Frees Herself," *Rolling Stone*, April 26, 2018. Available online: https://www.rollingstone.com/music/music-features/janelle-monae-frees-herself-629204/ (accessed July 3, 2022).

Street, M. (2022), "Janelle Monáe Comes Out as Nonbinary: I Am Everything," *The Advocate*, April 21, 2022. Available online: https://www.advocate.com/people/2022/4/21/janelle-monae-comes-out-nonbinary-i-am-everything (accessed July 3, 2022).

Chapter 24: The One in Front of the Gun Lives Forever: Kendrick Lamar's *good kid, m.A.A.d city*

Ahmed, I. (2012), "The Making of Kendrick Lamar's "good kid, m.A.A.d City," *Complex*, October 23, 2012. Available online: https://www.complex.com/music/2012/10/the-making-of-kendrick-lamars-good-kid-maad-city/ (accessed June 30, 2022).

Badu, E. (2013), "Kendrick Lamar by Erykah Badu," *Interview*, April 23, 2013. Available online: https://www.interviewmagazine.com/music/kendrick-lamar (accessed June 30, 2022).

Hiatt, B. (2017), "Kendrick Lamar: The Rolling Stone Interview," *Rolling Stone*, August 9, 2017. Available online: https://www.rollingstone.com/music/music-features/kendrick-lamar-the-rolling-stone-interview-199817/ (accessed June 26, 2022).

Hopper, J. (2012), "Kendrick Lamar: Not Your Average Everyday Rap Savoir," *SPIN*, October 9, 2012. Available online: https://www.spin.com/2012/10/kendrick-lamar-not-your-average-everyday-rap-savior/ (accessed June 29, 2022).

Lewis, M.M. (2021), *Promise That You Will Sing About Me*, New York: St. Martin's Press.

Reeves, M., et al. (2022), "The 50 Greatest Concept Albums of All Time," *Rolling Stone*, October 12, 2022. Available online: https://www.rollingstone.com/music/music-lists/best-concept-albums-1234604040/styx-5-1234604537/ (accessed December 30, 2022).

Chapter 25: Won't Let My Freedom Rot in Hell: Beyoncé's *Lemonade*

Gottesman, T. (2016), "EXCLUSIVE: Beyoncé Wants to Change the Conversation," *ELLE*, April 4, 2016. Available online: https://www.elle.com/fashion/a35286/beyonce-elle-cover-photos/ (accessed July 19, 2022).

Lozano, K. (2016), "James Blake Reveals He Ignored Beyoncé's Lyrics and Turned Down Drake," *Pitchfork*, July 13, 2016. Available online: https://pitchfork.com/news/66772-james-blake-reveals-he-ignored-beyonce-lyrics-and-turned-down-drake/ (accessed July 21, 2022).

NPR Staff (2016), "Jack White on Detroit, Beyoncé and Where His Songs Come From," NPR, September 10, 2016. Available online: https://www.npr.org/2016/09/10/493177019/jack-white-on-detroit-beyonc-and-where-songs-come-from (accessed July 19, 2022).

Russonello, G. (2017), "Beyoncé's and Adele's Grammy Speeches: Transcripts," *The New York Times*, February 12, 2017. Available online: https://www.nytimes.com/2017/02/12/arts/music/beyonce-speech-grammys-trump.html?searchResultPosition=4 (accessed July 21, 2022).

Sheffield, R. (2006), "Lemonade," *Rolling Stone*, April 25, 2016. Available online: https://www.rollingstone.com/music/music-album-reviews/lemonade-204663/ (accessed July 17, 2022).

Spanos, B. (2016), "Beyoncé Releases New Album 'Lemonade' on Tidal," *Rolling Stone*, April 24, 2016. Available online: https://www.rollingstone.com/music/music-news/beyonce-releases-new-album-lemonade-on-tidal-57155/ (accessed July 17, 2022).

Taraborrelli, J.R. (2016), *Becoming Beyoncé: The Untold Story*, New York: Grand Central Publishing.

Conclusion: When Everybody Who Is Lonely Will Be Free

Bromell, N. (2000). *Tomorrow Never Knows: Rock and Psychedelics in the 1960s*, Chicago: University of Chicago Press.

Caulfield, K. (2023). "Bad Bunny's 'Un Verano Sin Ti' Is Luminate's Top Album of 2022 in U.S.," Billboard, January 11, 2023. Available online: https://www.billboard.com/

music/chart-beat/2022-us-year-end-music-report-luminate-top-album-bad-bunny-un-verano-sin-ti-1235196736/ (accessed January 27, 2023).

Gilmore, M. (1998). *Night Beat: A Shadow History of Rock & Roll*. New York: Random House, Inc.

Norman, P. (1981), *Shout!: The Beatles in Their Generation*, New York: Fireside.

Valentine, P. (1972), "Joni Mitchell Interview," *Sounds Magazine*, June 3, 1972. Available online: https://jonimitchell.com/library/view.cfm?id=344 (accessed October 13, 2022).

Index

3 Feet High and Rising (De La Soul), 124–31, 218, 219
 "Buddy", 129
 "Can U Keep a Secret", 126
 "Change in Speak", 126
 "Contestant #1, do you have the answers?", 126
 "Contestant #4, do you have the answers?", 129
 "D.A.I.S.Y. Age", 129–30
 "De La Orgee", 129
 "Description", 129
 ending, 130
 "Eye Know", 127, 130
 game show concept, 124–5
 "Ghetto Thang", 127
 "I Can Do Anything (Delacratic)", 129
 "Jenifa Taught Me (Derwin's Revenge)", 127, 128
 "The Magic Number", 126, 130, 131
 "Me, Myself and I", 129, 130
 "Okay Contestant #2, do you have the answers?", 128
 opening, 125–6
 "Plug Tunin", 130
 reviews, 127
 "Say No Go", 128, 130
 skits, 126, 127–8, 129
 "Take It Of,", 127–8
 "This Is a Recording 4 Living in a Fulltime Era (L.I.F.E.)", 129
 "Transmitting Live from Mars", 124, 127
 "Tread Water", 128
 use of samples, 125
21st Century Breakdown (Green Day), 190
120 Minutes, 135

A Love Supreme (Coltrane), 7
"A Quick One While He's Away", (The Who), 72, 74
"A Whiter Shade of Pale" (Moody Blues), 25

The Advocate, 185
Afrofuturism, 46, 98, 193–8
Aftermath (Rolling Stones), 16, 22
Aftermath Entertainment, 200
The Age, 190
album as, show the, 17–8
album concept, 6
album-side song length, 72
Aletti, Vince, 62, 104
Alice's Restaurant (Guthrie), 72
alienation, 158–64
"All Along the Watchtower" (Hendrix), 45
American Idiot (Green Day), 6, 184–90, 218, 220, 222
 "American Idiot", 185
 "Are We the Waiting", 187
 "Boulevard of Broken Dreams", 187
 Broadway musical version, 190
 "Extraordinary Girl", 188
 "Give Me Novacaine", 188
 "Holiday", 186–7
 "Homecoming", 189
 "Jesus of Suburbia", 185–6, 189
 "Letterbomb", 188
 loss of focus, 190
 reviews, 190
 "She's a Rebel", 188
 "Wake Me Up When September Ends", 188–9
 "Whatsername", 189
 wooden drum interlude, 188
Americana, 178–83
Anderson, Ian, 72, 73–4, 74–5, 77, 78
Angelou, Maya, 204
antiheroes, 218
Aqualung (Jethro Tull), 73
The ArchAndroid (Monáe), 192–8, 220, 222
 "57821", 197
 "BabopbyeYa", 197
 "Cold War", 194, 198

"Come Alive (War of the Roses)", 195
concept, 195
"Dance or Die", 194
"Faster", 194
"Locked Inside", 194
"Make the Bus", 196
"Mushrooms & Roses", 195–6
"Neon Gumbo", 195
"Neon Valley Street", 196
"Oh, Maker", 195
origins, 192–3
release, 193
reviews, 192, 196
"Say You'll Go", 197
"Sir Greendown". 194
status, 198
"Suite II Overture", 193–4
"Suite III Overture", 196
"Tightrope (feat. Big Boi)", 195, 198
title, 192
"Wondaland", 196
Are You Experienced (Hendrix), 40
arena-ready rock, 189
Armstrong, Billie Joe, 184–5, 186, 187, 188, 190
Arnold, Gina, 138
artistic space, 22
artwork, 8–9
Asher, Tony, 182
autobiography, 109, 151–7, 166–72, 208–14, 218, 220
Axis: Bold as Love (Hendrix), 40
Azerrad, Michael, 115

Baez, Joan, 99
Barlow, Barriemore, 75
Barnes, Kevin, 196
Barnes, Mike, 29–30
Barrett, Roger "Syd", 86, 91, 92
Beach Boys, 1, 8–9, 15, 16, 22, 162–3, 177, 183, 189
Beatles, 8, 9–10, 60, 65, 113–4, 143, 161, 162, 210, 222
"Penny Lane", 16
Revolver, 15, 16, 216
Rubber Soul, 8
Sgt. Pepper's Lonely Hearts Club Band, 1–2, 15–22, 24, 32–4, 103, 124, 182, 216–8, 219

"She's Leaving Home.", 1
"Strawberry Fields Forever", 16
White Album, 41
Beck, 4
Beethoven, Ludwig van, 24
Beggars Banquet (Rolling Stones), 73, 118
Bellotte, Pete, 103–4, 105
Benson, Renaldo, 59, 60
Bergman, Ingmar, 118–9
Berliner, Emile, 3
Berry, Chuck, 24, 99
Beyoncé
  Beyoncé, 208
  Lemonade, 208–14, 218, 220, 222
Beyoncé (Beyoncé), 208
Billboard, 5–6, 6, 30, 39, 63, 70, 78, 86, 89, 104, 108, 109, 122, 141, 143, 149, 154, 155, 168, 187, 189, 198, 206, 214
Black Flag, 110
#BlackLivesMatter movement, 203, 214
Blake, James, 212
Blake, Peter, 21
Blige, Mary J., 169–70
Blonde on Blonde (Dylan), 16, 72
Blue (Mitchell), 65–71, 217, 220
  "A Case of You", 69–70, 70
  "All I Really Want", 66–7, 70
  "Blue", 68, 70
  "California", 68, 70
  "Carey", 67–8, 70
  emotion, 70
  inspiration, 66–7
  introspection, 66, 69–70
  "The Last Time I Saw Richard", 70
  "Little Green", 67, 70
  "My Old Man", 67, 70
  reviews, 70–1
  "River", 69, 70
  status, 70–1
  "This Flight Tonight", 68–9, 70
Bob Marley Museum, 167
Bogart, Paul, 104
Bolan, Marc, 82
Book of Revelations, 119
Boston Orpheum, 183
Bowie, David, 147

The Rise and Fall of Ziggy Stardust and the Spiders from Mars, 79–85, 217–8, 218, 220
"Space Oddity", 79
Boyz in the Hood (film), 201
Brailey, Jerome, 100–1
Brian Wilson Presents SMiLE, 178
Broken (Nine Inch Nails), 143–4
"Broken Home, Broken Heart", 111
Bromell, Nick, 218–9
Brown, James, 95
Browning, Tod, 34
Bush, George W., 187

Calvert, John, 193
Canned Applause, 162
Cannon, Geffrey, 46
capitalism, 89
Capitol Records, 5, 6, 177, 178
car songs, 42
caricature, 117
Casablanca Records, 104
Cash, Johnny, 4, 7, 148
CashBox, 1–2, 124
Cassady, Jack, 42
Castaneda, Carlos, *The Teachings of Don Juan*, 58
Cavallo, Rob, 185
change, 200–6
The Chicago Tribune, 2, 149
Chocolate City (Parliament), 100
Christgau, Robert, 182
Christmas songs, 69
The Cincinnati Enquirer, 65
"Clair De Lune" (Debussy), 197
Clapton, Eric, 34
clarity, 104–5
Clarke, Tony, 25–6, 29
Cleveland, Al, 59, 60
Clinton, George, 95–6, 98, 99–100, 100, 101
The Clones of Dr. Funkenstein (Parliament), 96, 101
Cohn, Nik, 50, 51
Cole, Nat King, *Wild Is Love*, 6, 7
Coleman, Ray, 84
Collins, Bootsy, 96, 100
Coltrane, John, *A Love Supreme*, 7

Columbia Records, 5, 166
Columbine High School massacre, 147
Combs, Sean, 151–2, 156
comic book heroes, 76
community, 219–21
compact discs, 24
concept albums
    change, 221–2
    definition, 2, 8–9, 57
    earliest use of term, 2
    implications, 2–3
    key element, 10
    origin, 1–3
    right to have, 197–8
    roots, 3–8
conceptual rock, 117
conceptual structure, 1
confession, 166–72
conformity, 197–8
contradiction, 195
Cooke, Sam, 99
Cool, Tré, 184
counter-culture movement, 16, 32, 33, 39
country music, 6–7
Cradle Will Rock, The, 3
creativity, 60
Creem, 78
Crouse, Timothy, 70–1
Cummings, Sue, 141
cynicism, 33, 70

Da Capo (Love), 72
Daltrey, Roger, 47, 48–9
The Dark Side of the Moon (Pink Floyd), 86–92, 218, 220
    "Any Colour You Like", 90, 92
    "Brain Damage", 88, 90–1, 92
    "Breathe", 88, 89, 92
    chart run, 86
    concepts, 92
    cover, 92
    "Eclipse", 91–2, 92
    "The Great Gig in the Sky", 89, 92
    "Money", 88, 89, 92
    "On the Run", 88, 92
    opening, 87–8
    planning, 87
    sound, 88

"Time", 88–9, 92
"Us and Them", 89–90, 92
wordless vocal, 89
David, Marlo, 193
Davies, Ron, 81
Davis, Angela, 138
Davis, Miles, 7
Davis, Ray, 100
Dawes, Chrisopher, 127
Days of Future Passed (Moody Blues), 24–30, 218, 219
  closing poem, 28–9
  "Dawn: Is a Feeling", 26–7
  "The Day Begins", 26
  fusion of classical and rock music, 29–30
  inspiration, 25–6
  liner notes, 29
  "Lunch Break: Peak Hour", 27
  "The Morning: Another Morning", 27
  "Nights in White Satin", 28–9, 30
  opening sound, 26
  "The Sunset", 28
  "Time to Get Away", 27–8
  total album concept, 30
De La Soul, *3 Feet High and Rising*, 124–31, 218, 219
death, 89, 122–3, 155, 156, 156–7, 163, 216
Debussy, Claude, "Clair De Lune", 197
Decca Records, 25, 29
Dery, Mark, 98
dialogue, 135–41
Dick, Alan, 122–3
Dickinson, Bruce, 117–8, 119, 120–1, 122
Dirnt, Mike, 184
Dirty Computer (Monáe), 198
disco, 104
dislocation, 159
The Downward Spiral (Nine Inch Nails), 143–9, 220
  "A Warm Place", 147
  "The Becoming", 146
  "Big Man with a Gun", 146–7
  "Closer", 143, 145–6, 148
  concept, 143–4
  "The Downward Spiral", 148
  ending, 148
  "Eraser", 147
  "Heresy", 145
  "Hurt", 148, 149
  "I Do Not Want This", 146
  inspiration, 144
  "March of the Pigs", 145
  "Mr. Self Destruct", 144
  "Piggy", 144–5
  "Reptile", 147
  reviews, 148–9
  "Ruiner", 146
  satire, 146–7
  song structure, 147
  themes, 144
drugs and drug use, 10, 16, 18, 30, 32–3, 52, 59, 60, 96, 114, 128, 151, 155, 188, 202, 203, 216, 219
Du Bois, W.E.B., 62–3
duality, 195
Dust Bowl Ballads (Guthrie), 4
Dylan, Bob, 4, 8, 9–10, 45, 160
  Blonde on Blonde, 16, 72
  "Sad-Eyed Lady of the Lowlands", 72
  Self-Portrait, 3
Dyson, Eric, 59–60
dystopia, 105, 114, 192–8

Edge, Graeme, 24, 26, 28, 29
Edison, Thomas, 3
education, 166–72
The Education of Sonny Carson (film), 166
The Electric Lady (Monáe), 198
Electric Ladyland (Hendrix), 40–6, 98, 217, 218, 219
  "…And the Gods Made Love", 41
  "1983 (A Merman I Should Turn to Be)", 43–4
  "All Along the Watchtower", 45
  "Burning of the Midnight Lamp", 43
  "Come on (And Let the Good Times Roll)", 43
  cover, 45–6
  "Crosstown Traffic", 41
  "Gypsy Eyes", 43
  "Have You Ever Been (to Electric Lady-land)?", 41
  "House Burning Down", 44–5
  "Little Miss Strange", 42–3
  "Long Hot Summer Night", 43

"Rainy Day, Dream Away", 43, 44
reviews, 46
"Still Raining, Still Dreaming", 44
structure, 41
"Voodoo Child (Slight Return)", 45
"Voodoo Chile", 42
Elijah, gospel of, 99
Ellington, Duke, 7
emotion, 70
endless road motif, 43
Entertainment Weekly, 214
Entwistle, John, 48
Essence, 172
estrangement, 218
Exile in Guyville (Phair), 135–41, 143, 218, 220
  "6'1'", 136
  "Canary", 138
  concept, 136
  "Dance of the Seven Veils", 137
  dialogue, 135–41
  "Divorce Song", 139
  "Explain It to Me", 138
  final words, 140
  "Flower", 139
  "Fuck and Run", 138–9
  "Glory", 137
  "Gunshy", 140
  "Help Me Mary", 136–7
  influence, 141
  inspiration, 135–6
  interactivity, 136
  "Johnny Sunshine", 140
  "Mesmerizing", 138
  "Never Said", 137
  opening, 136
  reviews, 140–1
  "Shatter", 139
  "Soap Star Joe", 137–8
  "Strange Loop", 140
  "Stratford-on-Guy", 140
Exile on Main St (Rolling Stones), 74, 78
  "All Down the Line", 140
  "Casino Boogie, 137
  Exile in Guyville (Phair) dialogue with, 135–41
  "Happy", 138–9
  "I Just Want to See His Face", 139
  "Let It Loose", 139
  "Rip This Joint", 136–7
  "Rocks Off", 136, 138
  "Shake Your Hips,", 137
  "Shine a Light", 140
  "Soul Survivor", 140
  "Stop Breaking Down", 140
  "Sweet Black Angel", 138
  "Sweet Virginia", 137–8
  "Torn and Frayed", 138
  "Tumbling Dice", 137
  "Turd on the Run", 139
  "Ventilator Blues", 139

fairytales, 103–9
fascism, 187
feminism, 210–1
focus, loss of, 190
fragmented technique, 177
Freak Out! (Zappa), 72
Freaks (film), 34
free-association, 61
freedom, 66–7, 197–8, 198, 214, 217–8
Fugees, the, 166
Funkadelic, 95–6, 102, 129
Funkentelechy vs. the Placebo Syndrome (Parliament), 102

gangsta rap, 200–6
Gates, Henry Louis, Jr, 153
Gaye, Frankie, 60
Gaye, Marvin, 15
  "I Heard It Through the Grapevine", 58
  What's Going On, 57–64, 71, 218, 219–20
gender, 135–41, 198
Genesis, 73
Genovese, Eugene D., 42
Gerson, Ben, 77–8
Gilmour, David, 86, 89, 90
Glover, Tony, 41
Godrich, Nigel, 158, 162
Gold, Jonathan, 143
Goldstein, Richard, 24
good kid, m.A.A.d city (Lamar), 200–6, 218, 220, 222
  "The Art of Peer Pressure", 202, 203, 204, 205

"Backseat Freestyle", 202, 205
"Bitch Don't Kill My Vibe", 201–2, 205, 206
chronological order, 205–6
"Compton", 205, 206
cover, 201
"m.A.A.d. city", 203–4, 206
"Money Trees", 202, 206
opening, 201
"Poetic Justice", 203, 205, 206
"Real", 205, 206
realism, 201
release, 206
reviews, 206
"Sherane a.k.a Master Splinter's Daughter", 201, 205, 206
"Sing About Me, I'm Dying of Thirst.", 204–5, 206
"Swimming Pools (Drank)", 204, 206
"Good Vibrations" (Beach Boys), 177
Goodman, Benny, 7
Gordy, Berry, 57, 58
grand theater, 79–85
Great American Songbook, The, 4
Great Migration, the, 63
Green, Richard, 52
Green Day
    21st Century Breakdown, 190
    American Idiot, 6, 184–90, 218, 220, 222
Greenwood, Colin, 158, 159
Greenwood, Jonny, 158, 159, 160
The Guardian, 46, 190
gun-as-phallic imagery, 146–7
Gunfighter Ballads and Trail Songs (Robbins), 7
Guthrie, Arlo, *Alice's Restaurant*, 72
Guthrie, Woody, 4, 9

Hair, 103
Hammond, Jeffrey, 75
Hanna, Kathleen, 188
Hansen, Barret, 41
Harris, Steve, 117–8, 118, 119, 120–1, 121, 122
Harrison, George, 16, 19–20, 33
Hart, Grant, 110, 112, 113, 113–4, 115
Hayward, Justin, 24, 25, 27, 28–9
heavy metal, 117

Hendrix, Jimi, 97
    Are You Experienced, 40
    Axis: Bold as Love, 40
    Electric Ladyland, 40–6, 98, 217, 218, 219
high art, 52
high fidelity, 25
Hill, Laury
    The Miseducation of Lauryn Hill, 166–72, 218, 220
    MTV Unplugged No. 2.0, 172
hip-hop, 124, 125, 130–1, 171
Hit Parader, 41
Hüsker Dü
    Land Speed Record, 110
    Zen Arcade, 110–6, 218, 220
hypocrisy, 156

"I Heard It Through the Grapevine" (Gaye), 58
idea albums, 5–6
identity, 208–14
In the Wee Small Hours (Sinatra), 5
independence, 210–1
individualism, 196, 197–8
Inside Pop: The Rock Revolution (TV show), 180–1
inspiration
    Blue (Mitchell), 66–7
    Days of Future Passed (Moody Blues), 25–6
    The Downward Spiral (Nine Inch Nails), 144
    Exile in Guyville (Phair), 135–6
    The Miseducation of Lauryn Hill (Hill), 166–7
    Mothership Connection (Parliament), 95–6
    OK Computer (Radiohead), 159
    Seventh Son of a Seventh Son (Iron Maiden), 117–8
    Sgt. Pepper's Lonely Hearts Club Band (Beatles), 16–8
interactivity, 136
International Times, 51–2
introspection, 66, 69–70
Iraq War, 187
Iron Maiden

The Number of the Beast, 122
Seventh Son of a Seventh Son, 117–23, 218, 220
isolation, 220
iTunes, 208, 209

Jackson, Janet, 203
Jackson, Kate, 57
Jagger, Mick, 72, 135, 137, 141
Jay Z, 209
jazz, 7–8
Jean, Wyclef, 166, 167, 168, 169
Jeffery, Alex, 105–6
Jethro Tull, 97
    Aqualung, 73
    Thick as a Brick, 72–8, 218, 220
    Thick as a Brick 2, 78
Jimi Hendrix Experience, 40
John Lennon/Plastic Ono Band (Lennon), 65
Johnson, Robert, 9, 10, 42, 46, 140
Johnson, Tommy, 43
Jones, Floyd, 43
Jones, LeRoi, 62
Jones, Nick, 32
juvenilia, 38

Kellgren, Gary, 34–5
King, B. B., 63
King, Carole, 65, 71
King, Diana, 156
King, Peggy, *Wish Upon a Star*, 6
King Crimson, 73
Klebold, Dylan, 147
Knight, Peter, 25, 30
Knowles, Mathew, 211

La Guardia, Fiorella, 126
LA Weekly, 141
Lamar, Kendrick
    good kid, m.A.A.d city, 200–6, 218, 220, 222
    Overly Dedicated, 200
Land Speed Record (Hüsker Dü), 110
Leary, Timothy, 216
Led Zeppelin, 74
Legendary Stardust Cowboy, 83
Lemonade (Beyoncé), 208–14, 209, 218, 220, 222

"6 Inch", 211
"All Night", 213
awards, 214
"Daddy Lessons", 211
"Don't Hurt Yourself", 210, 214
"Formation", 208, 213–4, 214
"Forward", 212
"Freedom", 213, 214
funding, 214
"Hold Up", 210
"Love Drought", 212
"Pray You Catch Me", 209
reviews, 214
samples, 210, 213
"Sandcastles", 212
"Sorry", 210–1
Lemonade (film), 209
Lennon, John, 16, 18–9, 19, 20–1, 24, 65, 216
Lewis, Miles Marshall, 200
Life After Death (The Notorious B.I.G), 156–7
Little Richard, 17
Lodge, John, 24, 27, 27–8
London Festival Orchestra, 26, 27–8
London Times, 190
loneliness, 148, 218
The Los Angeles Times, 69, 149, 214
Louvin Brothers, *Satan Is Real*, 7
love, 67, 69–70, 80–1, 108, 167–8, 169–70
Love, Mike, 182
LSD, 30, 33, 60, 216, 219
Luypaerts, Guy, *Music of the Danube*, 6
Lynskey, Dorian, 190

McBrain, Nico, 118, 122
McCarter, Jeremy, 192
McCartney, Paul, 1, 16, 16–7, 18, 19, 20–1, 33, 177, 181
McDonald, Ian, 18, 33
McGuire, Walt, 29
madness, descent into, 143–9
Malagaris, Topy, 2
male chauvinism, 100
Marcus, Greil, 3, 136
Marley, Bob, 167, 170
Marley, Rohan, 168
Marsh, Dave, 78

Martin, George, 8, 16, 17–8
Martin, Trayvon, killing of, 202–3
Mason, Nick, 86, 87, 89, 90–1, 92
Matador Records, 135
Mayer, Michael, 190
Mayfield, Curtis, 101
Mellotron, the, 25, 26–7, 27
Melody Maker, 32, 41, 45, 74, 84, 111, 127, 147
Mendl, Hugh, 26, 29
Method Man, 154
Metropolis (film), 192
Metropolis: Suite I (The Chase) (Monáe), 192–3
MGM, 34
Michel, Jean and Prakazrel, 166
Miles, Barry, 51–2
Mingus, Charles, 7
Minor Threat, 110
The Miseducation of Lauryn Hill (Hill), 166–72, 218, 220
  "Can't Take My Eyes Off of You", 171
  "Doo Wop (That Thing)", 168
  "Every Ghetto, Every City", 170
  "Everything Is Everything", 171
  "Ex-Factor", 168
  "Final Hour", 169
  "Forgive Them Father", 170
  "I Used to Love Him", 169–70
  inspiration, 166–7
  lawsuit, 172
  "Lost Ones", 166, 167
  "The Miseducation of Lauryn Hill", 171
  "Nothing Even Matters", 171
  opening, 167
  release, 172
  status, 172
  "Superstar", 169
  "Tell Him", 171–2
  title, 166
  "To Zion", 168
  "When It Hurts So Bad", 169
Mitchell, Joni
  Blue, 65–71, 217, 218, 220
  "Woodstock", 217
Mitchell, Mitch, 40, 42
Monáe, Janelle
  The ArchAndroid, 192–8, 220, 222

Dirty Computer, 198
The Electric Lady, 198
Metropolis: Suite I (The Chase), 192–3
Moody Blues
  "A Whiter Shade of Pale", 25
  Days of Future Passed, 24–30, 218, 219
Moon, Keith, 47
Morgan, Joan, 172
Moroder, Giorgio, 103–4, 105, 107
Mosson, Cardell, 96
Mothers of Invention, 32, 33, 38, 217
Mothership Connection (Parliament), 95–102, 193, 219
  concept, 96–7
  DJ's patter, 97–8
  ending, 101
  "Give Up the Funk (Tear the Roof off the Sucker)", 99, 100–1, 102
  "Handcuffs", 100
  inspiration, 95–6
  "Night of the Thumpasorus Peoples", 101
  opening, 97
  "P. Funk (Wants to Get Funked Up)", 97, 99
  reviews, 98
  "Star Child", 98–9
  "Supergroovalisticprosifunkstication", 99–100
  "Unfunky UFO", 99
Motown 25: Yesterday, Today, Forever (television special), 61
Motown Records, 57–8, 107
Mould, Bob, 110, 111, 112, 112–3, 113–4, 115, 115–6, 116
MTV, 135
MTV Unplugged No. 2.0, 172
Muddy Waters, 9, 46, 63
Murfett, Andrew, 190
Murray, Dave, 118, 120–1, 122
music consumption, 221–2
Music of the Danube (Luypaerts), 6
Musicraft Records, 3
musique concrète, 72, 162

Napster, 221
Nash, Graham, 67
National Recording Registry, 130–1

Nelson, Paul, 2
New Musical Express, 15, 52, 125
The New York Times, 51, 214
The New Yorker, 66, 159
Newsweek, 192
Nine Inch Nails
    Broken, 143–4
    The Downward Spiral, 143–9, 220
    Pretty Hate Machine, 143
Nirvana, 15
NME, 158
Norton, Greg, 110, 111, 113, 115
Notorious B.I.G., 218
    death, 156–7
    Life After Death, 156–7
    Ready to Die, 151–7
The Number of the Beast (Iron Maiden), 122

O'Brien, Ed, 158, 161
O'Driscoll, Gerry, 91–2
OK Computer (Radiohead), 158–64, 160–1, 164, 218, 220
    "Airbag", 159, 164
    "Climbing Up the Walls", 162, 164
    concept, 158–9
    "Electioneering", 162, 164
    "Fitter, Happier", 161–2, 164
    inspiration, 159
    "Karma Police", 161, 164
    "Let Down", 161, 164
    "Lucky", 163, 164
    "No Surprises", 162–3, 164
    "Paranoid Android", 159–60
    release, 164
    reputation, 164
    sales, 164
    structure, 164
    "Subterranean Homesick Alien", 160, 164
    "The Tourist", 163–4, 164
Oklahoma!, 3–4
Oldham, James, 158
Once Upon a Time . . . (Summer), 103–9, 218
    "A Man Like You", 107
    clarity, 104–5
    "Dance into My Life", 107

"Fairy Tale High", 105
"Faster and Faster to Nowhere", 105
"Happily Ever After", 108
"I Love You", 108
"If You Got It Flaunt It", 107
"Now I Need You", 106
"Once Upon a Time", 105
"Queen for a Day", 106–7
release, 104
"Rumour Has It", 108
"Say Something Nice", 105–6
status, 108–9
"Sweet Romance", 107
"Working the Midnight Shift", 106
Overkill, Urge, 135
Overly Dedicated (Lamar), 200
ownership, 202

pain and loss, 208–14, 218
Parker, Maceo, 100
Parks, Van Dyke, 177, 178
Parliament, 128
    Chocolate City, 100
    The Clones of Dr. Funkenstein, 96, 101
    Funkentelechy vs. the Placebo Syndrome, 102
    Mothership Connection, 95–102, 193, 219
Parry, Dick, 89
Parsons, Alan, 88, 89
Parsons, Tim, 122–3
Pasemaster Mase (Vincent Mason), 124, 125, 126
Patton, Charley, 43
Paul, Prince, 124, 125, 126
Pet Sounds (Beach Boys), 1, 8–9, 15, 16, 22, 71, 162–3, 177, 189
Petrusich, Amanda, 159
Phair, Liz, *Exile in Guyville*, 135–41, 143, 218, 220
Pinder, Mike, 24–5, 25–6, 26–7, 27, 28
Pink Floyd
    The Dark Side of the Moon, 86–92, 218, 220
    The Piper at the Gates of Dawn, 86
    The Wall, 92, 144
The Piper at the Gates of Dawn (Pink Floyd), 86

Poetic Justice (film), 203
Posdnus (Kelvin Mercer), 124, 124–5, 128, 131
Presley, Elvis, 9, 82, 99, 218–9
pretension, 52, 73
Pretty Hate Machine (Nine Inch Nails), 143
pride, 113
progressive rock, 73
prophecy, 123
protest songs, 44–5
psychedelic rock, 17
punk rock, 184–90
punk rock opera, 184–5

R&B, 42
Radiohead, 15
   OK Computer, 158–64, 218, 220
Raditz, Cary, 67–8, 68
rambling tradition, 9
Ramones, 110, 111
Ready to Die (Notorious B.I.G), 151–7
   "Big Poppa", 155
   concept, 152
   "Everyday Struggle", 155
   "Friend of Mine", 156
   "Gimme the Loot", 153
   "Intro", 152
   "Juicy", 154
   "Me & My Bitch", 155
   "One More Chance", 154, 156
   power, 157
   "Ready to Die", 152, 153
   "Respect", 156
   samples, 152–3, 156
   "Suicidal Thoughts", 156
   "Things Done Changed", 152–3
   "Unbelievable", 156
   "Warning", 153
   "The What", 154
realism, 201
Record World, 2, 104
Recording Industry Association of America, 115
recording technology, 3
Redding, Noel, 40
reinvention, 106–7
relatability, 138

Revolver (Beatles), 15, 16, 216
Reznor, Trent, 143–4, 144–5, 146, 147, 148–9, 218
Rice, Casey, 137
Ride This Train (Cash), 7
The Rise and Fall of Ziggy Stardust and the Spiders from Mars (Bowie), 79–85, 217–8, 218, 220
   "Five Years", 80
   "Hang on to Yourself", 82–3, 84
   "It Ain't Easy", 81
   "Lady Stardust", 82, 83
   "Moonage Daydream", 81
   narrative, 79
   reviews, 84
   "Rock and Roll Suicide", 84, 85
   "Soul Love", 80–1
   "Star", 82
   "Starman", 80, 81
   "Suffragette City", 83
   "Ziggy Stardust", 83
Robbins, Marty, *Gunfighter Ballads and Trail Songs*, 7
Robot Jox (film), 146
Rodgers, Jimmy, 9
Rolling Stone, 3, 15, 41, 47, 48, 59, 62, 63, 70–1, 77–8, 110, 128, 143, 154, 159, 182, 186, 190, 193, 200–1, 206, 214
Rolling Stones, 72
   Aftermath, 16, 22
   Beggars Banquet, 73, 118
   Exile on Main St, 74, 78, 135–41
   "Sympathy for the Devil", 118
   Their Satanic Majesties Request, 2, 73
The Rolling Stones' Rock and Roll Circus, 72–3
Romeo + Juliet (film), 160–1, 164
Ronson, Mick, 80
Royal Festival Hall, 84, 178
Rubber Soul (Beatles), 8–9
Rudis, Al, 65
Ruffhouse Records, 166

Sahanaja, Damian, 178
sampling, 125, 152–3, 156, 210, 213
Santana, Carlos, 168
Satan, 118–9
Satan Is Real (Louvin Brothers), 7

satire, 146–7, 220
schizophrenia, 90–1, 177–8
scream therapy, 65
Self-Portrait (Dylan), 3
self-worth, 105–6
Selway, Phil, 158, 159
The Seventh Seal (film), 118–9
Seventh Son of a Seventh Son (Iron Maiden), 117–23, 218, 220
   "Can I Play with Madness", 119, 120, 121
   "The Clairvoyant", 117, 121–1
   close, 122
   "The Evil That Men Do", 119–20, 121
   "Infinite Dreams", 119
   inspiration, 117–8
   "Moonchild", 118–9
   "Only the Good Die Young", 122
   opening, 118
   "The Prophecy", 121
   "Seventh Son of a Seventh Son", 120–1
sexuality, 104
Sgt. Pepper's Lonely Hearts Club Band (Beatles), 15–22, 24, 30, 32–4, 52, 103, 124, 182, 216–8, 219
   "A Day in the Life", 20–1, 27
   "Being for the Benefit of Mr. Kite!", 19, 20
   "Fixing a Hole", 19
   "Getting Better", 19
   "Good Morning, Good Morning", 20
   inspiration, 16–8
   "Lovely Rita", 20
   "Lucy in the Sky with Diamonds", 18–9
   presentation, 21–2
   reception, 1–2
   release, 1
   sales, 22
   secret inner groove, 21
   "She's Leaving Home", 1, 19
   status, 15–6, 22
   structure, 24
   "With a Little Help from My Friends", 18, 19
   "Within You Without You", 19–20
Sheffield, Rob, 190
Shore, Dinah, 57
show, the album as, 17–8

Siggers, Landon, 122–3
Sinatra, Frank, 4–5
singer-songwriter movement, 65–6, 69–70
slavery, 62–3
Sly and the Family Stone, 95, 97, 101
SMiLE (Wilson), 1, 177–83, 218, 219
   "Barnyard", 179
   Boston Orpheum performance, 183
   "Cabin Essence", 179–80
   "Child Is Father of the Man", 180
   elements suite, 181–2
   "Good Vibrations", 182
   "Heroes and Villains", 178–9
   "I'm in Great Shape/I Wanna Be Around Workshop", 181
   "In Blue Hawaii", 182
   "Mrs. O'Leary's Cow (Fire)", 182, 183
   "Old Master Painter", 179
   "On a Holiday", 181
   "Our Prayer", 178, 179, 183
   release, 182–3
   reviews, 182
   "Roll Plymouth Rock", 179
   "Song for Children", 180
   "Surf's Up", 180–1
   theme, 178
   "Vege-Tables", 181, 183
   Wilson's schizophrenia, 177–8
   "Wind Chimes", 181
   "Wonderful", 180
Smith, Adam, 118
Smith, Adrian, 120–1, 122
social media, 106
Songs for Young Lovers (Sinatra), 5
Sorrow Songs, 62–3
sound pictures, 41
Spector, Phil, 8, 35, 161
SPIN, 158, 184, 187
spirituality, 62, 77, 197
Springsteen, Bruce, 4
SST Records, 115
Starr, Ringo, 16, 19
Stokes, Doris, 117
story and storytelling, 48, 151–7
streaming platforms, 131
stream-of-conscious, 37, 66
Summer, Donna, 198, 211
   Once Upon a Time . . ., 103–9, 218

Swing Easy! (Sinatra), 5
"Swing Low, Sweet Chariot", 99
symphony, the, 24

Tate, Sharon, 144–5
Taylor, James, 65, 71
technology, overreliance on, 158–64
Their Satanic Majesties Request (Rolling Stones), 2, 73
Thick as a Brick (Jethro Tull), 72–8, 218, 220
   comic book heroes, 76
   on iTunes, 74
   mythology, 73–4
   opening lines, 74–5
   origins, 73–4
   red herrings, 77
   release, 73
   reviews, 77–8
   sequel, 78
   themes, 74
   "Thick as a Brick, Part 1", 73
   "Thick as a Brick, Part 2", 73
   waning minutes, 77
Thick as a Brick 2 (Jethro Tull), 78
This Is Spinal Tap (film), 117, 118
Thomas, Ray, 24, 25, 27, 28
thrash-rock, 110
Three Dog Night, 81
Thunder, Shelly, 170
THX 1138 (film), 144
Tidal, 209
Time, 22
Tommy (The Who), 3, 6, 47–53, 218, 219
   "The Acid Queen", 49
   "Amazing Journey", 49
   "Christmas", 49, 52
   "Cousin Kevin", 49, 52
   "Do You Think it's Alright?", 50
   "Fiddle About", 50
   final refrain, 53
   "Go to the Mirror, Boy!", 50–1, 52
   group effort, 48–9
   "The Hawker", 49
   "I'm Free", 51
   live performances, 52
   "Miracle Cure", 51
   origins, 47–8

"Overture", 48
"Pinball Wizard", 50, 52
pretension, 52
reception, 51–2
release, 48, 51
"Sally Simpson", 51
"Smash the Mirror,", 51
"Sparks", 49
structure, 48
"There's a Doctor", 50
"Tommy's Holiday Camp", 51
Tommy's internal world, 49
"Underture", 49–50, 52
"We're Not Gonna Take It", 51, 52
Top of the Pops, 79, 81, 85
Torry, Clare, 89
total album concept, 30
Townshend, Pete, 2–3, 47, 47–8, 48, 52, 53
Trugoy the Dove (David Jude Jolicoeur),, 124, 128
Tuff Gong, 167
Tupac, 156–7, 200, 203, 206
Turtles, The, 124
The Turtles Present the Battle of the Bands, 124
Tynan, Kenneth, 22

U2, 189
unification, 95–102

Van DePitte, David, 59
Variety, 2
Varnals, Derek, 29
Velvet Underground, 80
video game designing, 116
Vietnam War, 57, 60
Voice of Frank Sinatra, The (Sinatra), 4–5
voodoo, 42, 46

The Wall (Pink Floyd), 92, 144
war, 89–90
The Washington Post, 131
Waters, Roger, 86–7, 88, 90
Weingarten, Christopher R., 125
Welch, Chris, 74
We're Only in It for the Money (Zappa), 32–9, 101, 217, 219
   "Absolutely Free", 36–7

"Are You Hung Up?", 34–5
"Bowtie Daddy", 36
"The Chrome-Plated Megaphone of Destiny", 38–9
"Concentration Moon", 35–6
cover, 33
"Flower Punk", 37
"Harry, You're a Beast", 36
"The Idiot Bastard Son", 38
"Let's Make the Water Turn Black,", 37–8
"Lonely Little Girl", 38
"Mom & Dad", 36
"Mother People", 37, 38
"Nasal Retentive Calliope Music", 37
release, 33
stream-of-conscious, 37
"Take Your Clothes Off When You Dance", 38
"Telephone Conversation", 36
"What's the Ugliest Part of Your Body?", 36, 38
"Who Needs the Peace Corps?", 35
Wesley, Fred, 100
Western Culture, 98
What's Going On (Gaye), 57–64, 71, 218, 219–20
 as concept album, 57
 first-day sales, 58
 "Flying High (in the Friendly Sky)", 60
 "God Is Love", 61
 "Inner City Blues (Make Me Wanna Holler)", 62–3, 64
 live performance, 1972, 63–4
 "Mercy, Mercy Me (The Ecology).", 61
 origins, 58–9
 release, 58
 reviews, 62
 "Right On", 61–2
 "Save the Children", 60–1
 spiritual center, 62
 status, 63
 themes, 57
 "What's Going On", 58, 59–60, 64
 "What's Happening Brother", 60
 "Wholy Holy", 62
White, Jack, 210
White Album (Beatles), 41

Who, The
 "A Quick One While He's Away", 72, 74
 Tommy, 3, 6, 47–53, 218, 219
 The Who Sell Out, 47–8, 50
The Who Sell Out (The Who), 47–8, 50
Wild Is Love (Cole), 6, 7
Williams, Hank, 9
Williams, Saul, 194
Willis, Ellen, 66
Wilson, Brian, 1, 8–9
 SMiLE, 177–83, 218, 219
Winthrop, John, 58–9
Winwood, Steve, 42
Wish Upon a Star (King), 6
Wondaland Arts Society, 196
Wondermints, 178
Wood, Brad, 136, 137
Woodson, Carter Godwin, 166–7
Woodstock Festival, 47, 52–3, 58, 99, 217
working poor, the, 106
Wright, Rick, 86, 89, 90
Wu-Tang Clan, 154

Yes, 73
Yorke, Thom, 158, 159, 160, 160–1, 161

Zappa, Frank, 97
 Freak Out!, 72
 "The Return of the Son of Monster Magnet (Unfinished Ballet in Two Tableaux)", 72
 We're Only in It for the Money, 32–9, 101, 217, 219
Zen Arcade (Hüsker Dü), 110–6, 218, 220
 "Beyond the Threshold", 112–3
 "The Biggest Lie", 113
 "Chartered Trips", 112
 concept, 115–6
 "Dreams Reoccurring", 112
 "Hare Krsna", 112
 "I'll Never Forget You", 113
 incidents, 111
 "Indecision Time", 112
 "Masochism World", 113
 "Monday Will Never Be the Same", 114
 "Never Talking to You Again", 111–2
 "Newest Industry", 114

"One Step at a Time", 114
"Pink Turns to Blue", 114
"Pride", 113
"Reoccurring Dreams", 114, 115, 116
reviews, 115
"Something I Learned Today", 111
"Somewhere", 113–4

"Standing by the Sea", 113
"The Tooth Fairy and the Princess", 114
transitions, 111
"Turn on the News", 114–5, 116
"Whatever", 114
"What's Going On", 113
Zimmerman, George, 202–3